Teaching

Shakespeare

in the

High

School

LITERARY HERITAGE
A *Macmillan Teacher's Handbook*

TEACHING THE NOVEL IN PAPERBACK   *Margaret Ryan*
TEACHING POETRY IN THE HIGH SCHOOL   *Morris Sweetkind*
TEACHING SHAKESPEARE IN THE HIGH SCHOOL   *Bertrand Evans*

Teaching Shakespeare in the High School

BERTRAND EVANS

Professor of English
University of California
Berkeley, California

The Macmillan Company   New York

Cover photo: Courtesy Friedman-Abeles.
    American Shakespeare Festival production
    of *Romeo and Juliet.*

The Macmillan Company, New York
Collier-Macmillan Canada, Ltd., Toronto, Ontario
Printed in the United States of America

Contents

To the great Variety of Readers.

. . . And so we leave you to other of his Friends, whom if you need, can bee your guides: if you neede them not, you can leade your selves, and others. And such Readers we wish him.

John Heminge
Henrie Condell
First Folio (1623)

Teaching

Shakespeare

in the

High

School

CHAPTER 1

Why Shakespeare?

IT IS DOUBTFUL THAT ANY GOOD PURPOSE WOULD BE SERVED BY my being less honest at the outset than later, and therefore I shall immediately define the point of view that has governed everything I have said in the following pages about Shakespeare in the high school English program.

I am convinced that Shakespeare is far and away the most important author who can be studied by high school students. I believe, in fact, not merely that he is the most important, but that he is indispensable. I believe that he deserves and should have more time than any other single author in the literature program. I believe that a reasonable number of his plays to be studied in class in four years is eight, not two or four, and that they should be studied by *all* students except those who are genuinely incapable of getting any significant value from them no matter how hard both they and their teacher may try. I have said at one point in a later chapter that even if it were necessary for a teacher and a particular class to work through the text of a play together word by word, like translating Virgil at twenty lines a day, they should do just that. I stand by that statement, because I have been unable to think of any way in which, as an English class, they could be spending their time to more advantage.

I shall try to answer this question on two very different planes; the first practical, the second, perhaps, somewhat idealistic.

Why is Shakespeare so important?

To speak practically, first. Any major Shakespeare play provides a class with a compact body of reading matter with which they can have all the kinds of experiences that formulators of high school English programs have ever thought worthy of inclusion.

1

Such a play covers, in effect, all the genres: it is short story, novel, drama, poetry, essay. It offers narration, exposition, description, argumentation. For teachers who believe in teaching "critical thinking," no better material exists. For teachers who want students to distinguish "propaganda," every play will provide exercises. For teachers who like to emphasize vocabulary study, Shakespeare offers a better list of words than any prepared booklet. For teachers who like a great deal of oral work—discussion, panel discussion, debate, formal speeches, oral reading, acting experiences—Shakespeare offers a plenitude of opportunity. For teachers who want to "extend students' horizons" through acquaintance with other times, other countries, other values, any play of Shakespeare's is a treasure house. For teachers who believe in a heavy writing program, one play of Shakespeare's can yield more writing assignments than could be used in a four-year program, and in a great variety of kinds—paraphrase, précis, summary, paragraph, critical essay, research paper, poem, short story, play. For traditional grammarians, semanticists, or linguistically oriented teachers, Shakespeare offers a gold mine of words with shifted meanings, grammatical usages, sentence patterns, and dialects.

It is evident enough that a single major play of Shakespeare's, very probably more handily than any other one work, can provide opportunity for everything that any teacher is likely to think appropriate to "do" in an English class.

Next, to speak "impractically." For many teachers all the opportunities listed above, will not even touch the "real" answer to the question "Why Shakespeare?" For them, and for me, the true answer is simply that Shakespeare is absolutely first-rate, with all that that implies.

In later chapters I shall be found often insisting that what is of quintessential importance for students to "get" from a play of Shakespeare's is the experience, by which I mean the aesthetic experience, of the play itself, as a work of art. I am not so much concerned to have student "learn about Shakespeare," about his age, stage, dramatic genres, as I am to have them see and respond to—in Hazlitt's phrase—"all that is finest in the play."

I believe it is this experience, if anything, that has the best chance of exercising a salutary effect on students, and therefore I think it is the best "good" that teachers can help students to get from the plays. I am convinced that this "good" is intimately associated with the *pleasure* that is to be had from artistic works —in fact, that it is the *pleasure*, if anything, that makes the "salutary effect" possible. It goes without saying that I am in favor of having students get all the pleasure they can from every play. I am not sure that just *any* pleasure can be identified with "good," but I believe that pleasure derived from perceiving "all that is finest" in a first-rate work of art can be so identified.

"How to" books on teaching are generally deplorable, and a "how to" book on teaching Shakespeare seems like a peculiarly revolting idea. I am afraid that I have included a good deal of "how to" in these chapters, and I apologize for all of it. My intention was to deal with *principles*, in the light of which all possible sorts of "how to" questions could be answered by the teacher in the classroom; but I found that my principles stood a good chance of being ambiguous or misleading unless I made some applications by way of illustration—and there, suddenly sprung up like weeds, have appeared pages of "how to."

My best hope, and only justification, for what follows is that teachers will be stirred to debate with themselves, with one another, and with me about every "answer" I have given. Under such headings as "Which Plays?", "In Which Years?", "What Form of Presentation?", and so on, I have taken up one by one the rather obvious divisions of the subject, and in every case I have reasoned through the problem to what I thought was the best answer. But my hope for this book will be utterly defeated if *any* teacher—even a teacher who has not yet taught and has never read more than two of Shakespeare's plays—takes a single one of my answers for gospel, adopts it forthwith, and thinks no more about the matter.

On the other hand, my purpose will be entirely achieved if the answers that I have given should start a continuing, nationwide professional debate, furious but honest, over which plays, when, to whom, and how. That way, no one can lose, and the richest gainers will be tomorrow's citizens.

CHAPTER 2

Which Plays and When?

1. WHICH PLAYS?

MODERN SCHOLARS ARE GENERALLY AGREED ON A SHAKESPEARE canon that includes 37 plays, 2 long poems, and 154 sonnets. If it were both feasible and desirable for high schools to include all the thirty-seven plays in their English programs, we could omit most of this chapter, for there would be no problem of selection, but only one of arrangement—how to parcel them out to grades nine, ten, eleven, and twelve. But even the most avid Shakespearean—though he might, indeed, argue that a few select high school students could well cover the canon "on their own" during the four years—would hardly recommend that whole classes study them all. Whether we like it or not, therefore, we are at once confronted with a problem of selection that is both very difficult and very important.

If, again, all the plays were equal in quality and readability we could treat the task of selection lightly. But, of course, the plays are not all equally appropriate, and it is only too easy to choose very badly indeed.

The necessity of selection by individual teachers has been greatly increased in recent years with the arrival of new trends in publishing. Not long ago, in most schools, teachers' choices were sharply limited—indeed, they hardly existed. "Choice" meant whatever was included in the school's adopted series of anthologies. But now the complete works of Shakespeare, presented in individual paperbacks, attractive and inexpensive, ably edited by first-rate scholars, are available everywhere. The teacher is privileged to choose not only which of many plays he wants, but which of many editions.

4

Finally, the task of selection is made peculiarly difficult by the fact that, although Shakespeare's plays are not all equally excellent and equally suitable, far more of them are truly excellent and eminently suitable than can be included in a four-year English program. It is therefore necessary not merely to choose the excellent and the suitable from among the total number, but to select from among the truly excellent and eminently suitable the smaller number that will actually be "best" for intensive classroom study.

Let us first, however, make a list of the plays that deserve serious consideration. How shall we proceed in drawing up this list? Let us begin by suggesting that this list should include only those plays that satisfy two general criteria. First, all should be excellent. Second, none should involve any of several kinds of truly compelling reasons why, in spite of its excellence, it should not be selected.

We are instantly in trouble, with both criteria. On the first, three challenges immediately confront us. Why must they all be excellent? Excellent *in what way*—as stage pieces, or as works of literature? And are not *all* Shakespeare's plays, in any event, excellent? And on the second, we are at once challenged with the sobering question, "What kinds of reasons can there *possibly* be for not including a work if it is undeniably excellent?"

Here is not the place, certainly, to reason out in full philosophical detail the basic question of why the *excellent* in Shakespeare, as in other works of literature, is preferable, as an item in a reading program, to the less excellent and to the less-than-excellent. Bluntly, therefore, it would seem reasonable to suppose that when a single work of literature is to claim from four to six weeks of intensive study—as it is here intended the study of a Shakespeare play shall claim—it should be a *distinguished* work, which fully deserves the amount of time and energy given to it.

As to the question of the sense in which "excellence" is used, whether pertaining to the quality of the work as an acting piece or as a work of literature, perhaps that has been sufficiently answered by the preceding chapter. In the classroom Shakespeare must necessarily be approached primarily as a problem of gaining understanding and appreciation from the printed page; hence, excellence of the play as a work of literature is of first importance, and excellence as a stage play is secondary. Obviously, if the plays that are found to be excellent works of literature prove also to be surpassing stage plays, so much the better; and the fact is that, with Shakespeare, that is generally the case.

With almost any answer to the third challenge, "Are not *all* of Shakespeare's plays excellent?" we risk offending all devout Shakespeareans who maintain the affirmative and will not be denied. We can concede that all Shakespeare is excellent—and at the same time can assert what no Shakespearean will dispute, namely, that Shakespeare's plays are not all of equal merit; some are much superior to others.

We come finally to the last challenge: On what grounds can we *possibly* eliminate certain plays from consideration, if they are of admitted excellence, fully as deserving on literary grounds as are certain others that are included in our list? But here we cannot profitably deal in generalities. It will be necessary to defer this matter until later, when a relatively small number of plays must be subjected to individual scrutiny.

Let us now try to draw up an initial list of "possibles." Our way to this "first-round" list will be surer and shorter if, relying entirely upon general critical opinion—which has now had three and a half centuries in which to be tested and proved—we begin by eliminating the obvious, and perhaps some not-quite-so-obvious, choices.

Like any other artist, Shakespeare first had to learn his craft, and learning it took time and practice. If his period of apprenticeship was shorter than that of almost any other master, he nevertheless had one. The plays of his apprenticeship can be removed from consideration without much risk of dissent from any knowledgeable quarter. These plays include the first histories, that is, the three parts of *Henry VI* and *Richard III*; the first comedies, *Comedy of Errors*, *Two Gentlemen of Verona*, and *Love's Labour's Lost*; and the melodramatic "drama of blood," *Titus Andronicus*. We have immediately, thus, reduced the range of choice from thirty-seven to twenty-nine plays.

Besides the plays of Shakespeare's apprenticeship, numerous others have been generally acknowledged as definitely inferior for one or another reason, and these, too, we can eliminate fairly handily. They include three histories: *King John*, a disappointing chronicle considered by some critics as one of Shakespeare's least satisfactory performances; *Henry IV, Part 2*, which suffers the usual fate of the "sequel"; and *Henry VIII*, which has only a few great moments and is generally taken as only partly by Shakespeare. Three other works, for roughly the same reasons, may be similarly eliminated from serious consideration: *Troilus and Cressida*, which twentieth-century critics have found fascinating for many reasons, but which remains structurally and otherwise an impossible choice for our purposes; *Timon of Athens*, a defective work of which it has been said that Shakespeare did not succeed in dragging his subject out into the light; and *Pericles*, a haunting but seriously defective work of which at least the first two acts are almost certainly not Shakespeare's.

We have now, in the second round, eliminated fourteen plays from serious consideration. But twenty-three remain—still far too many for our purpose.

In order to draw up our final list of "most excellent and suitable plays," we shall ultimately have to make some fine distinctions in the areas of both excellence and general suitability. But we may postpone making those distinctions a little longer by first considering which of the twenty-three remaining plays contain within themselves—and usually quite aside from the question of their excellence—elements of any kind that make them rather obviously unsuitable for close classroom study at the high school level.

Of the comedies, those which can immediately be questioned are the *Merry Wives of Windsor*, *All's Well That Ends Well*, and *Measure for Measure*.

The *Merry Wives of Windsor* turns upon a series of efforts by Falstaff to seduce the wives, or, more specifically, one of the wives, and its three scenes of climactic interest represent his successive frustrations. *All's Well That Ends Well* rests upon a single central problem: the heroine must somehow contrive to get herself with child by her unwilling husband. *Measure for Measure*, like *All's Well That Ends Well*, turns upon a bed-trick. In addition, its generally unwholesome atmosphere would almost certainly, in most communities, be considered as polluting the air of the classroom. All three plays are clearly unsuitable for class use.

The foregoing points are made not in defense of an attitude of prudery in the classroom, but in pursuit of our aim, which is to identify a relatively few Shakespeare plays, from among a large number, that will be both most excellent and most suitable.

Of the remaining comedies, one more may now be rejected on fairly obvious but very different grounds from those on which the preceding three were rejected. Without challenging the artistic merits of *Cymbeline*—which, as a matter of fact, has never been accorded a high place in the history of Shakespeare criticism, and may even be said to have remained somewhat more obscure than its merits deserve—we shall be wise in excluding the play on account of its extraordinary complexity. The multiplicity of the "things going on" at any one time in this play exceeds that in any other play, and perhaps may indeed be said to be excessive. For this reason among others, *Cymbeline* must be accounted an exquisite feast for Shakespeare gourmets, but not especially palatable for those just being initiated.

Less defensible reasons exist for rejecting a final one of the comedies, *Much Ado About Nothing*. As a romantic comedy, it has never been thought the equal, on stage or in study, of any other work remaining in the comedy column. If we reject it, we shall have to do so simply on the basis of comparison with the others. With three exceptions, the characters in *Much Ado About Nothing* are unimpressive. Only three portraits are memorable: Dogberry, the eternal example of the blundering, obtuse officer of the law, and Benedick and Beatrice, the sparkling wits whose brilliance dims Claudio and Hero "as daylight doth the lamp." Conspicuously lacking is a Touchstone, a Feste, even a Launcelot Gobbo: the play has no professional fool, and needs one badly.

We turn next to the history plays, among which, since we have previously rejected seven, a single one, *Richard II*, can be excluded—though reluctantly—on fairly firm grounds. A beautiful and sometimes moving history play, noted for the lyrical tribute to England expressed by John of Gaunt and for the richly musical outpourings from the heart of the falling king, *Richard II* represents definite progress in Shakespeare's powers of selecting and shaping historical events to suit the form and effects of drama. Even so, the play shows Shakespeare's art still in a transitional stage, and much that is represented in certain scenes is primarily of historical rather than dramatic interest. The appeal of the work depends mainly upon Richard himself; the play lacks the comedy and the host of rich human portraits that make the histories of *Henry IV, Part 1,* and *Henry V* so lavishly entertaining, exciting, and profoundly rewarding. In short, this play, which is less rich than its immediate successors, also, because its drama is more fettered by history, offers more bars to appreciative reading than do the others.

We have so far rejected only two tragedies, the bloody *Titus* and the abortive *Timon.* We are thus left with eight to be considered in this second round of elimination. It is here proposed that we reject three: *Othello, Antony and Cleopatra,* and *Coriolanus.* Because the last two may perhaps be put aside more summarily, if not with less pain, we shall begin with them.

Perhaps, in rejecting *Antony and Cleopatra,* we need not raise objection to its subject, which is neither more nor less than an illicit enslavement of the flesh that proves inevitably ruinous to both the flesh and the spirit. The very enormity of this play, which stands with one foot in Rome and the other in Alexandria, may be sufficient to intimidate the teacher who is well advised. The play is huge in all respects, and more than one studious reader has confessed his inability to take everything in and hold it in the grasp of his mind. Unless both class and teacher are uncommonly sophisticated and uncommonly experienced in reading Shakespeare, they will unquestionably do well to leave the play unattempted.

The last of Shakespeare's tragedies, *Coriolanus,* nearly turned out to be a political debate rather than a drama. Beside its great predecessors, tragedies of passion whose warmly human protagonists, antagonists, and bystanders caught up in intense experiences of the soul excite our emotions and involve us deeply in their personal fates, *Coriolanus* reads like an intellectual argument. Our interest is drawn to the issue the characters debate, rather than to themselves as human individuals. Add to this the fact that the argument of *Coriolanus* is presented in some of Shakespeare's toughest, knottiest, most incapsulated prose and blank verse, and we acknowledge formidable obstacles here that must place this play, among the tragedies, only just ahead of *Titus*

Andronicus and *Timon of Athens* in its suitability for our purposes. *Coriolanus* is a better play for political science than for a high school English class.

We come finally to the thankless task of insisting on the necessity of rejecting *Othello*. It is, by virtually universal agreement, one of the "Big Four." *Othello* has been called Shakespeare's "most perfect" tragedy on the grounds of its technical excellence. The degree of personal involvement that it claims from reader or spectator is second to none in Shakespeare: it is reported that during one performance a member of the audience rose up and shot the actor playing Othello, just as he was smothering Desdemona. Further, the play puts no such barriers in the way of reading as have been mentioned in discussion of *Coriolanus*, *Antony and Cleopatra*, and *Cymbeline*. It is not too gigantic to take in, like *Antony and Cleopatra*; indeed, in this respect it is not as formidable as either *King Lear* or *Hamlet*. In language and action it is, in fact, the most "open" of the "Big Four," excepting only *Macbeth*. Possessing, as it unmistakably does, these highest attributes of excellence and readability, how, then, can it reasonably be excluded from our final list of best possible choices?

In approaching an answer to this question, we shall here need to anticipate very briefly some points that are discussed in detail in later chapters under the general heading of "the presentation of Shakespeare in the classroom." Underlying all that is said in every chapter of this book is the assumption that when we speak of "the teaching of Shakespeare in the classroom" we mean that the plays will actually be *taught*, in diametric contrast to their being merely read independently and individually by students on their own. As will be made clear hereafter, teaching Shakespeare in high school means close cooperative efforts of teacher and students, detailed study throughout the play, with much reading aloud, discussion and analysis of the meanings in word, line, and passage. Given this view of how Shakespeare is to be taught, can we include *Othello* in our list of "best and most suitable plays"?

The difficulty with *Othello* is not simply that the plot turns on a question of marital infidelity. Neither is it that the dialogue contains occasional "objectionable" words and *double entendres*, such as abound in many of the plays that will remain on our final list, and of which we must speak hereafter. The difficulty arises from the very brilliance with which Shakespeare reveals the kind of man that Iago essentially is. Iago is Shakespeare's only full-length study of a man with a dirty mind. Falstaff's broad humor is earthy but healthy; so is Mercutio's often gross but always sparkling wit. But Iago's condition is pathological. His mind turns always and unhealthily not merely upon sex, but upon sexual doings; his obsession expresses itself all too naturally in unnatural, gross, physical imagery—

> . . . an old black ram
> Is tupping your white ewe.

> . . . you'll have your daughter covered
> with a Barbary horse.

> . . . your daughter and the Moor are now
> making the beast with two backs.

> . . . the gross clasps of a lascivious Moor.

These images are from Scene 1 alone, when the play is just beginning. Later scenes reveal even more clearly the problem in teaching *Othello*.

Iago's mind circles and hovers over physical acts of sexuality as a buzzard circles and hovers over carrion. The foulness of his own imagination makes these acts seem vile; he besmears all that he touches. In particular, he accentuates the basic provocative image of the play, that which through the centuries has simultaneously repulsed and fascinated audiences, the intimate physical relations of a "blackamoor" and a "pure white Venetian."

The problem of using *Othello* with high school classes *for close study, with steady oral reading and discussion,* is surely a severe one—so severe that no satisfactory solution is apparent.

One solution, but an unsatisfactory one, is to use an edition of *Othello* from which all such imagery has been deleted. These images, however, are the basis and means of Iago's inflammatory campaign against Othello. The tragedy itself depends upon them, and to eliminate them is to destroy the tragedy, to degrade it to the level of unmotivated melodrama. These reasons force the conclusion that *Othello* must be omitted from our final list of "best and most suitable" plays.

We have now reduced our list to fourteen plays, which are as follows:

COMEDIES	HISTORIES	TRAGEDIES
A *Midsummer Night's Dream*	*Henry IV, Part 1*	*Romeo and Juliet*
The Merchant of Venice	*Henry V*	*Julius Caesar*
The Taming of the Shrew		*Hamlet*
As You Like It		*King Lear*
Twelfth Night		*Macbeth*
The Winter's Tale		
The Tempest		

It appears reasonable to suggest that, allowances being made for all sorts of varying circumstances in the schools, all of these plays are sufficiently excellent to deserve serious consideration, and that none contains elements of such kind and degree as have forced the elimination of some plays already considered. This is not to say that none of these plays confronts the teacher with problems. *All* of them do so; but, again making allowance for varying circumstances, these problems are not insuperable. To show how these and other problems can be adequately handled by a well-advised teacher is a function of later chapters on the presentation of the plays.

More immediately, though we have now reduced the thirty-seven plays to fourteen that "will do," we must complete the hardest task of all, which is to identify yet smaller groups of plays —for certainly it will be a rare high school that will make place for the study of all fourteen, and it is a certain fact that though any of the fourteen "will do," not all have equal claim to be among *the* two, or *the* four, or *the* eight, or even *the* twelve plays that a given school will actually wish to use. We have reached a point, of course, at which the personal taste and available enthusiasm of the individual teacher can and should count heavily for or against specific plays. Perhaps, indeed, if all the fourteen plays *are* sufficiently excellent and suitable, we should not go so far as to *insist* on any particular plays beyond this point. It is, therefore, rather in the spirit of suggestion than of insistence that we proceed into the final rounds.

Fortunately, we are aided considerably, in choosing among the remaining plays, by extremely well-advised and long-tested school tradition. That tradition is not invariably right, we know well enough; but in the case of the choice of certain of these plays, it appears to have been unerring. We may therefore best begin by citing its preferences.

Let us suppose, at the outset, that the program of a given school has space for only two Shakespeare plays—adding hastily that if such is the case, it is a regrettable one. All the pages of the present book are dedicated to the conviction that two are not enough; but the fact is that in most high schools, throughout the United States, for a whole generation, no more than two of the plays have actually been studied, and it is a sad but unescapable truth that many schools will continue to use no more than two. Therefore, which two?

On the evidence of the several most widely used series of anthologies in the high schools of the United States, and, indeed, on other evidence at least as reliable, it is clear that the two plays most regularly used, and especially where *only* two plays are used, are *Julius Caesar* and *Macbeth*. If it can be argued that neither of these is Shakespeare's very greatest play, it must also be agreed that both are undeniably very great plays; and it is demonstrable that other factors enter the case which, when all are accounted for, make the claims of these two unassailable. Not only are they great plays, but they are also the two plays that allow the fewest arguments of any kind to be made against them. Anyone who wished to unseat them would need to invent excuses. Of all Shakespeare's plays, these two are probably the most "open," the most readily understood. They contain fewer "objectionable" features of any kind than do any of the other great plays. Characterizations are sharp, clear, memorable, and magnificent. Their subjects are eternal. The range of their appeal is extraordinary; the history of their use in the schools alone has so well demonstrated that fact as to make further words superfluous. More will be said of these two plays in later chapters. For the present, we should have to concede that if a high school were to limit its Shakespeare to the study of only two plays, *Julius Caesar* and

Macbeth should continue to be, as they have been, the choices.

But if the school is to use four, what additional two have the best claims? Here the problem is harder.

One kind of argument is that since the first two plays are tragedies, the second pair should not be; they might be comedies or histories. And, to press the logic of this argument a little farther, since comedy is more truly than history the antithesis of tragedy, they should be comedies. We may not be convinced that schools need to keep a perfect balance of tragedy and comedy, or even that the issue is relevant at all; nevertheless, the suggestion offers one approach to our problem. For the moment, at least, we thus narrow the question: Which two comedies will be best when only two are to be taught?

Among comedies, the traditional favorites of the schools, as shown by the anthologies and otherwise, have been *A Midsummer Night's Dream* and *As You Like It*. As with the two tragedies that are the traditional leaders, we shall have poor luck if we attempt to unseat these favorites on any reasonable grounds. Both are undeniable masterpieces, as their history in criticism, on the stage, and in the schools makes apparent. Further, both are relatively open and readable, and so far as "objectionable" elements are concerned, they are, with *Julius Caesar* and *Macbeth*, among the purest of all Shakespeare's plays. Further, they are not dull. Both have hilarious moments, and both move along proven, basically popular lines of action as their heroes and heroines seek to overcome the age-old obstacles that prevent the course of true love from running smooth—parents, rivals, shyness, misunderstandings, passing quarrels. Their essential materials are the unbeatable trio of youth, love, and beauty, and the pattern they weave is the perennial pattern of life and love that is ever old, ever new.

Exactly the same, it must be confessed, may be said of other comedies remaining on our list. Little may therefore be said in justification of our decision to sustain the traditional choices of *A Midsummer Night's Dream* and *As You Like It* as the two that make up the "first" four, except that whereas various sorts of arguments, strong or weak, can be brought against the remaining comedies, these two are unassailable.

We move next to consideration of a second set of four plays.

There is no need to regard these as second-best; in a school where eight plays are studied, they are simply added to the others to make up the total. In a school in which only four plays are to be studied, all four would make acceptable alternates for the list of four already named; or any one, two or three of these could stand in place of any others on the first list. Shakespeare is not so short on great plays as to make apologies necessary for any play in a second group of four.

Relying this time also, as far as possible, on a long tradition of use in high school classes, we come easily to the following plays: *The Merchant of Venice, Romeo and Juliet, Twelfth Night,* and *Hamlet.* Why are these a "second set" rather than a "first"? Are they artistically inferior? No. Do they have less appeal? No. It can be argued that they have the potentiality of more appeal. Are there more things "wrong" to count against them? It is natural to suppose that, since these four are in fact less frequently studied in high schools than those on the first list, they must contain some sorts of elements, aside from artistic merits, that have made them only runners-up. And, truly, these are not hard, either to identify positively or, at worst, to conjecture. Let us consider the facts simply as facts, without argument.

The Merchant of Venice raises an issue of Christians and Jews, and to many individuals of both faiths the very fact that it does so makes the appropriateness of the play in public classrooms questionable. Areas of the United States differ, and communities within broad areas also differ. In certain communities teachers have found use of this play unthinkable; in others teachers have taught it closely and have reported no offense to sensitivities. (More on this play and the issue it raises will be found in Chapter 11.)

Romeo and Juliet includes many passages of highly fanciful, highly elaborated figures of speech, or "literary conceits," which are indeed remote from the language of "real life." Shakespeare liked to play with words and ideas, especially in this period. These have been sufficient to discourage many teachers who either know or fear that realistic modern adolescents will reject the whole work because of its "sappy poetry." In addition, particularly from the mouths of Mercutio and the Nurse, the play abounds in images of a grosser sort and in *double entendres* which cannot be fully explained without the risk of some in-delicacy and consequent embarrassment. (This play is dealt with in detail in Chapter 10.)

Twelfth Night is complex and often subtle, with many strands of action intricately interwoven to form peculiarly rich artistic patterns. Though it contains much that is obviously funny—the antics of the drunken Sir Toby Belch and the foolish Sir Andrew Aguecheek, the absurd ambitions of Malvolio, "sick with self-love"—it also includes scenes which, for their finest effects, demand a degree of sophistication in the reader. It is, in short, a much "harder" play than, say, *As You Like It*. (For a detailed discussion of *Twelfth Night*, see Chapter 11.)

Hamlet is one of Shakespeare's longest plays, and thus it con-trasts sharply with its chief competitor, *Macbeth*, which is Shake-speare's shortest tragedy. *Hamlet* is also bottomless; the possible interpretations even of its most important aspects are, it appears, various virtually to infinity. Because of its length, its complexity, and the continuing lack of agreement on a "right" interpretation, *Hamlet* presents a more formidable teaching and reading task than *Macbeth*. (Of *Hamlet*, too, more is to be said in Chapter 10.)

We could conveniently stop at this point, for it is very clear that few high schools in the United States can be expected to find time and place for the study of more than eight of Shakespeare's plays. Nevertheless, we succeeded earlier in paring Shakespeare's total of thirty-seven down to only fourteen—of which we have six remaining to be dealt with in some fashion. We can hardly dis-miss them now, without some comment. But this time let us go by twos rather than fours.

Of *Henry IV, Part 1, Henry V, King Lear, The Tempest, The Taming of the Shrew,* and *The Winter's Tale,* which two have strongest claim to take precedence over the others? We can narrow the field somewhat by deciding an easier question first: which two should have least claim? Of all the fourteen plays that we have named as acceptable, undoubtedly, the "slightest" pair are *The Taming of the Shrew* and *The Winter's Tale.* But that these two plays deserve a place among the acceptable four-teen there seems little cause to doubt.

The Taming of the Shrew, a fine acting play, is among the

plays that are relatively easy to read, and *The Winter's Tale* is certainly the least difficult one of Shakespeare's last plays, the "dramatic romances." Further, each has its moments of high excellence: in the former, virtually the whole of the action that involves Petruchio and Kate is highly entertaining; in the latter, the scene of the shepherds' feast (Act IV, Scene 4), with its fairy-tale prince and princess and the songs of Autolycus, is a little masterpiece.

Thus the former offers, at its best, uproarious fun, and the latter, at its best, a haunting charm. But at the same time that they assuredly deserve a place among the fourteen, these plays also seem to have best claim to the last places among the fourteen. Both lack much of the rich abundance of the other plays, and each is, in its own way, a less satisfying "whole" than is any one of the others. (More about *The Taming of the Shrew* and about *The Winter's Tale* can be found in Chapter 11.)

In deciding which of the two remaining pairs of plays should have priority, we shall find it necessary for the first time in all our selections, to part company with the tradition of actual use in the schools. Both *The Tempest* and *King Lear* are far more often taught in the schools than are *Henry IV* and *Henry V*. In reversing the traditional judgment, and insisting, as we do, that the two history plays should have priority, we should make clear that our decision has nothing to do with comparative excellence; we should indeed be foolish to attempt a distinction on that basis. At the high level of excellence with which we are here dealing, individual readers of the plays must make their own choices of "best" and "next best." How, then, can we decide that one pair is to have priority?

Perhaps the best answer is simply this: that readers should ideally "take on" *King Lear* and *The Tempest* only after they have read a very considerable amount—as much as possible—of Shakespeare. It has been remarked that no one is really ready to undertake *The Tempest* until he has read *all* of Shakespeare up to that final work.

As for *King Lear*, it is, like *Antony and Cleopatra*, gigantic in scope, almost too big to "take in." It has often been argued that *King Lear* is particularly ill-suited to high school study because its central experience is an experience of parentage and old age, with which adolescents are insufficiently mature to sympathize—they cannot "identify" with old Lear in the sufferings of mind and spirit that result from his conflict with his unkind daughters. This argument, surely, is nonsense; there is no more need for us to be old in order to sympathize with Lear, to enter deeply into his experience, than there is need for us to be a horse in order to sympathize with Black Beauty. The problem is of an entirely different kind. It is simply that we need as much experience as we can get in reading Shakespeare before we tackle a work of such immensity. *Lear* and *The Tempest* are not plays to begin with or to place early in the order of reading; to come to these plays after ten others have been studied is to come to them soon enough. (More is to be said of both plays in Chapter 11.)

On approximately the same grounds, strong argument might be made for putting *Henry IV, Part 1* and *Henry V* ahead even of certain plays that we have included among the first eight. It is unlikely that either of these is as demanding as, in particular, *Twelfth Night* or *Hamlet*. Probably the neglect that they have suffered in the schools stems from the simple fact that they are classified as histories rather than tragedies or comedies, both of which genres sound more inviting.

But the marvel of these two plays, the greatest of Shakespeare's ten histories, is that they so admirably blend elements of history, comedy, and, if not tragedy, intense drama. Between them, they contain no fewer than a dozen first-rate character studies of extraordinary fullness, clarity, and interest, and each of them includes as great an accumulation of richly comic figures as does any other single play of Shakespeare's. Further, among these comic figures is one who looms larger in the full roster of Shakespearean comic characters than does any other; that any student should go through school, and perhaps through life, without coming to know Sir John Falstaff seems hardly less intolerable than that anyone should go through life without meeting Hamlet. It is, indeed, tempting to assert that it would be better to miss both than to miss either, for each is the necessary complement, in a full experience, of the other.

The language of both plays, both prose and verse, is uncommonly robust and vigorous, neither "pretty," as is often the case in Shakespeare's early plays, nor knotty and condensed, as is often the case in the late plays. And, finally, the two plays include that which should make them peculiarly attractive to students of high school age—the story that they tell of a boy growing up to be a man, of a prince growing up to be a king, of the wild and un- promising Hal turning into the ideal hero-king of Shakespeare's imagination, Henry V; the story of this transformation contains the same element of basic human appeal as the story of the Ugly Duckling that became the gorgeous white swan. (Of both these plays, more is to be said in Chapter 10.)

We have now reasoned our way, as honestly as we could, to a list of fourteen plays. But we have as yet said nothing of place- ment, with respect to grades nine, ten, eleven, and twelve; in fact, in our single-minded pursuit of the "best possible" choices, we have deliberately excluded the added complication that the problem of placement introduces. We are now obliged, therefore, to deal with this problem, for which reasonable solutions are just as necessary as the solutions to the initial problem of selection.

2. IN WHICH YEARS?

Though we have claimed that any of our fourteen plays will make a reasonable choice, we must hastily deny that one will make as reasonable a choice as another for any given year. In the brief characterizations that we have given individual plays in the course of identifying the best choices, enough has been said to make it clear that these fourteen are by no means all alike in the demands they make on students and teacher. A few are relatively open and may confidently be described as the least difficult to read and understand; a few others, at the opposite pole, can as readily be described as the most difficult. But in between these obvious extremes stand a larger number of plays the difficulty of which, in relation to one another, is something on which it is difficult to agree.

One play, let us say, is especially notable for its complexity of plot, or plots, with several lines of action going forward alter- nately, touching and influencing one another at certain points, and finally converging; yet this same play is presented in language that is comparatively open, its characterizations are accomplished fairly directly, it has no bottomless depths of meaning to fathom in which interpretation falters.

Another play, let us say, is relatively uncomplicated in plot structure, having a single main line of action; but its language is less open, its characterizations subtle, its meanings peculiarly deep, its possible interpretations limitless. Let us now say that, in broad terms, these descriptions apply respectively to *Twelfth Night* and *Hamlet*. Which is the more "difficult" play? Or, when the differences in *kinds* of difficulty are averaged out, is one about as difficult as the other?

We shall certainly do best to begin by making a general division that requires least precision in specifying degrees of difficulty. At it happens, the fourteen plays of our list fall into two equal groups of those tending to be less and those tending to be more difficult. Listed in approximately chronological order, without reference to degrees of difficulty, the two groups are as follows:

LESS DIFFICULT	MORE DIFFICULT
The Taming of the Shrew	*Henry IV, Part 1*
A Midsummer Night's Dream	*Henry V*
Romeo and Juliet	*Twelfth Night*
The Merchant of Venice	*Hamlet*
As You Like It	*King Lear*
Julius Caesar	*The Winter's Tale*
Macbeth	*The Tempest*

If we attempt to grade the plays of either list in their precise order of difficulty, we immediately get into hopeless problems. It will be safer, and probably just as useful, to attempt certain generalizations about the two groups and to offer certain more specific remarks on particular plays.

It is noteworthy, first, that these two groups, with the exception of a single play in each, are respectively from the first and second halves of Shakespeare's dramatic career. The dividing line is approximately 1599–1600. In the first group, all the plays except *Macbeth* come before this date, and in the second group all but *Henry IV* follow it. This is to say, then, that *in general* the plays of the first half of Shakespeare's career tend to be less demanding than those of the second half. This generalization, however, needs a few words of clarification and of qualification.

If the plays of the first half are indeed somewhat less demanding, they are so not because of their poetic language but because of their comparatively less weighty "matter." The fact is that the language in the early plays often tends to get in the way of the matter. In this period of Shakespeare's career, his characters like to play with ideas—to draw them out at length by means of elaborative imagery. They note and comment on subtle distinctions, become entranced with fanciful embroideries on the periphery of the central thought. The indispensable gist of the communication must, then, be sought amidst a tangle of finery; the unwary reader may lose the core entirely, or mistake a peripheral refinement for the center. Many characters in the early plays exhibit the kind of flaw that Lorenzo observes in Gratiano in *The Merchant of Venice*: "Gratiano speaks an infinite deal of nothing, more than any man in all Venice. His reasons are as two grains of wheat hid in two bushels of chaff: you shall seek all day ere you find them, and when you have them they are not worth the search."

On the other hand, what saves the early works from being intolerably difficult, because of their excessive verbal play, is that their matter tends to be less weighty than that in later plays. They have fewer characters of depth and complexity; they have less solid meat that needs time for chewing and digesting.

The plays of the middle group, generally speaking, have their essential ideas less obscured by elaborate language, and in that respect they are less difficult than the early plays. Nevertheless, they tend to be more demanding because of their greater meaning. The great passages of the middle plays are filled with substance that requires deep and careful thought. The great human portraits that abound in the middle plays approximate the complexity and subtlety that "real" human beings have.

Finally, the later and last plays tend to be the most difficult of all because in them great matter is compressed within tight capsules that must be unlocked and probed. Here ideas are more often suggested, or touched with a glancing blow, rather than expressed in explicit statements. In them the great lines always hold "infinite riches in a little room"—in too little room.

From this general review of the facts, we may now move up for a closer look at individual plays, with the purpose of suggesting reasonably accurate placements in a four-year program.

The possible combinations of these plays in a program are too numerous for all to be represenfed here. Rather, we shall aim to describe a limited number of combinations in such a way as to make clear to teachers who choose any one of them just what it is that they are getting.

To begin with, one principle seems obvious: that in normal circumstances, any plays chosen for grades nine and ten should come from the list of seven "less difficult" plays. But does the converse also hold true—that plays chosen for grades eleven and twelve should come from the list of seven "more difficult" plays? No, it certainly does not. Does this principle mean, then, that students should read *all* of the plays on the first list before they undertake any on the second list? No, it does not quite mean that either—though it would unquestionably be wise to have read all of them before undertaking certain plays on the second list, notably, *King Lear* and *The Tempest*. To read only, say, *Julius Caesar* and *The Taming of the Shrew* in grades nine and ten, and then to jump directly to these plays in grades eleven and twelve would be sheer folly.

Earlier in the present chapter, we fixed upon certain groups of plays—a "first four," a "second four," and six remaining plays in pairs. If we now return to those lists, we should find them useful in identifying several placement combinations. Our "first four," it can now be noted, are all from the list of seven plays that we have designated "less difficult": *A Midsummer Night's Dream*, *As You Like It*, *Julius Caesar*, and *Macbeth*. One reasonable arrangement of these plays, for a class that is to read only the four in four years, is as follows:

Grade 9   *A Midsummer Night's Dream*
Grade 10   *Julius Caesar*
Grade 11   *As You Like It*
Grade 12   *Macbeth*

This is a kind of basic, "best-bet" arrangement. It might be made a little easier by dropping *Macbeth*, moving each of the other plays up one year, and starting with *The Taming of the Shrew* in the ninth grade, or by dropping *Macbeth* and inserting *The Merchant of Venice* at some point. It might be made somewhat harder by omitting *As You Like It* and substituting *Romeo and Juliet*.

Let us now suppose that a class is to read eight plays in four years. One reasonable arrangement, adding our "second four" list, would be as follows:

Grade 9   *A Midsummer Night's Dream, The Merchant of Venice*
Grade 10   *As You Like It, Julius Caesar*
Grade 11   *Romeo and Juliet, Macbeth*
Grade 12   *Twelfth Night, Hamlet*

Here it will be noted that we have added two plays from the "more difficult" list. We might again make the list a little easier by inserting *The Taming of the Shrew* at some early point and omitting one of the later plays. But the possible jugglings here are very numerous. There is no good reason why *Julius Caesar*, for example, might not be moved down one grade, and *The Merchant of Venice* up one grade. Similarly, *Romeo and Juliet* might go down one grade to be paired with *As You Like It*.

The basic principle by which we are proceeding should now have become apparent. It is simply this: that some classes can and should go farther in Shakespeare than others. Some, in four years, will get only to *Macbeth*—indeed, if they make use of only the "easiest" plays, they may read four or five and not even get to *Macbeth*. Others may be able to go beyond *Macbeth* to *Twelfth Night* and *Hamlet*, as our eight-play arrangement just presented shows. But a second principle should also be apparent. It is a negative principle, *that no class ought to jump abruptly from least difficult plays to more or most difficult ones,* just as it obviously should not start with more difficult ones and move backward to less difficult ones.

If, now, we consider the possibility of going beyond eight plays, one arrangement is as follows:

Grade 9   *A Midsummer Night's Dream, The Merchant of Venice, Julius Caesar*

Grade 10   *As You Like It, Romeo and Juliet, Macbeth*
Grade 11   *Twelfth Night, Henry IV, Part 1, and Henry* V
Grade 12   *Hamlet, King Lear, The Tempest*

Somewhat less juggling would seem reasonable in this order than might be supposed. One might, for example, interchange *The Merchant of Venice* and *As You Like It*; but because of the common love theme, one comic, the other tragic, it would appear less than desirable to separate *As You Like It* from *Romeo and Juliet*. Similar objections might be raised to other efforts to rearrange. For example, *Hamlet* might go to grade eleven, trading places with *Henry* V; but to make that trade would be to lose the distinct advantage of reading the two history plays in quick succession.

Finally, if a class were to undertake all the fourteen plays that we have named as reasonable choices, it should be a relatively simple matter to add *The Taming of the Shrew* to either the ninth or tenth grade program, whichever could better accommodate it, and to add *The Winter's Tale* in either of the upper grades.

For the moment omitting the two plays just mentioned, we should now take note of a possibly fallacy in our method of proceeding. We have been assuming that each year is to include an equal number of plays; thus, our first arrangement gave one play to each year, our second gave two, and our third gave three. But perhaps this balanced system will not be feasible everywhere; perhaps it will even be undesirable in some cases, and certainly it is not necessary. It is conceivable that the program of a particular school might find space for a single Shakespeare play in the ninth grade, and for as many as six in the twelfth grade. Indeed, it may well be argued that all six of the plays that we have distributed between grades eleven and twelve would go best in grade twelve alone.

A strong word of caution seems proper here. If our suggested orders for presenting the plays have any validity, it will follow that schools which omit Shakespeare entirely in any year, or schedule a single play, should take care, in the next year, to avoid "skipping over" the plays that have seemed to us appropriate at that level in order to "catch up." To take up, say, only *A Midsummer Night's Dream* in grade nine, only *As You Like It* in grade ten, to omit Shakespeare entirely in grade eleven, and then to light upon

King Lear and *The Tempest* in grade twelve would surely be, at least, ill-advised. The present is perhaps as appropriate as any time to comment, in passing, on the two grades in which Shakespeare is most frequently omitted in American high schools. These grades are the ninth and the eleventh. Although it is a fact that in increasing numbers schools are supplementing their basic anthologies with paperbacks of various titles, including paperback editions of individual Shakespeare plays, it is also a fact that in many high schools, teachers report that they are limited to the use of the basic anthologies only—and the widely used anthologies of literature typically include only two Shakespeare plays, *Julius Caesar* in the tenth-grade volume and *Macbeth* in the twelfth-grade volume.

The reason for the omission of Shakespeare from eleventh-grade volumes is a fact of long but not necessarily respectable standing, and one that can be accounted for only too easily: the eleventh-grade volume of a typical series is limited to American literature, and Shakespeare, unfortunately for high school juniors, was English. The most common, and obvious justification offered for giving the eleventh grade to American literature is that American History is taught in this year. That there is something to be said in defense of this point of view seems indisputable; that much can also be said against it is implied by the very determination with which many eleventh grade teachers manage to "smuggle in" a Shakespeare play in spite of the geographical limitations imposed by the anthology. The availability of paperback editions of Shakespeare now makes this smuggling comparatively easy to accomplish.

The omission of Shakespeare from the ninth-grade volume is a phenomenon of somewhat more recent origin, and the reasons for it are not nearly so clear. It should be pointed out, however, that older anthologies regularly included *Julius Caesar* in the volume for the ninth grade, whereas it is now equally regularly placed in the volume for the tenth grade. The removal of Shakespeare from ninth-grade volumes was approximately coincidental with the rise and general spread of junior high schools, which in turn occasioned the publication of anthologies in series for grades seven, eight, and nine; it was presumably in the major shifts here involved that *Julius Caesar* was up-graded to the tenth grade, leaving the ninth grade with no Shakespeare play.

Fortunately, the present availability of paperbacks now makes the anthologists' elimination of Shakespeare from two high school grades—half of the student's high school career—a deficiency that can easily be remedied by teachers whose aims include a graduated and more substantial experience of the plays in their four-year programs.

3. FOR WHICH STUDENTS?

In Chapter 1, something was said and much more implied about the question of which students Shakespeare is "suitable for." Further discussion of this question will also be found in the following chapters that consider methods of presenting the plays in the classroom. Here, therefore, our purpose is only to suggest what advantages may be taken of the flexibility that is allowed within the frame of our arrangement of the fourteen plays. The possible combinations of these plays are many and should prove easily sufficient to accommodate virtually all levels of maturity and reading ability found in any high school.

It should be reasserted here that one essentially uncomplicated conviction is basic to all the arguments of this book: namely, that as much Shakespeare should be taught to *all* high schools students as time, means, and their own potentialities will allow. It is not at all unlikely that certain classes in some high schools, over a four-year period, will actually study all of the fourteen plays; others will study twelve, eight, four; and yet others will study, two, or one. The list that we have drawn up is most easily adaptable to classes that will read many plays in four years—indeed, for those that read all fourteen, it needs no adaptation at all. But what of the classes that read only a few?

For purposes of illustration, let us suppose that we are selecting and arranging the plays for a large high school which has worked out an elaborate system of English "tracks." At one extreme we have a class at each grade level for the most gifted; at the other extreme we have a class at each grade level for the truly least able students in the school; and in between these extremes, let us suppose—as long as we are being purely hypothetical—that we have not merely two or three, but four or six tracks on which will proceed students who have been placed according to subtle shades of difference in their capabilities. We waive, for present purposes, both the objection that there simply are no high schools with such elaborately tracked systems in operation and the objection that even if there were such systems in operation there should not be. Here we mean only to illustrate a principle.

In such a system, the uppermost track can surely be allowed to read all of our fourteen plays on schedule, using in each year all those we have listed for that grade. It is conceivable that the next track below this, which also includes students who are definitely superior, though not as distinctly gifted, will also, on schedule, read all fourteen plays. The next track, a little lower, will manage, in its four years, to go through, let us say, twelve of the plays; perhaps it will reach to all but *King Lear* and *The Tempest*. And so on down through other tracks, all of which have one element in common, namely, that each ninth-grade class begins on schedule with plays suggested as suitable for the ninth grade, but differing thereafter in the distance they travel, some getting as far as *Hamlet* in the twelfth grade, some only to *Macbeth*, and so on.

But now what of the several tracks that run below these—all of which have in common the fact that students on these levels are not found to be ready, as ninth graders, to undertake any Shakespeare at all? But let us suppose that the most capable class on these lower tracks is found ready, on reaching the tenth grade, to tackle its first Shakespeare play. With which play should this class start? With one of the plays that we have suggested for the tenth grade? No, presumably they will do better to start with a play that classes on higher tracks read in the ninth grade. And what Shakespeare play should this class have in the eleventh grade? The class might study a play chosen from those suggested for the tenth grade, or, if even that seems too formidable, may read a second play of those suggested for the ninth grade. And what should these students do when they reach the twelfth grade? If they have progressed considerably, they may take a play suggested for the eleventh grade; if they have progressed only a little, a play suggested for the tenth grade; if not at all, or very slightly, they may do best, even in the twelfth grade, to use the remaining play that we have suggested for the ninth grade. Thus, to make a final illustration in the case of this particular class, its program might follow any of these three schedules:

PLAN 1

Grade 9   No play
Grade 10   A *Midsummer Night's Dream*
Grade 11   *As You Like It*
Grade 12   *Romeo and Juliet*

PLAN 2

Grade 9   No play
Grade 10   A *Midsummer Night's Dream*
Grade 11   *The Merchant of Venice*
Grade 12   *As You Like It*

PLAN 3

Grade 9   No play
Grade 10   A *Midsummer Night's Dream*
Grade 11   *The Merchant of Venice*
Grade 12   *Julius Caesar*

Thus, by Plan 1, the class would end by reading an eleventh-grade play in the twelfth grade; by Plan 2, a tenth-grade play; and by Plan 3, a ninth-grade play.

If we now go one step farther, we can imagine a class which is not prepared for any Shakespeare in either the ninth or the tenth grade, but is found ready in the eleventh. By our principle, that class would then begin with one of the ninth-grade plays in the eleventh grade and would move to one of the tenth-grade plays in the twelfth grade—or, indeed a second ninth-grade play in the twelfth grade. And we may, finally, go one step farther to suppose that a class exists which cannot be found ready for any Shakespeare until the twelfth grade. By our principle it would then read one of the ninth-grade plays. Most readers of this book, it is hoped, will find it unimaginable that *any* high school class will finish the twelfth grade without ever being found ready to read even a single Shakespeare play. From the point of view of this book, a single ninth-grade play, taught in the twelfth grade, represents the irreducible minimum of Shakespeare that should be given to any high school class, no matter what "track" it is on, during its four years.

A few final remarks may be useful here, in order to summarize what has been suggested and to qualify, or even correct, certain points that, because they were made only to illustrate a principle, without regard to other considerations, will appear to contradict a point made earlier, in Part 2 of this chapter. It was there suggested that a class which could not or did not read *all* of the plays listed as especially suitable for the ninth grade might do well, in the tenth grade, to read the remaining ninth-grade play or plays before proceeding with the tenth-grade plays, and that this principle should follow through to the twelfth grade. To take an extreme illustration of this principle, a certain class, reading at the rate of a single play each year, might end its career in the twelfth grade with *As You Like It*—the first play listed for the tenth grade —having used the three earlier years to complete the three plays listed for the ninth grade. This principle is in apparent contradiction, in particular, of Plan 1 suggested previously, in which a class that began late is shown as moving up to a "harder" Shakespeare play each year. But Plan 1 is intended as only one possibility —and not necessarily the best one; it will be noted that Plan 3 accords completely with the principle earlier recommended as reasonable.

It should be noted that the foregoing discussion is an attempt not only to suggest how a variety of widely differing classes may be accommodated, but to accommodate also two fundamentally opposed points of view, each of which appears to have some merit. The first point of view is that a class ought to move up to a "harder" Shakespeare play each year; this point of view is illustrated by Plan 1, and would also be illustrated by the progress of a typical class that takes a ninth-grade play in the ninth grade, a tenth-grade play in the tenth grade, and so on up, even though it moves at the rate of a single play each year.

The second point of view has been implied by the suggestion that a given class should first finish all the listed ninth-grade plays, whether in a single year or in three years, before moving up to any play listed for the tenth grade; very simply stated, this point of view is that there is not *necessarily* any merit in moving on to a "harder" play, for a "harder" play of Shakespeare's is not necessarily a "better" play. We have scrupulously avoided comparing the merits of the plays included on our final list. What is involved in that list is only relative *difficulty*—and no claims of exactness, but only of generality, are made even for that. We suggest, thus, that *Romeo and Juliet* is a tenth-grade play because it is more difficult than *Julius Caesar*, not because it is better, and *The Tempest* is listed for the twelfth grade not because it is better than *A Midsummer Night's Dream*, which is listed for the ninth, but purely because it is more difficult. In short, if teachers feel obliged to have a class move up on our list from year to year, they should not do so under the illusion that they are necessarily getting to better plays in this way. They should do so, rather, if they believe that there is a special value in following a line of generally increasing difficulty.

It is not our task just now to declare that one of these points of view is right and the other wrong; it has already been suggested that both views have merit. Nevertheless, an earlier statement of principle may well be reasserted here, namely, that for any given class it would seem reasonable and desirable to start with the ninth-grade plays and go as far as it can by the end of the twelfth grade. If it gets only as far as *As You Like It*, very well; if it gets as far as *Twelfth Night*, so much the better; if it gets as far as *The Tempest*, and has even managed to tuck *The Taming of the Shrew* and *The Winter's Tale* into the schedule at appropriate times, it will have made itself a very literate class indeed. On the other hand, if a particular class has not even been able to start its Shakespeare until the twelfth grade, reading the first ninth-grade play in that year and getting no farther, it can at the least be assured that that play is not *inferior* to the final play it would read if it had managed to get through all fourteen in four years instead of only one. No apologies for teaching *A Midsummer Night's Dream* to seniors are ever in order. It is as worthy of their attention as *King Lear* is.

CHAPTER 3

What of the Edition and the Teacher?

1. WHAT KIND OF EDITION IS BEST?

DURING THE SEVENTEENTH, EIGHTEENTH, AND NINETEENTH centuries, the publication of each successive new *Complete Works of William Shakespeare* was an event of literary history.

The First Folio of 1623 will always remain the most important, indeed the only truly indispensable edition, since except for it we would simply be without eighteen of the plays that we have, including such monumental ones as *Julius Caesar, As You Like It, Twelfth Night, Macbeth, Antony and Cleopatra,* and *The Tempest.* Furthermore, most of the plays that we would have even if there had been no First Folio, but only quartos, would survive as inferior texts, some incomplete, some garbled, all inaccurate.

Editions of *The Complete Works* represent landmarks of laborious scholarly activity throughout the 18th century. In quick succession came the editions of Rowe (1709), Pope (1725), Theobald (1733), Hanmer (1744), Warburton (1747), Dr. Johnson (1765), Capell (1767), and Malone (1790). Sets of these impressive scholarly editions survive in major libraries throughout the world, and in private collections.

These editions do not really offer Shakespeare very attractively to the general modern reader. Filled with textual notes that tell countless stories of scholarly quarrels over both significant and relatively insignificant issues of text and interpretation, all have a forbidding look. They are often wrong-headed, intolerably garrulous, unbecomingly barbed with uncharitable comments of one

31

scholar upon another. But in the aggregate these editions, too, are indispensable, for out of their battles emerged the possibility of the great modern editions that are authoritative, complete, pleasantly readable—and that we take for granted.

The nineteenth century began inauspiciously with Bowdler's bowdlerized "Family Shakespeare" in four volumes (1807). But Collier (1842), Hudson (1851), and Clark (1863) progressed with ever increasing enlightenment, thanks to the labors of the eighteenth century, toward the establishment of a "definitive text." Though that "definitive text" has not yet appeared, and probably never will appear, the famed "Globe Edition" (1864), in one volume, based on Clark's edition of 1863, achieved a standard by which subsequent variations are conveniently measured. From the readings of this text, the many modern editions deviate in numerous but, in the last analysis, relatively minor details. This is not to say that the old scholarly wars have ceased. Every play has at least a textual crux or two, and certain plays have many trouble spots round which scholarly controversies either rage continually or flare up at intervals. Did Hamlet wish that his too, too "solid" or his too, too "sullied" flesh would melt? Did the elder Hamlet smite the "sledded Polacks" on the ice, or did he smite the "sleaded (leaded) pole-ax" on the ice? Is a line gone from the third speech of *Measure for Measure*—and if so what did it say? Did Juliet wish that "runaway," "runaway's," or "runaways'" eyes would wink—and what did she mean in any case?

Greater problems than these remain in the modern text, it is true; but it is also true that major modern editions of Shakespeare are generally trustworthy, authoritative, well-considered, and essentially alike in the details of text. Any reader or teacher can choose from among such editions with confidence, knowing that whichever edition he decides to choose will be approximately as "right" textually as any of the others.

The task of choosing an edition of a Shakespeare play for use in a high school English class is, however, a very special one, fraught with greater perils than that which confronts the general reader choosing for his own use or the college teacher choosing for his lecture course, his senior section, or his seminar.

It is a complex and difficult task, first of all, because of the very profusion of available editions. The time has been that "availability" was a problem in only one sense, that of severe limitation: one took what one could get, or what one's school° already had, and perhaps had had for a generation. The present problem of availability is just the opposite: availability now is without limit. Shakespeare now comes in single-volume editions of the *Complete Works*; in three volumes of comedies, histories, and tragedies; in four, eight, ten or twelve volumes; with one, two, three, six, eight, twelve, or twenty-three plays to the volume; as *Major Plays*, *Principal Plays*, or *Representative Plays*. Shakespeare, in short, is available now as never before in history—in single volumes and in series, in hard covers and paperbacks, with elaborate scholarly and critical apparatus or with little more than the bare text, in a great range of bright colors and at whatever price one may wish to pay.

Confronted by this superabundance, what is the high school teacher to do who, next September, wishes to teach *Macbeth*, or *Julius Caesar*, or *Hamlet*, or *As You Like It*, or any one, two, or more of the fourteen plays that may be considered as eminently suitable choices? The selection of edition is second only in importance to the selection of play; it is unfortunately possible to go just as wrong in choosing the one as in choosing the other.

Rather than attempt to survey the range of possibilities volume by volume and edition by edition—an undertaking that is obviously unfeasible here—we should approach the problem not by identifying all the available editions, but by classifying the available kinds of editions within a few large divisions. (We will exclude one-volume editions of the *Complete Works*, which are expensive and, of course, include many more plays than would be used in high school.) The following, then, appear to represent the possibilities:

1. College or "general reader's" editions (individual volumes).
2. Editions included in high school anthologies of literature.
3. "Adapted" editions for school use.
4. Non-anthologized, non-adapted school editions.

Let us consider these in order.

1. *The college or "general reader's" editions.* The college or general reader's edition will probably make either the best or the

second-best choice, depending on the class and the teacher's personal preference. The advantages of this kind of edition are definite and significant, and in enumerating these advantages we shall come close to saying all that we think a teacher should look for in choosing a Shakespeare text for classroom study.

First, the text can be counted on to be complete and accurate —the one *sine qua non* of any Shakespearean edition.

Second, the scholarly-critical apparatus of introduction, notes, etc., will be authoritative.

Third, the volume will feature the text itself and will not be cluttered with illustrations, added stage directions, gratuitous descriptions of settings, summaries of action, or lists of "suggested activities."

Fourth, the format will be attractive, the volume neat, pleasant to hold, agreeable to read from. (It is supposed, of course, that the teacher will take advantage of the best, in these respects, that is presently available in "series" volumes, whether paperback or hard-covers.)

Besides being generally sound and attractive, each of these editions has its special virtues, its special points of emphasis, which teachers should note and consider. Thus, for example, the Pelican edition features inconspicuous act and scene divisions, placed in the margin rather than at the top, with the intention that the experience of reading should be more like that of seeing the action flow without interruption, as on the Elizabethan stage. The new Signet edition reprints the full source, or salient parts of it, and includes generous samplings of representative criticism from the eighteenth century to the present. The Laurel edition features the Sisson text, which represents a studious effort to restore the Folio or quarto reading, wherever possible, in preference to emendations supplied by three centuries of editors. The Folger edition prints text on one page, with all notes on the facing page. The Kittredge series, which is incomplete but includes all the plays that are likely to be used in high school, is famous for its elaborate, erudite footnotes and textual interpretations. The New Arden series, which is nearly complete at this writing, attempts to do just about everything that can be done in a fully scholarly edition of Shakespeare. (Unfortunately, the volumes may be found too expensive for general classroom use, but they are indispensable for the serious teacher.)

Considered individually or considered as a group, all these editions have great merit. Is there anything, then, that can reasonably be argued against this general kind of edition of which some outstanding examples have been cited and of which all meet the one indispensable requirement, that of offering a full and authoritatively edited text?

Two contrasting kinds of dissatisfaction with these editions have been expressed by some experienced teachers: (1) on the one hand, dissatisfaction with their emphasis on "scholar's matters" in introduction and textual notes; (2) on the other hand, dissatisfaction with the lack of "teaching aids" of various sorts. (But it is fair to point out here that whereas some teachers deplore these editions on the grounds of both 1 and 2, other teachers applaud them on the same grounds; further, some teachers applaud them for 1 but deplore them for 2, and yet others applaud them for 2 but deplore them for 1. There is clearly no unanimity of opinion.) Let us consider the two points in order.

That these college editions do include, in widely varying amounts, "scholar's matters" of many kinds is, of course, a fact. The editor of a college text of Shakespeare is directly obligated to demonstrate his scholarly respectability, and with this fact there can surely be no serious quarrel. Perhaps the danger, if there is one, is that the teacher who chooses an edition that is overloaded with "scholar's matters" will allow them to define his emphasis —his approach, his presentation, even his purpose, with the result that, for the students, the study of Shakespeare becomes a process of acquiring "facts about" the work rather than experiencing the work itself. However, it should be asserted that the terms "scholar's matters" and "teaching materials" are not necessarily antithetical and mutually exclusive. In careful hands "scholar's matters" can become "teaching materials" of first importance. Wrongly used —i.e., as items of fact to be memorized and regurgitated on tests— they can surely be vicious.

The second source of dissatisfaction with the college editions, their lack of "teaching aids," will best be considered in connection with the various non-college editions, one characteristic of which is their great abundance of such materials. We may therefore postpone discussion of this matter.

2. *Editions included in high school anthologies.* These editions are usually unsatisfactory for two reasons: (1) a typical four-volume series includes only two plays by Shakespeare, *Julius Caesar* in the volume for the tenth grade and *Macbeth* in the volume for the twelfth grade; (2) even these two, which are among the "cleanest" and most open of all Shakespeare's plays, are regularly cut, sometimes slightly and sometimes heavily, and the texts show evidence of various kinds and degrees of editorial tampering.

In one of the most widely used of all anthologies, for example, the text of *Julius Caesar*, though labeled "complete," lacks four entire scenes (among them the scene of Cinna the Poet and his meeting with the Roman mob) and an enormous number of lines that have been removed singly, in pairs, or in passages of varying lengths up to sixteen lines. The reason for these cuttings is, without exception, inexplicable, and the damage done to the total play is, of course, disastrous.

Macbeth is never so viciously mutilated in typical anthology editions, but certain passages (for example, the Porter's disquisition on the effects of drink in Act II, Scene 3) are regularly omitted, and here and there individual lines are dropped.

Besides omissions, the texts of *Julius Caesar* and *Macbeth* that are included in the widely used anthologies are characterized by editorial additions in great number, often of considerable length, and of a great variety of kinds. Typically, these additions are inserted at the beginnings of acts and scenes, but often they occur also within the course of scenes and at the ends of scenes as well. They purport to "set the stage," describe the reactions of characters, comment on the action, specify stage business, interpret what has just happened or what is next to come, etc.—all as if Shakespeare himself had supplied the comments. A pair of examples taken from a single edition of *Julius Caesar* will at least represent their general character, if not their abundance. First, the opening of Act I, Scene 1:

> *It is early afternoon on February 15, 44 B.C., and beneath the clear Italian sky the lemon-colored buildings glint in the warm*

sunshine. An expectant mob of people have crowded the narrow streets and archways to celebrate two important events. The first is a grand military parade being held to commemorate Caesar's victory over the sons of Pompey in Spain, and the second is the annual feast of the Lupercal, an old Roman festival. While waiting for the parade, many of the crowd are putting wreaths on the statues of Roman heroes nearby. Suddenly, dramatically, two tribunes enter—Marullus and Flavius. When they see the common people putting garlands on a statue of Caesar, they scowl and begin to heckle the crowd.

—Adventures in Appreciation
Harcourt, Brace & World, 1963

Here is the opening of Act II, Scene 2:

It is early morning after the stormy night on which the conspirators met at Brutus' house. The heavens are still troubled, and Caesar's night, like Brutus', has been robbed of its rest.
Caesar's house is on the Palatine Hill overlooking the Forum. Heavy draperies, patterned floors of marble, statues on pedestals, and draped couches convey an atmosphere of magnificence. Tall candelabra shed a soft light.

Ibid., page 533

These examples, taken from a single anthology, typify the editorial additions not only of that one anthology but of most major anthologies available at the time of this writing.

Unlike the college editions, the editions included in high school anthologies are not overweighted with "scholar's matters," such as arguments over dating, tracing of source materials, comparison of good and bad quartos. Ordinarily, what they provide is a skeletal account of historical fact and traditional opinion, which in most cases appears adequate to set the play in its context of time and place.

Unlike the college editions, also, they supply student and teacher with an abundance of "teaching aids" in the form of study questions, questions for discussion, suggested activities, reviews of scenes and acts, names and addresses of film and record companies, etc. These materials vary widely in both quantity and quality from anthology to anthology, and so also do the opinions of teachers vary on their usefulness. Teachers who prefer to leave the reading of plays largely up to their students tend to like the inclusion of abundant study aids; those who prefer to work through scenes and acts directly with their students often like to devise their own questions, comments, and related activities as the class progresses and as occasion arises. The problems of supplying or using teaching materials are discussed in detail in following chapters on the presentation of Shakespeare in the classroom.

3. *"Adapted" editions for school use.* These volumes are commendable in one particular, namely, that the publishers present them honestly for what they are: adapted versions rather than straight Shakesperean texts. A sampling of these versions includes the following:

"*Julius Caesar.* In Modern English, Adapted from Shakespeare's Play." (Scott, Foresman and Company, 1957)

"Shakespeare's *Julius Caesar.* Adapted." (Globe Book Company, 1952)

"Shakespeare's *Julius Caesar, A Midsummer Night's Dream, Romeo and Juliet,* Modern Version." (Laidlaw Brothers, 1958)

To characterize the adapted versions for which those listed stand as fair representatives, it will be useful first to quote briefly from editors' explanations of what has been attempted. One of the fullest statements introduces Laidlaw Brothers' modern versions of *Julius Caesar, A Midsummer Night's Dream,* and *Romeo and Juliet.* Here follows a portion of "A Further Word of Explanation —intended especially for the teacher":

> This volume is not "just another *Julius Caesar.*" The editor has done boldly what has only been attempted before. Here is a modern version of the text in which the lines themselves have been altered—slightly, it is true, but definitely—and the stage directions have been creatively amplified to allow the drama as such to stand forth, unencumbered by footnotes and lengthy explanation. This is *a* Shakespeare the student can—and will— read!
>
> . . . The teacher may wish to know something more about

how this modern version differs from standard editions of Shakespeare. The easiest way to tell, of course, is to compare them line for line, a tedious undertaking. In all, there are about 1000 changes in *Julius Caesar* and a proportional number in the other two plays, perhaps two-thirds of these being changes in the dialogue and one-third in the stage directions.

. . . This edition has been prepared, not to debase Shakespeare, but to serve as a tool for the student's education. Through it *he will learn new words the natural way*. Words and word-senses and phrases that are strange to him are introduced when the *context* will make their meaning clear. Thus, after the "ides of March" has once been explained (in this case by altering a line in the dialogue), its meaning elsewhere will be clear. When a deer-hunting context has once been established by the word *stag*, then the strange word *hart* becomes meaningful (as naming the animal hunted) and the pun with *heart* is understood. (pp. 329–332)

Similar purpose is suggested by the editor of Scott, Foresman's "*Julius Caesar* in Modern English":

. . . (Shakespeare) wrote *Julius Caesar* and his other plays in the English of his own day—a language understood by the average man of that time. But ways of saying things change with the years. Today, as much as we admire his plays, we find his wording a little hard to understand. We can enjoy his plays more if we know ahead of time what they are about.

This book re-tells the play *Julius Caesar* in the English of today. Poetry has been changed to prose; five acts reduced to three; outdated words replaced by those in use today. With some scenes left out or regrouped, the play has been made easy to produce. . . .

Only four minor characters have been omitted. Some of the people in the play have been identified in new terms, however. The tribunes elected in Caesar's time to protect the rights and interests of the common people are called "officers of the law," since today their actions in Scene One would suggest policemen. Shakespeare's soothsayer is called a fortuneteller; the teacher of rhetoric, a schoolteacher. (pp. 5–6)

Space does not permit more than token representation of the treatment given Shakespeare in the adapted versions; yet some comparison is obviously necessary, and the most economical method will be to cite a few parallel readings in *Julius Caesar* that are especially famous. First, here is Shakespeare's version of Marullus' rebuke to the citizens in Act I, Scene 1:

> Wherefore rejoice? What conquest brings he home?
> What tributaries follow him to Rome,
> To grace in captive bonds his chariot wheels?
> You blocks, you stones, you worse than senseless things,
> O you hard hearts, you cruel men of Rome,
> Knew you not Pompey? Many a time and oft
> Have you climbed up to walls and battlements,
> To towers and windows, yea, to chimney tops,
> Your infants in your arms, and there have sat
> The livelong day, with patient expectation,
> To see great Pompey pass the streets of Rome.
> And when you saw his chariot but appear,
> Have you not made an universal shout,
> That Tiber trembled underneath her banks . . .

Here is the Globe Book Company's adaptation of this speech, with notable changes italicized:

> *Rejoice for what?* What conquest brings he home?
> What *conquered soldiers* follow him to Rome,
> To grace in captive chains his chariot wheels?
> You blocks, you stones, you worse than senseless things!
> O you hard hearts, you cruel men of Rome,
> Knew you not Pompey? Many a time, *I know*,
> *You have* climbed up to walls and battlements,
> To towers and windows, *yes*, to chimney tops,
> Your infants in your arms, and there have sat
> *Throughout the day*, with patient expectation
> To see great Pompey pass the streets of Rome;
> And when you saw his chariot appear,
> Have you not made *a* universal shout,
> That *shook the river Tiber in its banks?*

Next are two readings of Antony's oration to the citizens in Act III, Scene 2. First is Shakespeare's reading:

Friends, Romans, countrymen, lend me your ears;
I come to bury Caesar, not to praise him.
The evil that men do lives after them;
The good is oft interred with their bones;
So let it be with Caesar. The noble Brutus
Hath told you Caesar was ambitious:
If it were so, it was a grievous fault,
And grievously hath Caesar answer'd it.
Here, under leave of Brutus and the rest—
For Brutus is an honourable man;
So are they all, all honourable men—
Come I to speak in Caesar's funeral.
He was my friend, faithful and just to me:
But Brutus says he was ambitious;
And Brutus is an honourable man.
He hath brought many captives home to Rome,
Whose ransoms did the general coffers fill:
Did this in Caesar seem ambitious?
When that the poor have cried, Caesar hath wept:
Ambition should be made of sterner stuff:
Yet Brutus says he was ambitious;
And Brutus is an honourable man.
You all did see that on the Lupercal
I thrice presented him a kingly crown,
Which he did thrice refuse: was this ambition?
Yet Brutus says he was ambitious;
And, sure, he is an honourable man.

Here is the same passage in the Scott, Foresman   prose version
of the play, including editorial additions in the form of questions,
that typify such additions throughout this version. Since the
variations between the prose rendering and the original are extensive, no italics are used to mark them.

Friends, Romans, Countrymen, listen to me. I have come to
speak at Caesar's burial, not to praise him. The evil that men
do lives after them; the good is often buried with their bones.
Let it be so with Caesar. Brutus has told you Caesar was
ambitious. If it is true, it was a serious fault, and Caesar has

answered for it. Brutus is an honorable man. They are all honorable men. With their permission I speak to you.

(*Angry murmurs rise from the mob. The people do not want him to speak against Brutus. Antony quickly says something to win the people back.*)

Caesar was my friend, faithful and fair with me. But Brutus says he was ambitious, and Brutus is an honorable man.

What doubts does Antony raise in his listeners?

Caesar brought many prisoners home to Rome. Their ransoms filled our treasury. Was this ambitious? Caesar has wept for the poor. Ambition should be made of sterner stuff. Yet Brutus says he was ambitious, (*He speaks somewhat sarcastically.*) and Brutus is an honorable man.
You all saw me, a month ago, offer Caesar a crown. Three times he refused it. Was this ambition? Yet Brutus says he was ambitious; and, certainly, Brutus is an honorable man.

How do Antony's pauses and tears affect the crowd?

Next follow readings from Shakespeare's *Macbeth* and from the Scott, Foresman "modern" version; the passage is from Act V, Scene 5.

She should have died hereafter;
There would have been a time for such a word.
Tomorrow, and tomorrow, and tomorrow
Creeps in this petty pace from day to day
To the last syllable of recorded time,
And all our yesterdays have lighted fools
The way to dusty death. Out, out, brief candle!
Life's but a walking shadow, a poor player
That struts and frets his hour upon the stage
And then is heard no more; it is a tale
Told by an idiot, full of sound and fury,
Signifying nothing.

She should have died later on. There would have been a time
for such sad news. (*He sits down heavily at the table. A
candle throws his shadow on the wall behind him.*) Tomorrow and tomorrow and tomorrow creep on, day by day, to
the end of time. And all our yesterdays have shown fools
the way to dusty death. (*He looks at the candle.*) Out, out,
brief candle! (*He looks at his shadow.*) Life's nothing but a
shadow—a poor actor that struts and rages an hour upon the
stage, and then is heard no more. Life is a tale told by an
idiot, full of sound and fury, but meaning nothing! (*He
pinches the candle out.*)

In Laidlaw Brothers' volume of three plays in "modern" versions, changes are more sparing than in the other adapted versions.
Nevertheless, comparison of just two lines from this version with
the standard reading will show the gross transformation of Shakespeare that is wrought even by "minor" alteration. When Romeo
descends at the end of the second balcony scene (Act III, Scene
3), Juliet remarks that he looks pale, "As one dead in the bottom
of a tomb." Romeo replies:

> And trust me, love, in my eye so do you:
> Dry sorrow drinks our blood.

In Laidlaw's "modern" version, Romeo replies:

> And trust me, love, in my eye so do you.
> Thus sorrow drains our blood.

If the difference between "Dry sorrow drinks" and "Thus sorrow
drains" may figuratively stand for all that inevitably happens when
Shakespeare is "adapted," it may perhaps be taken also as a potent
argument on the side of the many teachers who insist that Shakespeare adapted is no longer Shakespeare. It is not to overstress the
case of these teachers to assert that one of the first reasons, if not
the very first reason, for teaching Shakespeare is that he so regularly writes lines like "Dry sorrow drinks" and so rarely writes lines
like "Thus sorrow drains." And if the very first reason for teaching
Shakespeare at all is rendered invalid by "adaptation"—indeed, if

Shakespeare "adapted" is no longer Shakespeare—then it follows that the claim of the "adaptations" to a place in a reading program is suspect and must be established on grounds that are independent of Shakespeare.

It is in any event debatable whether Shakespeare retold in any form has any unique merit. The point of view of the present book on the teaching of Shakespeare in the schools is precisely as follows. The teaching of Shakespeare does not mean the teaching of Shakespeare in any form or language but Shakespeare's own; it means the teaching of any standard modern text that is authoritatively derived from the original quarto and folio texts. If students cannot, with the close and steady direction of their teachers, read Shakespeare in this form, it is emphatically recommended that they not read "Shakespeare" in any form, but read instead other authors who can be read without adaptation. A good novel, for example, in the form in which it was originally written, is a better thing than a play "adapted" from Shakespeare by any such person as would be willing to adapt Shakespeare. The good novel is a legitimate literary work; *Macbeth* "adapted" is not.

It is therefore necessary to reject both the "adapted" editions and the versions contained in present widely used high school anthologies of literature as being inadequate and generally unsatisfactory. Reference is made to the fact that for nearly three hundred years the history of Shakespearean editing has been the record of scholarly attempts to establish an accurate and complete text of the plays, a text as close to what Shakespeare wrote as can be reasonably determined on the basis of the best and most relevant evidence. Though scholars have often disagreed with one another, and continue to disagree, their basic purpose has been the same: *to discover and preserve exactly the words that Shakespeare wrote*.

On the other hand, "adapters" and editors of high school anthologies have reversed this underlying principle: far from being devoted to the ideal of discovering and recording Shakespeare's precise words, they have often and too easily and deliberately discarded what were unquestionably Shakespeare's precise words in favor of their own words, or have simply omitted Shakespeare's words. They have made gross alterations and "minor" alterations, gross additions and "minor" additions, gross omissions and "minor" omissions. But from the point of view that directs the present book, *any* alteration of Shakespeare's wording must be accounted a gross alteration. Teachers and students alike have the right to assume that their school texts of Shakespeare are as accurate as modern knowledge can make them—a right that the teachers themselves are now asserting in increasing numbers.

4. *Non-anthologized, non-adapted school editions.* This final class includes a relatively small number of volumes, some of them now grown very old, that were edited primarily for school use but without any real violence being done to the standard text. They differ, in this all-important way, from the "adapted" versions just discussed. They differ from the versions included in major anthologies by being cut either not at all or only in certain words or lines which, to the editors' minds, posed real problems of propriety. And, finally, they differ from the "general" or college editions primarily by their inclusion of teaching aids in the form of questions for discussion, assignments for writing, etc.

As for "scholarly" materials such as source, date of composition, historical backgrounds, etc., some of the commonly used editions of this class do not differ significantly from the college editions; the emphasis of certain of their introductions clearly imitates that of the college editions.

Recent editions of this general class include the Macmillan Literary Heritage paperback series (1963), which includes two plays in each volume; an excellent *Macbeth* (1922, 1958) in Allyn and Bacon's Academy Classics; and equally excellent texts of *Macbeth* and *Julius Caesar* (1958) from Longmans, Green and Company (Swan Edition). These are examples only, but it is a fact that presently available school editions which include study and discussion questions and similar teaching aids and which at the same time have been edited with respect for the text of Shakespeare are, in comparison with the number of available college editions, exceedingly few.

Finally, to summarize this discussion of an important problem, the choice of edition for high school classes in which Shakespeare is to be studied more faithfully than heavily abbreviated or "adapted" texts allow is limited to two general classifications. First, the college or general editions are available in a wide range of format and price; all are authoritatively edited and most are tastefully attractive; the only objections to them, as expressed by some teachers, are that most or all emphasize "scholar's matters" and that none of them include the teaching aids that many teachers want. Second, the unadapted high school editions supply such aids abundantly, and thus, in the eyes of some teachers, have the advantage; but (except for the Macmillan paperback series) these are regularly "cut," even though only slightly: for example, both the Allyn and Bacon and the Longmans, Green editions of *Macbeth*, cited here for their general excellence, omit the Porter's disquisition on the effects of drink. It seems reasonable to suppose that the purposes of some teachers will be best served by one kind of edition and the purposes of others by another kind, and it is appropriate that teachers themselves choose according to these purposes.

2. WHAT KIND OF TEACHER?

It is conceivable that a brilliant English teacher may do a passable job of teaching a play of Shakespeare's though it is the only play she knows in detail from beginning to end. Each of the plays is, in an important sense, marvelously self-contained; even the interlocking history plays can be read as independent entities, for the dramatist has shrewdly built into opening scenes all the indispensable facts of what went before and has so wrought the closing scenes as to create an effect of finished action. Even, say, *Henry VI, Part 2*, could stand alone.

It is also a fact that many teachers who teach, say, no play but *Macbeth* year after year for twenty years find little leisure time to study or restudy any of the other thirty-six plays in all that time; and perhaps before they began to teach they had taken no more than a single college course in which only six or eight plays were examined, or in which a dozen plays were read rapidly.

We have all known exceptions, of course: teachers who are "hipped" on Shakespeare—who are, as it seems, always reading and rereading him; collecting new editions as they appear; taking additional Shakespeare courses, including seminars, during the summer or in night classes; never missing a chance to see Shakespeare on stage, screen, or television; accumulating a library of long-playing recordings, especially of the plays that are rarely seen on the stage; taking part in groups that meet to read the plays aloud, or actually inspiring and participating in local productions. But even though we grant that these welcome exceptions exist in numbers—and, contrary to what we might expect, the numbers appear to be increasing—the fact is that most of the Shakespeare that is being taught in high schools throughout the United States is being taught by teachers who are "getting along" on a recent acquaintance with only the play or plays they actually teach. It has already been stated that a superior teacher may do a passable job with no wider acquaintance, and, there is ample evidence that many superior teachers *do* just that. But not all teachers are "superior," and even so a "passable" job of teaching Shakespeare is less than high school students deserve.

Ideally, all English teachers who have occasion to teach Shakespeare would know all of the plays intimately—each play within itself, in its relationships with other plays of the Shakespeare canon, and in the contexts of its genre and the age. They would know Shakespeare's dramatic predecessors, his contemporaries, and his immediate successors, the frames of convention and tradition within which he worked and which he sometimes broke out of, the sources on which he drew, the facts of theater, acting, audience. They would be versed in Shakespeare criticism from Ben Jonson to L. C. Knights; in the history of text and the editorial problem from the quartos and the First Folio to Sisson and Hinman; in the theatrical histories of the plays in England and America.

This ideal is, of course, largely an unattainable goal with present-day English teachers. Practically, however, it is particularly desirable that a teacher know most of Shakespeare's plays, certainly twelve to fifteen of the major plays, well. For though, as has been stated, each play is a self-contained and independent work of art, each is also *a part of the whole that is Shakespeare.* All the plays came from one mind, and in a truly profound sense, while each play is an individual piece, all the plays are also "of a piece." Certain invaluable kinds of illumination of individual plays can best be drawn, or can be drawn only, from an acquaintance with the whole or most of the *corpus.* Basic ideas about man, time, the universe, sovereign and subject, life and death, good and evil recur again and again in the plays. Sometimes, in a given play, a basic idea is merely touched obliquely, as if full understanding were assumed and could be evoked by a passing allusion, whereas the full idea is adumbrated in another play.

Again, Shakespeare abounds with recurrent images, recurrent themes, recurrent rhetorical patterns; he has certain habits of dramatic technique that he indulges repeatedly; he uses essentially the same dramatic devices again and again to evoke laughter, excitement, a sense of foreboding. Rosalind's adventures in boy's garb in *As You Like It*, the circumstances of her undertaking the disguise, her special style of "carrying off" the male role can be made richer for students by a teacher who knows that the plots of the romantic comedies regularly turn upon the heroine's masquerade as a man and who can speak, when appropriate, of parallel incidents in the masquerades of Julia, Portia, and Viola; can contrast the motives of these heroines in their decision to don men's clothes, and can compare their "masculine" performances. Thus Rosalind's brilliant exuberance in playing the "saucy lackey" with Orlando can be best appreciated when set against the ultrafeminine Viola's difficulty and distress in man's role, just as the comic force of Viola's near failure is enhanced by being set against Rosalind's bold success. Through this kind of illumination comes a fuller realization of what fantastically great artistic achievements these two heroines represent.

Macbeth's self-debate before the murder of Duncan can be understood in terms of itself, within the context of the single protagonist and the single play; but the sense of it as a "point" in the course of a Shakespearean tragedy is enhanced by knowledge of the comparable moments in which Brutus, Hamlet, Othello, Lear, Antony, and Coriolanus subject *their* souls to private scrutiny.

To paraphrase a line from John Donne that Hemingway made famous, no play of Shakespeare's is an island. Though a ninth-grade student who reads well but has never read another play can take up *Julius Caesar* and in due time make his way through it unaided and gain a good general sense of "what happened," no teacher whose acquaintance with Shakespeare is limited to *Julius Caesar* and a few other plays perhaps read long ago can do more than a "passable" job of conducting a class through that play; and a passable job is not good enough.

These are harsh words, but they are justified by an even harsher fact: whenever a play like *Macbeth* or *Julius Caesar* has failed really to excite, stimulate, or even interest a class, or the majority of a class—and if we are honest we must agree that even these most nearly failure-proof plays have failed in the classroom more often than they have succeeded—the fault, at bottom, has been the teacher's insufficient acquaintance with Shakespeare. Occasionally, for unusual students, the force of these plays has come through in spite of the teacher's inadequacy; but the assumption of the present book is that Shakespeare is not for "unusual" students only.

The teacher's insufficient acquaintance with Shakespeare can lead, unfortunately, to worse things than merely the failure to illuminate certain lines and passages in one play by the light of other plays. It leads, for example, to methods of approach to and presentation of the play that can be described only as perverse, and virtually certain to give the play its slimmest chance of "getting to" students. Though faulty methods of approach and presentation unquestionably stem from other causes as well, there can be no serious doubt about the underlying cause: it is simply insufficient acquaintance with the plays.

Besides first-hand acquaintance with the plays, teachers need an acquaintance with a reasonably wide range of Shakespeare criticism. The most astute reader, reading for a lifetime unaided, will not become aware of all that is to be seen and thought about in these plays. No Shakespeare critic was ever so brilliant that he had no insights to gain from other critics; indeed, the most brilliant have been those who learned most from others and wisely used what they learned to amplify their own views. This is not to say that a critic's, teacher's, student's, or general reader's views of Shakespeare ought to be only a composite of other people's views and none of his own. What alone matters at last is how he himself sees the plays. But he will see much better if others—many others—have helped him to see.

The history of Shakespeare criticism is long, and the volume is enormous and daily increasing. For most people it is impossible to keep up, let alone catch up; hence it is necessary to be selective.

It is also presumptuous for anyone to dictate a brief list of "indispensable" critical works, for estimates of books about the plays vary almost as widely as do critical interpretations of the plays themselves. Nevertheless, a very short list comprising an "irreducible minimum" may not be totally lacking in usefulness. (An expanded, but also highly selective bibliography will be found on page 294.)

Bradley, A. C. *Shakespearean Tragedy*. London: Macmillan & Company, Ltd., 1904. (Also available in paperback.)

Charlton, H. B. *Shakespearean Comedy*. London: Methuen, 1938.

Charlton, H. B. *Shakespearean Tragedy*. New York and London: Cambridge University Press, 1948. (Also available in paperback.)

Clemen, Wolfgang H. *The Development of Shakespeare's Imagery*. Cambridge, Mass.: Harvard University Press, 1951.

Coleridge, Samuel Taylor. *Shakespearean Criticism*, ed. Thomas Middleton Raysor. New York: E. P. Dutton & Co., Inc., 1960; London: J. M. Dent & Sons, Ltd., 1961. 2 vols. (Also available in paperback.)

Craig, Hardin. *An Interpretation of Shakespeare*. New York: Citadel Press, 1948.

Granville-Barker, Harley. *Prefaces to Shakespeare*. Princeton, N. J.: Princeton University Press, 1946–47. 2 vols. (Also available in paperback.)

Hazlitt, William. *Characters of Shakespeare's Plays*. London, 1817.

Spencer, Theodore. *Shakespeare and the Nature of Man*. New York: The Macmillan Company, 1942.

Spurgeon, Caroline F. E. *Shakespeare's Imagery and What It Tells Us*. London: Cambridge University Press, 1935. (Also available in paperback.)

Van Doren, Mark. *Shakespeare*. New York: Henry Holt & Company, Inc., 1939.

Finally, what does the teacher need besides a wide acquaintance with the plays at first hand and an active working knowledge of

Shakespeare criticism? The final requisite is far and away the most important of all: it is an abiding passion for the plays and a desire to have students share this passion. This is the most important qualification, but at the same time the mere mention of it is redundant because the teacher who has the first two qualifications will also have the third; and, conversely, if he does not have at least the one, he cannot possibly have the third except in a way that Holden Caulfield would instantly identify as "phony."

The editors of the First Folio, Heminge and Condell, in their preface "To the great Variety of Readers," gave a memorable admonition:

> But it is not our province, who onely gather his works, and give them to you, to praise him. It is yours that reade him. And there we hope, to your divers capacities, you will find enough, both to draw, and hold you: for his wit can no more lie hid, then it could be lost. Reade him, therefore; and againe, and againe: And if then you doe not like him, surely you are in some manifest danger, not to understand him.

It is a demonstrable fact, provable by all sorts of means, that throughout the world those who best *know* Shakespeare and those who best *like* Shakespeare are one and the same; there are no exceptions. Ultimately, for all genuine Shakespeareans, the end can be no other than that acknowledged by Logan Pearsall Smith in the last sentence of *On Reading Shakespeare*:

> . . . And if, lingering too long to listen, spell-bound, to this voice, surely the most magical, the most musical of all voices, I too have lost my reason, it is not amid the shouting theorists that you shall find me, but babbling, among the imbecile adorers, my praise. (p. 179)

This same humane critic and teacher of Shakespeare, elsewhere in the same volume, confides something that will be alarming to all those who are too well-adjusted to teach Shakespeare:

> Of the inhabitants of the insane asylums of Great Britain, it has been calculated that, after the religious maniacs, the

two next largest classes consist of those who rave about the Royal Family, or those who, by thinking about Shakespeare, have unhinged their minds. (p. 30)

It is not necessary to be mad to teach Shakespeare—at least at the high school level; but any teacher of Shakespeare needs to be a little mad in order even to know what Logan Pearsall Smith meant, and he can have reached that point only by reading Shakespeare "againe, and againe," until he saw what was "there," and realized the impossibility of ever getting anyone else to see *all* of it unless the other, too, could be brought to read "againe, and againe."

CHAPTER 4

What Unit and What Approach?

1. WHAT KIND OF UNIT?

WE HAVE EARLIER DISCUSSED SOME OF THE PROBLEMS OF ASSIGNING the plays to particular high school years and have suggested four-year arrangements of such flexibility that, hopefully, all teachers will be able to stay somewhere within the general scheme and yet find the play they want to teach in the year in which they want to teach it.

But we have been concerned only with year-by-year distribution and have left untouched another, and difficult, problem of arrangement: where should Shakespeare come *within* any given year? Should the play (or plays) come in the first or the second semester? Should it come early or late in the semester? Should it be part of some kind of "unit"? If so, what kind? Should Shakespeare's play be one in a unit "on drama"—with one or two one-act plays, a Greek play, a television play, a Broadway hit, an O'Neill play, a Shaw play, an Ibsen play, a Miller play, a Wilder play?

Should it be part of a thematic unit, along with whatever other plays, poems, short stories, novels, essays "fit" with it by being concerned with love, courage, justice, loyalty, ambition?

Should it be part of a geographical-chronological unit—taught with other works of the English Renaissance?

Should it be part of a unit "on comedy" or "on tragedy," placed with other representatives of its genre from various times and

53

countries? Or should *Julius Caesar*, say, be taught as an "example" of tragedy in a two-play unit, the other play being a comedy?

If *two* Shakespeare plays are taught in one year, should they be taught one after the other, as a "Shakespeare unit"? And in that event should some of Shakespeare's sonnets be included in the units?

As everyone knows, such questions as these are most often "answered" not by principle but by practical circumstance: "I teach my Shakespeare play," says a teacher, "whenever the other class gets through with the set of copies." "And I teach it," says another, "when we get to it in the anthology." Teachers who use standard twelfth-grade anthologies all know very well when *Macbeth* comes: it follows historically, after something from Chaucer, something from Spenser, and sundry Elizabethan lyrics. That puts it in the first semester, around November.

Practical necessities will continue to exist, and it will never be feasible to say a categorical "no" to every one of them. Further, the organizational principle of the full year's program will no doubt continue to "fix" the place of the Shakespeare play for many teachers. Thus if the class moves by genres throughout the year, Shakespeare's play alone or in company with other dramatic works will presumably follow or come somewhere between units on the short story, poetry, the novel, biography, the essay; if the class moves geographically, it will come whenever the tour of "world literature" arrives in England; if the class moves chronologically, it will come when the tour reaches the Elizabethan Renaissance.

But the fact that such practicalities, without benefit of *any* sort of rationale, will continue to determine the placement of a Shakespearean play in relation to other works and to the time of year should not excuse a teacher from the obligation to think seriously on the question of what placement will be *best* for the play. And certainly they cannot excuse us here from pondering that question. It would be easiest and simplest to say, "Since English literature is taught chronologically in the twelfth grade, *Macbeth* is taught along with other works of the Elizabethan-Jacobean Period," or "Since world history is taught in the tenth grade, *Julius Caesar* is taught at or just after the time the history class is studying the Roman Empire." But neither of these answers is based on a rationale. Both of them ignore the basic question, "What is the *best* placement for these plays?"

By "best" can we reasonably mean anything other than *that placement which will most favor the chance that students will experience the play itself, as a work of art?* This sense of purpose is fundamentally different from that of having the play come through as an "example" of tragedy. It is different from having it come through as an "example" of literature in the English Renaissance. It is different from having it serve to supplement students' knowledge of the Roman Empire. *If* teaching Macbeth with other works of the Elizabethan-Jacobean Period will provide the best chance for students to experience the play itself, then, by our principle, the historical placement is clearly right. *If* teaching *Julius Caesar* at the time the history class is studying the Roman Empire will best ensure that students will experience the play as a work of art, then clearly that placement is right. But *if* teaching *Macbeth* in a "unit" with other works that develop the theme of ambition will give it the best chance to come through as an experience of art, then, by our principle, *that* placement is best for it; and *if* teaching *Julius Caesar* in a unit with other works that develop the theme of honor will give it the best chance to affect students as an artistic experience, then that placement is best for it.

In the following section of this chapter we shall be concerned with the question of "approach"—i.e., what kind of introductory material or activities, if any, will best prepare a class for the reading of a Shakespearean play. That question is very intimately related to the present one, since the nature of the "approach" will necessarily be much influenced or even determined by the kind of "unit" the play is set in. For the present, therefore, it seems appropriate to leave open the questions that we have just raised about placement. Though they are questions only, and not answers, they at least may point the way to a general principle. In addition to whatever light the following discussion of "approach" may cast on the problem, specific recommendations will be found in the final chapters, where plays and the problems of teaching them are discussed individually.

We should say here only, by way of summarizing the drift of the foregoing discussion, that, as most teachers know, there *are* dangers in placing a Shakespearean play, or any other large complex work of art, in *any* special "frame," be it typological, geographical, chronological, or thematic. There is danger that the artistic force of the work will be somehow impaired, that the experience of the work as a work of art will be subordinated, as a purpose, to something else that is less important. At worst, *Macbeth* will stand as an "example" of Jacobean tragedy, or its complexity and multiplicity of meaning will be narrowly cramped to fit into a unit treating the single theme of, say, ambition. The danger is certainly far less when the teacher is well aware that the danger exists and takes deliberate care to prevent the play from being dominated by the frame it is placed in, though even then its effectiveness will probably be somewhat impaired. But when the teacher does not know that the danger exists, and takes no precautions against it, the experience of the work as a whole work of art can be virtually suffocated by the "unit" that frames it. Rather than risk that appalling waste, it may be best to leave a Shakespearean play, or any other great literary work, free of any frame, to teach it as an independent entity at whatever time in the semester or year a class is found readiest for the experience it affords.

2. WHAT KIND OF APPROACH?

"Approach" as used here means something other than the critical form that signifies "emphasis of study"—as an historical, linguistic, "appreciative," sociological, psychological, bibliographical, textual, or other emphasis. It refers to the introduction or preparation given by the teacher just before beginning the actual reading of a work. What should the teacher do?

Lecture on the life of Shakespeare? On the Renaissance? On the physical characteristics of the Elizabethan theater? On the genre of the play to be read—comedy, history, tragedy? On the costumes of Elizabethans? On the reputation of Shakespeare? On the conditions of London society? On blank verse? On the plot, character, and meaning of the play to be read? On the costumes, customs, political and social conditions of the time represented in the play?

Assign reports on the life of Shakespeare? On the Renaissance?

On the physical characteristics of the Elizabethan theater? On the genre of the play to be read? On the costumes of Elizabethans? On the reputation of Shakespeare? etc.

Show a film on the life of Shakespeare? On the Renaissance? On the Elizabethan theater? etc.

The following is an experienced high school English teacher's account of her regular method of "approaching" the tragedy of *Julius Caesar*. It is presented because it virtually exhausts the many possibilities:

Some weeks before the study of *Julius Caesar* is to begin, I make arrangements to have on hand as many of the following materials as possible:

    I. Films
        Julius Caesar (IFB)
        Julius Caesar Act III, Sc. ii (BIS)
        Julius Caesar Act IV, Sc. iii (United World)

    II. Filmstrips
        Introduction to Wm. Shakespeare (Young America)
        Shakespeare's Theater (Young America)
        Julius Caesar—set of two filmstrips (Young America)

    III. Recordings
        Julius Caesar (CRS)
        Julius Caesar Act III, Sc. ii (BIS)

    IV. Exhibits
        Roman Life picture display—photographic
        Elizabethan England picture display (History Service)
        Costume Dolls of Queen Elizabeth and the English Court (County Schools A.V.Dept.)

    V. Books
        Marchette Chute, *Shakespeare of London*
        Julian Markel, *Shakespeare's Julius Caesar*
        Mark Van Doren, *Shakespeare*

I place the Roman Life display on one bulletin board and the Elizabethan England display on the other.

Since this is an historical play, before the actual reading begins the students need to be prepared with a backround of history and politics which, while not too comprehensive, will give them an understanding of the setting of *Julius Caesar*. They will also need some background to prepare a favorable climate for the play's presentation.

This is a good place to use student reports. I assign groups to prepare oral presentations on such topics as:

- (a) The early history of Rome
- (b) The political situation in Rome in the 1st Century B.C.
- (c) The conspiracy against Caesar
- (d) The places of Brutus, Antony, and Octavius in the politics of the day.

I encourage students to read North's translation of Plutarch's *Lives* for source material.

I assign other groups to tell about Shakespeare's life and times, and the kind of theater for which he wrote with its bare stage open to the sky, its lack of curtains, the rabble in the pit eating and shouting, and the dandies on the stage demanding and getting entertainment.

If there are any artists in the class, I encourage them to draw pictures of the Elizabethan theater, its stage, its elaborate costumes, etc., to supplement the bulletin board displays.

After the assignments are given and arrangements made to spend the next class period in the library gathering material for the reports, I lecture about the play, keeping in mind always that my own enthusiasm will go a long way towards kindling a like enthusiasm in my students. I tell them that Shakespeare's reason for writing plays was much the same as that of most playwrights today—money—and that he was a particularly successful playwright. Indeed, Marchette Chute tells us that young people flocked to his plays as they do to movies and football games today.

I tell them, too, that this is a play about great men and great issues and, whereas in the history we read of the murder of Caesar by the conspirators, in the play we can hear them speak. And, as they express their fears and doubts they come alive for us and we realize that their problems are much like our problems today, that men in those times joined in causes for every reason from super-patriotism to a desire for personal gain, just as they do today.

After the class presentations, which could be panel discussions or summaries by one member of the group, I arrange to have them see or hear the play as a whole. Ideal, of course, would be a stage production, but it is certainly a coincidence if one is being given at this particular time. Second choice would be the viewing of the movie starring Marlon Brando. But, failing this, there is always a good recording available; and while hearing is not as good an experience as seeing, it is still very valuable.

Then, just as soon as these advance activities have been completed, the class will be ready to start the reading of the play.

The teacher who prepared this account of her approach to *Julius Caesar* with a tenth-grade class would appear to have covered nearly all of the possibilities in the way of both materials and means. She has introduced her students to the life and times of Shakespeare, the Elizabethan theater, the source of the play, Roman history and the political situation; she has likened the Roman problems to modern problems and thus shown the play to be "timely." She has pointed out the advantages of dramatic over expository presentation of historical events. Further, she has availed herself of all, or nearly all, possible means of inculcating the many and varied aspects of background in students' minds, using films and filmstrips, recordings, bulletin board exhibits, individual and group study, panel discussion, individual reports, lecture, art work, and costume dolls.

It is not unlikely that this representative teacher would insist that what she genuinely wants above all else is to have her students "experience" the play of *Julius Caesar*. But her approach suggests that what she really values, and wants her students to get, is "acquaintance" with Shakespeare, his life and times, the Elizabethan theater, and so on, and information on Roman history, politics, customs. She wants her students to "know about" Shakespeare and his times and Caesar and his times. Since this is what she wants, and since the approach itself is calculated to provide all the information, what need is there to add *Julius Caesar*? That masterpiece can at best add a few more bits of information to suit her purpose, and at worst it will be superfluous. And in any event it is certain to be a tedious bore, no matter how enthusiastically the teacher may talk about how great Shakespeare was, how popular he was in his day, how much money he made, and how much the Romans' problems were like our own.

If what a teacher chiefly wants is to have her class "learn about" Shakespeare, Elizabethan England, and Rome, there are better ways, more efficient ways, than having them read *Julius Caesar*. As for Rome, Shakespeare knew comparatively little about it himself. He read Plutarch on Caesar, Antony, and Brutus, and that was enough for his play. The high school student who faithfully plods through the "approach" to *Julius Caesar* that the teacher has laid out for him will very likely know more about Rome before he gets to the play itself than Shakespeare knew about it when he wrote the play. And then the play may be a real disappointment to him because the "approach" has led him to expect to find in it even more and somehow better information about Rome.

The teacher who devised the elaborate approach that we are considering would no doubt deny that her underlying purpose was to introduce students to Caesar and his times and Shakespeare and his times. She would insist that she devised the approach as preparation for the play that is to be read. She would insist that they need to "know about" these men and their periods in order to appreciate the play. And no doubt she would genuinely believe that what she says is true.

But that, then, is to admit that she has no real confidence in Shakespeare and his play. She reveals the same lack of confidence when she anticipates the reading of the play by repeatedly saying how great Shakespeare was, how great his play is, how the problems of Caesar's times were much like the problems of our times, how politicians of those times were like politicians today. She makes the same confession when she embellishes her "approach" to the play with the entertainment of films, filmstrips, pictures, drawings, and costume dolls. She does not really trust Shakespeare or his play.

Shakespeare is worth more trust. He himself provides, normally in the first scene of a play, the "background" that is needed to understand the situation and the persons who are involved in it. He needs no crutches in the form of insistence on how great he is, no displays on bulletin boards, blackboards, tables, or in corners. The teacher has approached him as if she secretly doubted that he holds enough to make it on his own, as if he must be helped out by all manner of eye-catching devices.

That the approach here outlined and discussed is indeed typical may be (and has been) confirmed in a variety of ways: by conversations with teachers, visits to classrooms, talks with students; by examination of lesson plans; and possibly most of all by study of introductions and "suggestions for activities" included in widely used anthologies and other school editions of plays and of the "Teachers' Handbook" kind of publication that often accompanies the textbooks. It is unnecessary to go into detail here about these, but typical items should be mentioned. Under some such heading as "Before the Assignment," i.e., before the reading of the play is begun, are regularly listed such suggestions as the following:

1. Selection of student committee to make a bulletin-board display, with pictures of Shakespeare, the Globe Theater, famous Shakespearean actors, illustrations of Elizabethan costumes, etc.
2. Preparation by students of short talks or panel discussion on the life of Shakespeare.
3. Preparation of talks, illustrations, and models to represent Shakespeare's theater.
4. Arrangements for showing filmstrips relating to Shakespeare and his times.
5. Short talks on historical backgrounds of the play to be read.
6. Discussion of other plays by Shakespeare and his contemporaries.

After these more general preparations, typical suggestions call for teacher and class to move somewhat closer to the actual reading of the play; such means as the following are usual:

1. Narration (by the teacher or from the "headnote" included in the edition being used) of "the story of the play."
2. Preliminary examination of the Dramatis Personae, and advance discussion of the characters in the play.
3. Preliminary inspection of the text of the play, including pictures, footnotes, number of lines, act and scene division, suggested activities, etc.
4. Reading or other presentation of material (but not Shakespeare's) that is introductory to the first scene—general situation, setting, purpose, etc.

5. Assignment of parts to be prepared for oral reading by students.

Though practices vary, representative school editions allow from two to three weeks for these and similar activities that antecede the actual beginning of the reading. When the introductory materials provided by the particular edition are detailed and substantial, teachers are often advised to give tests covering various matters before the play is begun; some introductions, for example, include rather full descriptions of the principal characters of the play, and on the basis of these students are sometimes asked to characterize Brutus, Cassius, Caesar, and Antony *before they have read Shakespeare's opening scene*, and, of course, before they have met them "dramatically."

The editions often provide also for other forms of preliminary writing. In one somewhat older but still widely used edition of separate plays, the text of the play is preceded by a series of short chapters, or sections, with the total Introduction amounting to nearly one hundred pages. Each chapter—treating the usual topics of "Shakespeare's Theater," "Language and Versification," "The Characters of the Play," etc.—is followed by a list of twelve to twenty questions covering details of the chapter. This edition was a long-term favorite of English teachers across the country. At least in part it was so because of these questions, which students were sometimes required to answer in writing as homework or classwork, or both. Thus, if the teacher who used this text was one who desired a full and systematic coverage, students would have worked about two weeks in writing the answers to one hundred or one hundred fifty questions on various aspects of background before they actually reached the promised land of, say, *A Midsummer Night's Dream*.

It appears reasonable to doubt that even *A Midsummer Night's Dream* could survive this kind of approach. And what is truly sad is that students tend to blame Shakespeare himself for the boredom that has been inflicted on them.

In the preceding review of prevailing approaches to the reading of a Shakespeare play, two main, and mutually contradictory, tendencies can be distinguished:

1. The tendency to make the study of Shakespeare a long-

drawn out and deadly tedious process. Acquiring "background knowledge" while one has not yet met the thing itself for which the background is being acquired is as inevitably deadly as the method is perverse.

2. The tendency to make (or to attempt to make) Shakespeare "interesting and alive" by means of side-show effects—filmstrips, dolls, art work, etc. Such interest as may be aroused by these activities will be largely false, for it will not be interest in the *play*, but in the activity itself, or, at best, in what is peripheral to the play.

In the past few years, however, many high school teachers have recoiled violently from the first practice. They refuse to launch their classes upon long and tedious study of backgrounds before beginning the play, and they shudder at such a procedure as that just named, in which students are made to write out answers to historical questions for a week or two in advance of the reading. Yet among these rebel teachers are many of the most avid devotees of the second practice. By changing from library to filmstrip, the teacher has probably made the learning process more entertaining, and possibly students will even learn more about the age by this less painful means. But merely to exchange one elaborate fashion of approach for another is to miss the main point.

The main point is this: *the place to begin with a Shakespeare play is right where Shakespeare began—with the first scene.*

Not with filmstrips, library study, panel discussion, lectures on the greatness of Shakespeare, drawings, dolls, cardboard Globe Theaters, narration of "the story of the play," pre-tests on principal characters, or photographs of The Shakespeare Country, but *with the first scene*: let Shakespeare make his own introduction of the play; he knew how to do it better than any other dramatist, and certainly better than teachers can devise.

Thus the place to begin *Julius Caesar* is here:

> FLAVIUS. Hence! Home, you idle creatures, get you home.
> Is this a holiday? What! Know you not,
> Being mechanical, you ought not walk
> Upon a laboring day without the sign
> Of your profession? Speak, what trade art thou?

And the place to begin *Hamlet* is precisely here:

BERNARDO. Who's there?

FRANCISCO. Nay, answer me! Stand and unfold yourself.

Does this approach—or, rather, this complete absence of approach—mean, then, that students are *never* to learn that *Julius Caesar* and *Hamlet* are tragedies, and what tragedy is? Are they never to learn that Shakespeare was a great dramatist? That he lived and wrote during the reigns of Elizabeth and James I? That these two plays were derived respectively from Plutarch and Saxo Grammaticus? That they are written mainly in blank verse? That the Elizabethan stage had a projecting platform and no front curtain? That boys played women's roles?

No, it means no such thing. On the contrary, it can mean that students will eventually gain a greater knowledge of all such matters than if they had been made to study them for three weeks before reading the opening lines of the play. But they will have gained it not as an end in itself, but as one of the means to the real end, the experience of the play.

When are they to acquire these wide-ranging pieces of helpful information, if not prior to the actual reading? They will gain most of them *when and as they become relevant in the course of the reading*, and possibly some of them after the first reading has been finished. What has all too often bulked huge and forbidding as an approach thus becomes a functional part of the actual presentation (the reading) of the play, and of the activities that accompany and follow the presentation. When, for example, a scene ends with a command to carry off the body of a character who has been struck down during the action, the fact that the platform lacked a front curtain becomes highly relevant and can be told in such a way that it is unlikely ever to be forgotten. When the heroine of a comedy dons boy's clothes and identity and starts her masquerade, the fact that the *player* was a boy to start with can be told so that it too will be fixed permanently in the memory. When there is a sudden change of scene, from a street to a duke's chamber or from a queen's boudoir to a forest, the facts of multiple playing areas on the Elizabethan stage and the absence of stage scenery can be told most pointedly. When dialogue changes from blank verse to prose or prose to blank verse, or when a rhymed couplet first appears, the technical facts of Shakespeare's basic form and his frequent variations can be introduced. Preliminary lecture can do nothing as effectively or as memorably.

But we have begun to touch on matters that must be dealt with as occasion arises in the course of the actual presentation, and it is to this subject that we now turn.

CHAPTER 5

What Form of Presentation?

As it is used here and throughout this book, "presentation" means *the initial, actual reading of the play*, by whatever methods this is accomplished.

The possible means are many, and before we attempt to identify one of them as "best" we should have them all before us. Classification of the basic possibilities is a rather obvious first necessity. In the most general terms, they are as follows:

Silent reading
   Out of class
   In class
   Combination

Oral reading
   By members of the class
   By the teacher
   Combination

Recording

This outline is presumably complete. Notably absent are any devices that do not involve actual reading, which is required by our definition of presentation. Hence watching a play on film or in any kind of "live" production is not included. Recording is included, but only on the assumption that students will follow in their texts; merely listening, like watching or watching and listening, is not reading. Similarly, oral reading is included as a form of "actual reading" because it is assumed that, whether teacher or individual students read aloud, the whole class will follow, i.e., *read*—in the texts.

We must soon consider in detail the relative merits of the basic forms of presentation with the aim of determining which has best claim to be the teacher's mainstay, which should be secondary, and which should be avoided. But first we must take up a vexing question that we cannot trust to lie quiet if we simply ignore it. The question has already been exposed, unfortunately but necessarily, by our summary rejection above of films and live productions as legitimate forms of "presentation" on the grounds that they do not involve actual reading. Whether or not they *do* involve actual reading is not our question, for of course they do not: the question is whether, even so, they should not have a claim to be regarded as legitimate forms of presentation. If so, we have defined "presentation" too narrowly. Let us first divide the question:

1. Should witnessing a performance of a play on film or on the stage be regarded as an appropriate *substitute* for reading the play?
2. Should witnessing a performance be regarded as an appropriate *initial* presentation to be followed by the actual reading of the play?

(We have partly begged the question with the second wording, for we have already defined presentation as the "initial, actual reading." But for the present let us suspend that technical subtlety.) The question whether it is better to see or to read one of Shakespeare's plays is a very old one and does not require detailed review here. Moreover, as we shall show, it is not precisely the issue here, though it is intimately related. In any event, the question is important and requires comment.

It requires comment, first of all, because editors of Shakespeare's plays for use in school generally appear to have *assumed* an unqualified answer without troubling to debate the question with themselves. Most school editions of the plays start off with a prefatory remark which directly or by implication apologizes to students for asking them to read rather than see the play. To anyone who has a reasonably close acquaintance with Shakespeare's plays, gained by study, this apologetic tone seems foolish, unnecessary, and offensive.

Typically, the editor begins with a statement of indisputable fact—that Shakespeare's plays were written for the stage; written, that is to say, to be seen, not read.

But, the editor then continues, we (teacher and students) are regrettably limited to classroom facilities, and there is nothing to do but make the best of our second-best situation. We shall have to *read* our *Julius Caesar* from our books! So let us all knuckle down and have great fun; for after all *something* can be made of Shakespeare even from the printed page. But of course we would see the play instead, if we could. . . .

In insisting that no editor (or teacher) needs to adopt this tone of abject apology, we need not go as far as Charles Lamb went in his essay, "On the Tragedies of Shakespeare." Lamb maintained that Shakespeare's plays were "less calculated for performance on a stage, than those of almost any other dramatist whatever." According to Lamb, what in reading the plays appeals to the imagination is, in seeing them, transformed to ugly physical reality:

> . . . The state of sublime emotion into which we are elevated by those images of night and horror which Macbeth is made to utter, that solemn prelude with which he entertains the time till the bell shall strike which is to call him to murder Duncan, —when we no longer read it in a book, when we have given up that vantage-ground of abstraction which reading possesses over seeing, and come to see a man in his bodily shape before our eyes actually preparing to commit a murder . . . the painful anxiety about the act, the natural longing to prevent it while it yet seems unperpetrated, the too close pressing semblance of reality, give a pain and an uneasiness which totally destroy all the delight which the words in the book convey. . . . The sublime images, the poetry alone, is that which is present to our minds in the reading.

And, further, in seeing the play, the eyes mislead the mind as to what is important:

> . . . The shewing of every thing, levels all things: it makes

tricks, bows, and curtesies, of importance. Mrs. S. [Sarah Siddons] never got more fame by any thing than by the manner in which she dismisses the guests in the banquet-scene in Macbeth. . . . But does such a trifle as this enter into the imaginations of the readers of that wild and wonderful scene? Does not the mind dismiss the feasters as rapidly as it can? Does it care about the gracefulness of the doing it? But by acting . . . all these non-essentials are raised into an importance, injurious to the main interest of the play.

In the course of his extensive review, Lamb cites many of the greatest scenes in Shakespeare's plays, and always to the same purpose of showing that *the experience of seeing them is an inferior, gross, and distorted experience beside that of reading.* Probably the most famous outburst of his entire essay concerns *King Lear:*

But the Lear of Shakespeare cannot be acted. The contemptible machinery by which they mimic the storm which he goes out in, is not more inadequate to represent the horrors of the real elements, than any actor can be to represent Lear: they might more easily propose to personate the Satan of Milton upon a stage, or one of Michael Angelo's terrible figures. The greatness of Lear is not in corporal dimension, but in intellectual: the explosions of his passion are terrible as a volcano; they are storms turning up and disclosing to the bottom that sea, his mind, with all its vast riches. It is his mind which is laid bare. This case of flesh and blood seems too insignificant to be thought on; even as he himself neglects it. On the stage we see nothing but corporal infirmities and weakness, the impotence of rage. While we read it, we see not Lear, but we are Lear: we are in his mind, we are sustained by a grandeur which baffles the malice of daughters and storms. . . .

William Hazlitt and Lamb agreed on a view of Shakespeare that may be best summed up in Hazlitt's verdict on a performance of A *Midsummer Night's Dream:* "All that is finest in the play is lost in the representation." Here is Hazlitt more fully:

The Midsummer Night's Dream, when acted, is converted from a delightful fiction into a dull pantomime. . . . Poetry and the

stage do not agree well together. The attempt to reconcile
them . . . fails not only of effect, but of decorum. The *ideal*
can have no place upon the stage, which is a picture without
perspective; everything there is in the foreground. That which
was merely an airy shape, a dream, a passing thought, immediately becomes an unmanageable reality. . . . Any offence
given to the eye is not to be got rid of by explanation. Thus
Bottom's head in the play is a fantastic illusion, produced by
magic spells; on the stage it is an ass's head, and nothing more;
certainly a very strange costume for a gentleman to appear in.
. . . Fairies are not incredible, but fairies six feet high are
so. . . . The boards of a theatre and the regions of fancy are
not the same thing.

Hazlitt and Lamb are famous Romantics and, on the question
of stage versus study, famous heretics. They would, it seems,
almost persuade us that Shakespeare should never be acted, and
that if, unfortunately, he *were* acted, nobody should go to see
him. In this view they do not stand alone, by any means, in the
history of Shakespeare criticism; others, including T. S. Eliot,
have objected to the intrusion of director-actor-setting, with
the "interpretation" that these imply between themselves and
Shakespeare's text—an objection that approximates Hazlitt's
admonition that the stage is no place to study Shakespeare's
characters, for there what one studies is only actors' interpretations.

Yet though these views are extreme they have value here as
counterbalances to the opposite attitude that is expressed in the
apologetic tones of editors (and sometimes teachers) who suggest
to students that reading Shakespeare is at best only second-best
and should not be endured at all if only a performance were available. Is any reconciliation of these extremes possible? We have
earlier insisted that teachers see Shakespeare's plays wherever and
whenever they can, as often as they can; that recommendation is
herewith extended to include the students of these same teachers:
no teacher is quite alert enough who fails to encourage students to
see the plays anywhere, anytime, on any stage or screen, with any
sort of actors, professional, amateur, or puppets.

But does this recommendation place us with editors who regard
reading Shakespeare as second-best? It certainly does not. Seeing

Shakespeare on the stage and reading Shakespeare's text are *two essentially different kinds of experience*—and especially they are so for the beginner. We can agree emphatically with the argument that there is no substitute for seeing Shakespeare acted, that it is impossible, or next to impossible, to perceive all that Shakespeare *is* until one sees him acted. But then we must insist just as emphatically that there is also no substitute for reading Shakespeare, no substitute for the leisurely, deliberate, and *imaginative* study of the plays. It is the English teacher's primary responsibility and privilege to provide this latter experience: the teacher's main resource is the printed page.

But let us reconstruct, in token form, what our beginner—who has never read the play—"gets" from a performance of, say, *Julius Caesar*, the "easiest" of the great plays. And to make all things fairer than probability would admit, let us suppose that the performance seen was a superlative production executed by a superlative cast—the finest *Julius Caesar* ever presented since, say, 1599; furthermore, let us hear our best ninth-grader report on the performance:

> When the curtain went up this mob of rough looking people in some kind of sheets were all over the stage, and then these two fellows came in and really told them off because they were fixing to welcome Caesar back from fighting this other fellow. Then they all went off and pretty soon a whole bunch came in with Caesar and his wife out front, and they met a really queer old guy who looked like he was blind, and he told Caesar he'd better watch out for the Ides of March, or something. Caesar didn't pay any attention to him. Caesar was wearing a wreath of some kind on his head, and his wife had on a lot of shiny jewelry and a long purple or red gown that dragged on the stage. Caesar looked like a kind of a snob, and his wife was all painted up, like someone who would do anything. She was pretty, though, except her eyes were a little too close together and her hair was too done up.
>
> After Caesar and everyone else went off, Brutus and Cassius stayed and talked about things for a long time. Brutus was a short man, with a puzzled look most of the time. Cassius was tall and skinny, and kept squinting his eyes; he seemed to have a slight limp in his left leg, too. I liked the actor who played Cassius the best, because he had a sharp way of talking so that

you could hear every word. Brutus sometimes turned his back and you didn't catch all the words. Also, I think Cassius looked more like a Roman than anyone except Antony.

> (Excerpt from student report;
> minor mechanical corrections)

It is surely unnecessary to reproduce more of this report. The essential character of the student's total experience is sufficiently represented by the excerpt. The rest may be summarized: he saw fine actors on a stage, liked some of them and disliked others; he gained a fairly good sense of "what happened" and how it all came out; he laughed at the antics of some of the Citizens and the grimaces of Casca; he was impressed by the elocution of Antony in the funeral oration and by the physical appearance of Antony, who looked "the most like a Roman"; he thought Brutus and Cassius were actually going to kill one another in the quarrel scene; he enjoyed the skirmishes of the final scenes, especially the expert use of swords and shields; he marvelled at the realism achieved by the actors with their daggers and swords at the deaths of Caesar, Cassius, and Brutus. No doubt he gained unconsciously much more than this, for he heard the magnificent music of Shakespeare's blank verse spoken by first-rate actors with well-trained voices—though at the same time he wished they "had just talked more like people do." He agrees most enthusiastically that the trip to the theater was worth it and wants to know when the class can go again.

"All that is finest in the play," said Hazlitt, "is lost in the representation."

For the novice, Hazlitt's statement is largely true. For what the novice "gets" from watching the play on the stage is, quite literally, nothing at all of that enormous, one may even say inexhaustible, potentiality that makes Shakespeare Shakespeare and is the reason for emphasizing him in the school program. This can be tapped, up to the student's own expanding capacity, only by study of the printed lines, by deliberate contemplation, and exercise of the individual imagination.

Hence our answer to the initial question, "Should watching a performance be considered an appropriate substitute for reading?" is necessarily a loud and categorical No. Not only the high school student, but the intelligent adult who is unfamiliar with the particular play of Shakespeare's that is being performed misses "all that is finest in the play."

This is by no means to suggest that the adult who has not read the play should therefore refrain from seeing it. It is not to suggest that if he has not read it he will get nothing from it. He will get plenty: he will follow the course of the story and know in a very general way what is being said and what is happening at any given moment; he will enjoy the sounds of the language, be pleased by the visual beauties of costumes and living figures, and sometimes be excited or moved by the action; he will admire this actor and that, laugh at the grimaces of the comic figures, applaud scenes that are obviously well executed, and all in all pronounce it a full entertainment. But none of this that he gets is what makes Shakespeare Shakespeare. It is certainly far better to see one of Shakespeare's plays than *not* to see it, and it is far better to see it if one is *not* going to read it. But for the beginner, whether ninth grader or adult, it is certainly not better to see it than to read it in the classroom with an able teacher.

The novice, of course, will disagree violently with these statements. It is even possible that he will continue to disagree *after* he has also read the play that he has previously seen: he may be positive that he "got more" out of seeing it. Or, if he has seen one play well done on the stage and has thereafter read through another play of approximately equal quality, he will swear that there is simply no comparison between the two experiences: he had a fine, exciting time in seeing the one play, and he had a laborious time in reading the other. What is more, it is very probable that his assessment of the two experiences is, in a sense, correct: he may indeed have "got more" from seeing than from reading. But more what? Not, certainly, more of what makes Shakespeare Shakespeare.

On the other hand, if the beginner who is imagined in this comparison reads the play "on his own," without benefits of an able teacher, his assessment of the two experiences of seeing and reading will be correct in a very different sense: in seeing, he got a great deal, even though it had little to do with what makes Shakespeare Shakespeare; but in reading "on his own" he not only failed to get what makes Shakespeare Shakespeare but, in all probability, failed to get anything at all.

It is precisely therefore that the role of the teacher in the reading of Shakespeare is crucial; for the beginner, the teacher must make the difference between getting "all that is finest in the play" and getting something else, or nothing.

But, to return briefly, why is it that the novice in the theater fails to get "what makes Shakespeare Shakespeare"? If one follows the argument of Hazlitt and Lamb, he concludes that, far from helping the beginner to get the best that is there, the stage spectacle impedes him; the physical eye, darting about over all sorts of objects and actions equally displayed for it to see, distracts the mind from what is most important. But if one balks at this extreme argument, he must still reach the same conclusion by another route. What is most important in a play by Shakespeare is the *incredible wealth of ideas bodied forth in the incredible profusion of imagery*. If one misses this, or a large part of it, Shakespeare is neither better nor worse than any competent playwright, and there is no really sound reason to see or read him instead of any other playwright. And in the theater it is just this that the beginner—who has not previously plumbed the depths by deliberate study—*does* miss. However skilled is the actor in expressing lines so that meaning comes clear, Shakespeare's riches spill out in such abundance, with such rapidity, that the mind of the unread hearer simply cannot keep up. At the end of Macbeth's "If it were done" soliloquy, the mind has managed to hold on to little more than that Macbeth was deciding whether or not to kill Duncan. At the end of Hamlet's "To be or not to be" soliloquy, it retains only the idea that Hamlet thought of killing himself but feared the life after death. As for passages that produce a machine-gun fire of subtle word-and-idea play, how can the mind keep up with those?

> BARDOLPH. My Lord, do you see these meteors? Do you
>   behold these exhalations?
> PRINCE. I do.
> BARDOLPH. What think you they portend?
> PRINCE. Hot livers and cold purses.
> BARDOLPH. Choler, my lord, if rightly taken.
> PRINCE. No, if rightly taken, halter.
>
> *Henry IV, Part 1* (II, 4)

The answer is that it does nothing at all with them. The novice in the audience laughs at the bright red nose and the "whelks and bubukles" that have been applied to Bardolph's face with makeup and to which gestures and dialogue draw attention; but "all that is finest" in the exchange of remarks is missed by the mind and might as well not be there. And that is to say that one had as well be watching a play by some other playwright.

Yes Shakespeare wrote for the theater of his time, and presumably had no thought of printed text and deliberate study. Do we, then, imply that Shakespeare's audiences, seeing the plays for the first time and never having read them, "got" much more of what is in them than does a modern audience of first-timers?

Of course the Elizabethan audience was more familiar with the language than is the modern audience, and that fact would account for much difference in the ease with which it would "take in" what was said. But when one looks closely at the language of the great, crucial passages in the plays, he may be surprised by how few really significant differences between Shakespeare's language and ours he can detect. In Macbeth's "If it were done" speech one does not find a single word with which he can be sure the typical Elizabethan theatergoer was more familiar than his modern equivalent. If "this bank and shoal of time" eludes the mind of the modern theatergoer, what reason is there to think the Elizabethan in the pit took it in? It was just as highly figurative then as now. The same precisely is true of Hamlet's "To be or not to be" speech. The average modern spectator may not be acquainted with "coil," "contumely," "quietus," "bodkin," and "fardels"; but is there any reason to suppose that the average Elizabethan could apprehend their literal and figurative meanings any faster?

However we may have been led to suppose otherwise, the mere *language* that Shakespeare used does not differ essentially from our own, and it certainly was not so much more familiar to Elizabethan audiences as to make the plays easy for them while they are hard for us. The most frequent differences in language occur in words that are not crucial to understanding, words that are not keys to the meanings of sentences. If the Elizabethan theatergoer was familiar with "in sooth"—a frequent parenthetical expression in the plays—whereas the modern theatergoer is not, the Elizabethan's advantage was still negligible—for the meaning of lines does not lie in expressions like "in sooth." If the Elizabethan was entirely accustomed to the use of "an" for "if," his advantage over us was still not worth mentioning. When one inspects passage after passage in this way, he is forced to conclude that the Elizabethan audience had no profound advantage in understanding the plays by virtue of closer familiarity with the language.

If not his language, then were Shakespeare's *ideas* significantly more familiar to Elizabethan audiences? No doubt some were—ideas that were "local" in character, that depend on references to timely events and familiar places. Current jokes, references to Moor Ditch, allusions to horns and the French disease—most of the plays include a sprinkling of such matters in a wide variety. But these are not the matters on which the plays turn; they are things of the moment, spoken in passing.

As for Shakespeare's "big ideas"—of God, man, the universe, the state, honor, justice, mercy, loyalty, love, friendship, etc.—it would appear, without much thought given to the matter, that these should have been more familiar to his contemporaries than to us. But the fact is that the ideas of great authors are likely to be much "harder" for the author's contemporaries than for later ages. A writer of the *avant garde* is rarely understood in his own time by more than a handful who form his special cult, while later periods may find his ideas not only readily understandable but ordinary. It is true that no critics have classed Shakespeare as *avant garde*—except in limited, special ways. On the contrary, it is usual to say that he expressed the great central attitudes of his time, and excelled because he expressed them better than others did. Nevertheless, these same great central attitudes or ideas are unquestionably more familiar to the average theatergoer today than they were to his equivalent in Shakespeare's day. They have had nearly four hundred years in which to pervade the atmosphere of our lives; as nearly as such things can be, they have become a part of modern man's inherited "intelligence." In short, we shall argue in vain if we seek to prove that Shakespeare's plays were, because of their ideas, more readily accessible to the Elizabethan than the modern audience.

If it was neither language nor ideas, then was it the syntax of blank verse that enabled Elizabethan audiences to comprehend him more quickly than we can? Obviously, blank verse was blank verse to Shakespeare's audiences as much as to modern audiences. The Elizabethan's ears may have been more enthralled by it because of its freshness and newness, but his mind could not take in its meanings more swiftly than ours can.

Only one possibility remains, and if that fails, we shall be forced to conclude that the spectator in Shakespeare's theater who had not previously studied the play got little more of what Shakespeare packed into it than does his modern equivalent. Was the Elizabethan theatergoer so much *brighter* than we are that his mind apprehended and digested in an instant—or quickly enough to be ready for the next line—what our own poor wits must have leisure to turn over and over, to examine from every side, and to probe? This possibility, like the last, is absurd and needs no consideration. Of course there were quick wits in the galleries, and perhaps among the gallants sitting on the platform within reach of the actors. But the average Elizabethan theatergoer was a brute in comparison to the modern one. He came in off the street for a penny and stood in the pit gawking and gesticulating and nudging his fellows, cracking nuts, drinking beer, and loudly applauding the obvious. It may be exaggeration to say that he was

> incapable of nothing but inexplicable dumb-show
> and noise

—but he was surely incapable of much more.

Much more importantly, though this fellow had perhaps come to think Will Shakespeare "the greatest" for the fun and excitement he provided, he had no reason to guess that there were enormous riches to be plumbed beneath the surface of sound and action; nobody had told him. All the odds, thus, favor the modern theatergoer, even the one who has not read the play. He goes to the theater on his best behavior, sits quietly, and makes a valiant effort to get all that is to be had—for he is more than enough familiar with Shakespeare's reputation to know that there is much to *be* had. He is at least as bright as the Elizabethan, and he is much more sophisticated. He works hard at the task of understanding, because he knows he has a kind of cultural obligation to understand Shakespeare. And in spite of all, he misses everything but the most obvious.

Did Shakespeare, then, put into his plays a vast deal more than was necessary, considering that even his immediate audiences were to perceive so little of what was there? He certainly did; and studious readers, together with theatergoers who have been studious readers, are the beneficiaries. But why did he do it? He did it, presumably, because he was Shakespeare and must satisfy himself. And, though he certainly never guessed that at a future date scholars, teachers, and classroom pupils would be digging deep, combining their energies in efforts to unlock "all that is finest in the play," and thus redeem his own labors of putting it there in the first place, yet he doubtless was impelled to his best by a care for "the judicious few" in the audiences of his day.

This is not to say, however, that he wrote with only the few "judicious" in mind, and only for them. Universal applause has proved that there is something for everyone in Shakespeare. However, the virtue of the classroom study of Shakespeare is that it can unlock "all that is finest in the play," which, in the theater, is accessible—at very best—to only the rarely gifted few, the super-judicious—and, of course, to others who have already made an intelligent study of the play in classroom or study.

Though Shakespeare was warmly applauded in his own time by audiences that had not read a word of the plays they applauded, and though he continued to be applauded after his death, it was not until men began to *read* him that his true worth became apparent. Further, the growth of his popularity on the stage—growth in the sense of ever widening audiences in the countries of the civilized world—during the past two centuries has been an *effect*, not a cause, of the rapidly widening distribution of Shakespeare in printed texts during this period, and, accordingly, of the rapidly widening reading public implied by the availability of these texts. Theatrical productions, in short, have multiplied because the publication and the reading of texts have enormously widened the base. The present abundance of Elizabethan theaters, Shakespeare festivals, and individual productions, amateur, community, commercial, "off-Broadway," and all others, rests on this base. In short, the stage did not make the printed text popular; the printed text made the theatrical production popular.

To argue, thus, for the priority of *reading* Shakespeare in the classroom is not at all to identify oneself as an enemy of Shakespeare on the stage, but to make oneself, ultimately, the staunchest support of Shakespeare on the stage. English teachers who, in the classroom, do well by the printed text of the play are the foundation that makes the theatrical production possible. Without their work, Shakespeare on the stage would be dead in the space of a generation.

But that is not at all the same as saying that to keep Shakespeare alive on the stage they should take their students to see him on the stage instead of reading him in the classroom. To keep him flourishing on the stage, as he is flourishing at present, they must zealously strive to show their students "all that is finest in the play"—and that means studying the text.

We turn next to our second question, whether seeing the play is an appropriate "initial presentation," to be followed by reading.

Teachers are sometimes heard to say, with high enthusiasm, that "fortunately," just as they were preparing to start their classroom study of *Julius Caesar*, the film with James Mason and Marlon Brando came to town again; or "fortunately," as they were ready to start A *Midsummer Night's Dream*, the old Reinhardt film with Mickey Rooney as Puck was shown on television; or the Orson Welles version of *Macbeth* popped up again just in time; or the Olivier *Hamlet*, etc. Indeed, teachers have been known to seek information far in advance of a film or television showing or of the opening of a play and to plan their semesters in such a way as to "take advantage" of the production, *just at the point of beginning study in the classroom*. Sometimes teachers recommend that students attend the production; sometimes they insist that they do so, making attendance a class assignment; sometimes they arrange for seats and the class attends the theater as a group. The main purpose, as teachers conceive it, is motivational and introductory: the production will prepare the students for study by "exciting them about the play" and familiarizing them with settings, characters, and plot. But, in fact, to have students see a play, in any form of full production, is to do much more than motivate and introduce its study; witnessing a production, whether the teacher intends it so or not, actually becomes, for the students, the "initial presentation."

But what if it does? What is the matter with using a production as the initial form of presentation? On the surface, this would appear an ideal order of events: to see the full spectacle of the play, acted by skilled actors in the space of two or three hours, and then to follow this agreeable, often exciting experience with study and discussion of the text.

Though we must certainly agree that seeing a play and then reading it is better than seeing it and *never* reading it, we must insist also that to see a play of Shakespeare's before reading it is to damage the experience of reading it. To see one play and then to read a *different* one is good, and to read the play and *thereafter* to see it is even better—in fact, it is best of all. But to see the play and then to read it is not even as good as merely to read it.

What is so desperately "wrong" about seeing a production of, say, *Hamlet*, before studying the text is briefly this: seeing the production first robs the student of the experience—the high privilege—of creating his own "production" in his own mind's eye. To deprive a student of this experience is worse than unfortunate; it is positively wicked!

Such romantic heretics as Lamb and Hazlitt thought that no actor playing Lear, or Hamlet, or Macbeth, or Prospero could possibly equal the hero that *their own imaginations*, inspired by the bare text, could create. Speaking only for themselves, they were no doubt quite right, for their imaginations were rarely gifted and educated. It would be faulty to suppose that the imaginations of most students are equally capable; almost certainly, the Hamlets that immature students can "produce" even under ideal conditions of study will be absurdly inferior to the Hamlets they might see on the stage acted by a Gielgud, an Olivier, or a Burton. On the surface, then, that obvious fact would seem to constitute an argument for letting them *see* a great Hamlet instead of trying, inadequately, to invent their own: if what they can get, ready-made on the stage and free for the watching, is far better than they can *imagine*, let them get it, and stop there.

But that is not the point at all. The point is that *the experience of the getting is at least as valuable as what is got*. The vague, incomplete, distorted, inconsistent, impossible Hamlet that the student's struggling imagination manages to conjure up for his mind's eye to see represents a better experience for him, because he did it himself, than the superb but ready-made Hamlet of Gielgud, fitted out with all the complete details of hair, nose, voice, dimension, motion, attitude, and black doublet and hose.

What happens when, say, Hamlet is seen before it is studied is that the imagination is temporarily rendered inactive. There is no need for it to be otherwise. While the student who has recently seen the play reads the text, his mind is not busily engaged in forming its own image of Hamlet, as it ideally should be; for an image has already been thrust upon it by the actor on the stage. The mind's eye has no need to search for glimpses and strive to piece together a whole plausible image—for there before it, ever present and palpable, intruding between mind and text, are all the physical features of—Gielgud.

And as with the protagonist, so also with all the rest of the play: other characters, settings, movements have all been supplied and need not be imagined. Gertrude is the bosomy woman in the flame-colored, low-necked gown, Polonius the plump little figure with legs too puny for his body; the Queen's boudoir is dominated by a canopied bed with bright red coverlet; the Ghost enters from upper left stage while the lighting catches rifts of fog wafted out of the wings; Hamlet finally kills the King by leaping down on him from a table, his weight on the foil. Thus the physical details of the particular production stand between student and text, and the mind's activity becomes mere recollection of these details—an activity which is a shoddy substitute indeed for the activity of the mind striving to build its own solid images of persons, settings, actions from the abstractions on the printed page.

It should also be pointed out that we have been assuming that the available theatrical production was of the highest order, with actors of international reputation and all other features comparably distinguished. But as a practical matter of fact, the productions available for students to see *cannot* generally be counted on to be of this high order. Some will be mediocre, or worse. Some will be "timely" distortions—*The Taming of the Shrew* played in cowboy milieu; *Julius Caesar* with black shirts, brown shirts, and pistols; *Romeo and Juliet* as a twentieth-century "sociological document," plainly influenced by *West Side Story; Hamlet* in modern dress, the hero a pale Freudian, sexually mixed up; *Twelfth Night* played in an eighteenth-century setting. If, as we have insisted, even absolutely first-rate productions are inadequate substitutes for first readings, weak or distorted productions must be accounted intolerable as substitutes. The thought that a leather-jacketed Romeo might become the student's involuntary and permanent image of Shakespeare's Romeo should appall every teacher of English.

CHAPTER 6

The Forms of Presentation Examined

1. RECORDINGS

WE HAVE REJECTED THEATRICAL PERFORMANCE AS AN APPROPRIATE initial presentation of a Shakespearean play. One argument not previously raised is that the teacher has no *control* over the performance, but is only, like the student, a spectator. The performance runs along at its own fast pace, and is finished in one hour or three hours, depending on the completeness of the script. The teacher cannot shout from the audience, "Stop! Speak that passage again, and let us think about it!" A similar objection must be raised to the use of phonograph records. It is true, of course, that the teacher can exercise much more control of these than of live or filmed productions. The machine can be stopped at will, for discussion; the arm can be lifted and moved back to play a passage or a scene again. But this kind of manipulation, hard on records, is even harder on nerves. To move through an entire play in this manner, making as many stops and restarts as necessary to ensure the full understanding of a class, is clearly intolerable. The use of a tape recorder is obviously preferable in this respect. By pressing or releasing a single lever, the teacher can stop or start the tape at will, and can, by managing a succession of buttons, stop, back up, and go ahead again.

But though recordings can be controlled in these ways, and though they have the great advantage of allowing students to hear Shakespeare's lines spoken by distinguished actors, they are far from wholly satisfactory as a method of initial presentation. It *is* necessary, in the course of the serious study of a Shakespearean play, to stop, back up, wait, go ahead, back up, wait, go ahead again—not merely a very great many times, but almost constantly, and to do so quietly, inconspicuously, without the distracting effects of mechanical noises. The most expert operators of tape recorders, compelled to move backward and forward incessantly, unavoidably call attention to the mere mechanics of the whole operation. Coleridge's "willing suspension of disbelief" simply cannot take place when a student's attention is repeatedly claimed by the operation of a machine—indeed, by the very *fact* of the machine. Furthermore, because of the necessity for repeated stopping and starting, the one great advantage offered by the machine—hearing great actors read the passages—is largely lost.

Since that is the case, why not simply play the tape or record through *without* stopping and restarting? The answer is the same as that for which we rejected the use of any staged production as an appropriate substitute for reading—namely, that the mind, being thus exposed to the riches of the text for the first time, is incapable of taking them in fast enough to keep up. But, then, why not play the recording straight through, and *then* begin the careful study of the text? We have objected to the use of film or stage production prior to study of the play—that is, to its use as a form of "initial presentation"—on the grounds that it robs students of the high privilege of exercising their imaginations. Not quite the same objection can be made to use of the recording, which furnishes no physical details of setting and action to the eye, but only accomplished voices.

The use of a recording, then, played straight through, with students following in their texts, of course, may appear to deserve serious consideration as an appropriate form of initial presentation: it is rapid, it provides the special values of skilled actors reading the lines, and it does not rob the students of the right to imagine. Supposing—for the moment at least—that it is the best possible form, let us consider what kind of study should follow. Since, as we have repeatedly insisted, the mind is incapable of taking in "all that is finest in the play" when the lines rush swiftly by and without time for contemplation of meaning, it is evident that the initial presentation—the recording—must be followed by slower, more painstaking examination, with frequent pauses for thought, discussion, and rereading—indeed, sometimes multiple rereadings—of lines and passages. Presumably this activity will take place in class, involving teacher and students, with only occasional recourse to the recording. Though special passages of the recording might sometimes be re-played, probably the teacher should refrain from re-playing any individual passages until students have exhausted their own resources in attempting to resolve questions of interpretation. The danger of too-easy reference to the recording is as serious as it is obvious: the recording can become *the* authority for the "right" interpretation; worse than this, it can stifle students' efforts to solve problems of interpretation. Having the professional reading always at hand is like having "the answers" in the back of the book.

Possibly, with these latter cautions, we have now raised some doubts about the appropriateness of the recording as the initial form of presentation: its "authority" can tarnish the honest independence of a class's efforts to dig out "all that is finest" in the play. We shall return to the question hereafter, when we make a final assessment of all the possible methods of initial presentation.

But now a second question about the use of a recording for initial presentation confronts us. We have supposed that such a first presentation will be followed by a close, careful study of the text. But this "close, deliberate study" will require from three to five weeks, and its effect will be to fragmentize the play; the whole will be lost somewhere among all the pieces. It would be sad indeed to leave things in this condition—*Hamlet*, for example, remembered primarily as an assortment of great lines, purple passages, metaphors of disease, and examples of dramatic techniques, rather than as an artistic whole. Some way of reassembling this whole is imperative. One way is to require students to sit and read the play straight through, at home, without getting up from their chairs, or to give them two or three class meetings for fast, uninterrupted silent reading; a second way—unfortunately, much more often unavailable than available—is to send them to a film or a stage production; and a third way is to repeat the recording that was used for the initial presentation.

Generally speaking, recordings make the best possible way of "putting the play together again" at the close of detailed study. Theatrical performances may be unavailable, and if available may be cut or otherwise inadequate. Some students reading alone may, even after the detailed study, be unable to read well enough and fast enough to sense the artistic wholeness of the play. That leaves the recording as best. Does the fact, then, of its great usefulness at the *end* of study, constitute an argument against use of the recording for initial presentation? To this question, too, we return later.

2. INDIVIDUAL (SILENT) READING

Should students be assigned the task of reading a play first on their own? If so, should they read in class, or at home, or both? And should they be supplied with study questions to guide their reading? Finally, may independent reading be an appropriate form of initial presentation for, say, eleventh and twelfth grades but not for ninth and tenth grades? It is supposed that, if teachers adopt the practice of assigning individual silent reading as the means of first getting through a play, the greater part of each class hour will be spent in discussion, probably with considerable rereading of scenes that have been assigned; otherwise, though the play may have been "read," it will certainly not have been "taught," and an underlying assumption of this book is that with any play of Shakespeare's students need steady and close attention from the teacher.

The method that has just been raised for scrutiny—namely, assignment of scenes for silent reading, followed by class discussion of what has been read—is the most widely used method of teaching Shakespeare in the United States. Variations of this popular method have to do with length of assignments and with the use or non-use of study questions. Teachers sometimes assign small "chunks"—single scenes, or a given number of lines or pages—for overnight reading. They sometimes move through the play rapidly the first time in five assignments, one act to be read each night. Sometimes they ask that classes give the whole play an even faster first reading, using a class period and an overnight or week-end assignment, after which discussion of the play, scene by scene, begins. The one common denominator appears to be the basic principle of having students read first, whether part or whole, and then discuss. It is with the wisdom of this basic order, then, that we should be primarily concerned; the variations are of minor importance.

Though this is indeed the basic method most frequently used in American high schools, it has not been generally successful, and is, in fact, quite unsatisfactory. Probably more than any other one factor, the use of this method is responsible for the complete extinction of Shakespeare in a very large number of English classes throughout the United States, and for this virtual extinction in a great many more, and, what is worse, for the very existence of the "adapted" texts reviewed earlier.

In an enormous number of schools, only "college prep" classes get any Shakespeare at all, and many of these, as we have seen, get only two plays, usually one in the tenth grade and one in the twelfth; and even these classes, in many cases, are given Shakespeare not because the students, as a whole, show any great interest, but because Shakespeare "must" be included in "college prep" classes.

As for the average and "lower track" classes, which have rarely had any Shakespeare since about the mid-1930's, the reason for the disappearance of the plays from their reading lists can be heard in a chorus of voices at any time one may choose to listen. Speaking individually, in the conversation of private groups, on panels and platforms at large and small meetings, or writing in professional journals, teachers have been saying the same thing for many years: "The students can't read him, they don't understand him, they get nothing out of him, they don't like him, they won't read him." And, indeed, teachers of a year's experience are conditioned to expect, in response to the announcement that "We shall start *A Midsummer Night's Dream* next Monday," a rumble of general protest made up of groans, sighs, and muttered "Ugh's!" What is more, teachers who have taught at several levels never fail to comment that the rumble of dissent grows louder each year from the ninth through the twelfth, not because children's lungs grow larger but because their dislike of Shakespeare grows stronger.

While allowing for many exceptions, we have no choice, then, but to yield to the volume of evidence: high school students, in general, cannot read Shakespeare with any significant amount of understanding or with any real pleasure at all. It is not our purpose here to assign blame for this unfortunate fact. It has often been said that the system by which students have been taught to read leaves them unequipped to read Shakespeare, and it has been said just as often that the *kinds* of reading materials given them during the elementary school years have done nothing for either their ability to tackle great works of imaginative literature or their interest in doing so. In short, many secondary teachers blame their elementary colleagues—and they sometimes do so with genuine bitterness—for their students' inability to read Shakespeare. We may best set these quarrels aside for the moment by means of a statement that will at first—in the present context of a book that insists on much Shakespeare in high school—appear startling: it is doubtful that students, in general, would be able to "read Shakespeare" by the time they reach high school, no matter how they had been taught to read and no matter what kind of "reading materials" they exercised themselves on during the elementary school years. Under ideal conditions, doubtless many more would read more successfully than they now do; but the likelihood that very many would read Shakespeare *well enough*, on their own, to perceive much of what is finest in the play is slim. And if they are to perceive little or none of this, there seems no compelling reason for them to be given Shakespeare at all. For the moment, then, we seem to have aligned ourselves with English professors who advocate omitting Shakespeare from high school programs lest students be alienated forever.

We are not, however, ready to argue that Shakespeare should be abandoned in the high school years, early or late. What must be abandoned is the usual way of going at the reading of Shakespeare.

When teachers who have given up Shakespeare's plays entirely, or are at the point of doing so, or, worse, are ready to turn to "adapted" versions are questioned about their method of teaching, their answers are monotonously similar: *they have assigned students to read independently first, in smaller or larger chunks, and have discussed afterwards.* A typical statement is the following, supplied by a ninth-grade teacher:

> I told them to read A *Midsummer Night's Dream* through once over the week end so that we could start discussing on Monday. On Monday only about half the class had managed to get to the end; some of the others had given up before the end of Act II. But what was more discouraging was that those who finished, or said they had, knew really nothing about the play except what they had read in the Introduction. They could not tell me how it all "came out." They did not think the artisans' play was funny, and only a few even remembered it. They had no understanding of why the lovers act the way they do in the forest. They disliked all the poetry and simply skipped over most of it. They were completely indifferent to the fairies. Only one boy could point to a specific scene where he thought Bottom was "funny." After a completely frustrating week of discussion, I decided that Shakespeare was not for this class.

When assignments have been made in shorter "doses," reports are not all quite so bad: students have dutifully plowed through the required number of lines or scenes, though they have taken no joy in doing so; they have found much that was meaningless in spite of the footnotes and the glossary; they have found the poetry "icky," the action "mixed up." When they have been assigned to write answers to study questions in connection with their reading, they have done their lesson as if they were plodding through mire.

The evidence, then, appears to be conclusive: not only ninth graders, but high school students in general cannot read Shakespeare—cannot read, that is, with understanding, with perception, and with pleasure. It has already been stated that perhaps it is really unreasonable to expect that they *should* be able to do so. But to say so much is not to agree that Shakespeare is not for them; it is only to say that the basic method of "read first—discuss afterwards" is unsatisfactory.

3. READING ALOUD BY STUDENTS

Before getting into the question whether reading aloud by students in class is a desirable form of initial presentation, we should

avoid possible misunderstanding by making one categorical statement with which few teachers are likely to disagree: *reading
aloud of Shakespeare by students is not only highly desirable, but
indispensable; the study of no play should be considered finished
until every student in the class has had his chance and made the
most of it.*

But whether reading aloud by students is a desirable form of
initial presentation is quite another question. Here we should
also point out that in all probability this basic method of first
"getting through" the play is second only to the method just
discussed in the frequency of its use by teachers.

Several variations of the basic method are possible and are
used. Some teachers, starting the play, call on students at random
to read parts, changing readers at intervals during the hour. Some
teachers tend to choose the best readers, at least for major roles;
others—preferring to give experience to those who most need it—
pick out the timid or the least able. Sometimes readers are chosen
a day ahead and asked to prepare to read specified parts in the
next scene; for these students, thus, the "initial presentation"
will not be the oral reading they perform in class, but the independent reading they do at home. Sometimes teachers break into
the reading at frequent intervals for explanation or discussion;
sometimes they wait until a scene has been completed, then
discuss the whole before moving to the next scene. And yet
again, teachers sometimes assign a "cast" of students to make
more elaborate preparation, including rehearsal, for reading a
scene aloud in front of the class with token action and props;
occasionally students are asked to read a scene in this fashion
without the preparation of prior reading or rehearsal. But the
variations devised by ingenious teachers are many, and we need
not catalogue them all.

The advantages usually claimed for this basic method in any
or all of its variations are fairly obvious, and their values are
so real as to make dispute fruitless. Reading aloud by students,
especially in front of the class with a suggestion of action, is
said to "liven up" the plays, to "bring Shakespeare to life." Vis-
ible, audible, actual persons are thus supplied to fill up what
would otherwise, for most students, be only a void of words.
Dramatic poetry, in this way, is first *heard*, as it was meant to

be. The method involves student participation in the fullest sense, and all members of the class can, by turns, enjoy this active participation. Classes, allowing for the inevitable individual exceptions, usually enjoy this kind of participation. And, finally, the experience of reading Shakespeare aloud as part of even the most inept "cast" is in itself a rewarding one. What is more, just as acting in a wretchedly performed Shakespearean play can be a splendid experience for the actors even though it is a bore for the audience, so the experience of reading Shakespeare aloud badly can be exciting to students though listening may be painful to the teacher. But the fact is that teachers, too, often enjoy this method because students seem to enjoy it and things appear to be "going so well."

Is nothing, then, to be said against a basic method for which such high claims, all quite legitimate, are made? Or is this truly the best possible solution to the problem of initial presentation?

Before we conclude that it is, we should put the question somewhat differently: Is this the way that will most likely enable students to perceive "all that is finest in the play"?

We should also consider a point made by some teachers who have tried and abruptly abandoned the method—a point that, incidentally, is more than likely to be emphatically seconded by professional Shakespeareans. Summed up in the form of an admonition, the argument is as follows: "If you truly value Shakespeare and want students to learn to do the same, never allow them to hear *for the first time* the lines of a play read aloud by their classmates."

What is implied is that, in general, high school students read Shakespeare so poorly that a major obstacle is thereby raised between the hearer and appreciation of the play. To this, one reply is that students do, indeed, read Shakespeare aloud badly—which is all the more reason they should have as much practice as they can get in reading him. But the reply to this, in turn, seems unanswerable: true, but not at the expense of their classmates' perception of what is to be valued in Shakespeare.

Though the inadequacy of students' reading is certainly lessened somewhat when students are first asked to "prepare" their parts, the improvement is not enough to make any material difference in the performance. If students have prepared on their own, they will have encountered the same difficulties that were pointed out in our discussion of independent, individual reading as a form of initial presentation. They will not have understood. And that is to say that they will not be appreciably better prepared to read aloud than if they have not prepared at all, since reading well assumes understanding of what is being read. The fact is that if students in general cannot read Shakespeare well enough on their own to understand and value what is finest in the plays, they most certainly cannot succeed in the far harder task of reading aloud in such a way that their classmates will understand and value what is in the plays.

How then can it be that so very many teachers continue to use this method year after year? Some "always" use it. Others use it "mainly," and add that "if there were time" they would go through the whole play in this manner—implying their conviction that this is the ideal method, which only the limitation of time prevents their using exclusively. Teaching manuals that accompany textbook editions generally lend a kind of authority for the method, recommending its use in whole or part, and textbooks on the teaching of English—with some notable exceptions—also sanction it.

On the whole, we shall no doubt be right if we assume that most teachers who regularly use this method do so because they honestly believe in it. On the surface, the evidence appears conclusive: all students are busy, some reading aloud while others listen and watch their texts; students are also plainly enjoying the hour, laughing on occasion; often addressing good-humored comments at readers who have finished their "turn" for the moment, rarely doing anything that requires any disciplinary action or cross word from the teacher; and, meanwhile, the lines, passages, scenes, and acts are sliding past at a satisfactory clip. To all appearances, they are genuinely enjoying the study of Shakespeare. Could the most uncompromsing Shakespearean ask for more than just that?

But is this really "the study of Shakespeare," and is it really Shakespeare that is being enjoyed? Or is this in fact merely "playing at" the study of Shakespeare? Is it Shakespeare who is really the center of attention and interest? Are the minds of the listeners fixed on the lines being read, or are they fixed on the reading of the lines by Dorothy, or Fred, or Harry? When they laugh, is it more often because of a Shakespearean joke or because of the "goof" that Harry just made in pronunciation? When they are moved to comment admiringly, is it because they truly appreciated the passage just read, or because they have an eye for Dorothy, who came through her stint without a fumble? Is Fred, who has just read a speech, now intently following the meaning of the lines being read by the next reader, or is he slyly peeking ahead at his own next speech to find what formidable words it contains?

When the hour is done and they all go out, talking happily and impatient for more of the same tomorrow, was it Shakespeare who gave them their good time—or had he, really, any more than an incidental part in it? Was the highest and most memorable moment of the hour *really* supplied by the masterful ironies of Antony's eloquence in the funeral oration—or was it, in fact, supplied by the happy accident that "Friends, Romans, countrymen, lend me your ears" was read by Joe, whose enormous ears have always been the butt of the joke and in this case made the whole speech hilarious and sent the class into hysterics?

It would be merely perverse to insist that a class hour spent so happily as this one (which is a sketch drawn from life) was without some sort of educational value; the very camaraderie inspired by the accident of the ears might alone be worth something. But it seems in order to suggest that, whatever these values amount to, they are different in kind from those potential in a Shakespearean play. They may be fine values, but they are not Shakespearean values. During the two decades, roughly, of the 1940's and 1950's we should hardly have dared to commit the heresy even of questioning, when students were having "fun" with the classroom activity they were engaged in, whether that activity was necessarily the best possible one for them to be engaged in. During those decades the fun *was* the value. But in the 1960's, perhaps we dare to suggest that the obvious fun of reading Shakespeare aloud is not the best value to gain from the study of Shakespeare. And certainly we may risk asserting that the two values are not synonymous, that in fact they may not even have any real connection with each other. And it is, in any event,

Shakespearean values that teacher and class should strive to gain from the study of Shakespeare.

Here, lest we seem to disprize the experience of reading aloud, we should reassert what we said at the outset—namely, that reading Shakespeare aloud is an indispensable experience for students and that no study of a play should be considered finished until all have had their chance. *But the right time is not at the beginning.* Reading aloud by students is an unsatisfactory form of "initial presentation" because it substitutes a different kind of experience for the experience of "all that is finest" in the play. The time to have students read aloud is any time after the initial presentation has been finished.

Finally, before turning to other matters, we should add that the objections we have raised to this basic and popular method of initial presentation are not necessarily applicable to other plays than Shakespeare's. Probably this method is nearly as unsatisfactory for the Greek tragedies that are read in some high schools, and for some other plays that are often read, such as those of Ibsen and Shaw. But it is very likely not only satisfactory but eminently appropriate for the general run of Broadway plays. Just as most plays are better seen on the stage, and never read at all, so these latter, if they *are* read, will probably yield most if they are read aloud by a cast of students; most of "what is in them" is thus opened to understanding and enjoyment. But Shakespeare's plays stand quite apart from these. If their wealth in depth is merely skimmed over, left untapped, as it is when students "take parts" there is no really sound reason for preferring Shakespeare to *Our Town.*

4. READING ALOUD BY THE TEACHER

We have now considered three possible methods of initial presentation and have found two to be unsatisfactory for the same underlying reason, namely, that they fail to unlock "all that is finest in the play" to the understanding and enjoyment of students. Only one method—use of recordings, with students following in the text—was not rejected flatly, like the others, but was reserved for comparison with the fourth and final method.

This remaining method presumes *line-by-line reading of the entire play by the teacher with students following in their own texts*. It does not, however, presume that the reading will be uninterrupted—like "a dramatic reading," or performance by the teacher; on the contrary, it involves a combination of reading, re-reading, comment, question, and discussion carried on as a single operation—an operation that precludes the possibility of "dramatic reading." It might aptly be described as the "joint progress" of teacher and students through the text of a play, with the teacher always in control of pace, depth, and emphasis.

Though certain teachers—including, very probably, a high percentage of those who "know Shakespeare" best—have continued to use this method year after year with no significant variation, the fact is that it has been generally out of favor during the past twenty-five to thirty years. Its period of disfavor, that is to say, has coincided with the period of an English philosophy that advocated "free" reading, individualized reading, breadth rather than depth, quantity rather than quality, multiple activity. This point of view favored having students read mainly on their own, and chose to provide "readable" materials of graded difficulty that students could indeed read without a teacher.

Now this era has passed, or is passing. Both Shakespeare and the basic principle of close reading of first-rate literary texts by teachers and students together are rapidly, even abruptly, regaining favor. And indeed there can be no serious doubt that the return of Shakespeare to truly general use in classrooms and schools where he has been absent or represented in bastard versions is contingent on the adoption of this basic method. This is hardly a debatable issue; it is a statement of a truth that teachers who are sufficiently acquainted with both Shakespeare and students have never doubted.

But before discussing the advantages of this method and the details of its use, we are obliged to deal systematically with the principal objections that are or have been made to it. These are numerous, and many are ferociously advanced. Further, some are weighty, and if they prove valid, we may have to agree that they outbalance the sum of the advantages that can be named. Briefly, these objections are as follows; we shall name them and then discuss each.

1. This method is too slow; it takes too long to read through a play aloud line by line.

2. It invites inattention, boredom, shirking of individual responsibility by students.

3. It is a piecemeal approach which fragmentizes the play, destroying the sense of continuity and the dramatic force of the action.

4. It holds all students to the same pace, delaying some and rushing others.

5. It is "spoon feeding"; it gives students no choice to learn to read Shakespeare independently.

6. It reduces or eliminates opportunities for group activities of many kinds, etc.

7. It denies to students the experience of reading aloud and "taking parts."

8. It presumes an ability that not all teachers can be expected to have—that of reading Shakespeare well aloud.

9. It demands too much of teachers physically, taxing both voice and general energy unreasonably.

10. It forces on students the teacher's own interpretations, attitudes, conceptions of character, etc.

In short, as these major objections make apparent, this method of initial presentation of a play runs counter to almost everything about teaching methods that English teachers have read, heard, or been actively taught during, roughly, the past thirty years. For it does not involve wide and free reading at as rapid rate as possible, with a premium placed on quantity, in graded materials of calculated difficulty that can be covered "on the student's own." It does not involve the use of "dynamically functioning" groups of students gathered about tables or in little circles. It does not involve, at least immediately, the use of any audio-visual aids except the textbooks and the teacher's voice. And it involves no busy participation in the form of panels, committees, class clubs, or polls. It does not, in fact, involve any of the favored procedures that long threatened the total extinction of Shakespeare in American high schools, actually did eliminate him in many schools except for elite classes, and fathered a host of bastard editions—

"forty-minute" plays, modern English "adaptations," and even prose retellings—because only these could be managed by the methods advocated.

We should now examine, one by one, the listed objections. In the course of dealing with these, we shall necessarily also expose much of the actual working of this method of teaching Shakespeare and most of the advantages that can be claimed for it. Thereafter a bare summary should suffice to conclude the discussion.

1. *Too slow, takes too long.* That line-by-line reading and discussion of a play with a class is a speedy operation, no teacher who has ever used the method will be likely to contend. But that it is "too" slow and takes "too" long does not necessarily follow—and in this case it does not follow at all. How slow is "too" slow, if what is being read is absolutely first-rate, as Shakespeare is? How long is "too" long, if what is being read is absolutely first-rate? To say that "too" long was spent on a certain work is to suggest that teacher and class could have spent their time, or the saved portion of it, to better advantage on something else. But then we must ask, a little snappishly, just precisely *how* teacher and class could better spend their time than in the close study of a supremely great work. Finish *Hamlet* in a week in order to move on to something else? *What* else?

These questions do not imply, however, that there can be no such thing as spending "too" long on one of Shakespeare's plays. Teacher and class spend "too" long when—to borrow a term from economics—they go past the point of "diminishing returns." The determination of this critical point is never easy or certain; but the teacher who works line by line with students, using a method of such flexibility that it permits "playing by ear," is in a better position than anyone else to determine when it is reached —and to act accordingly.

The need is for sensitivity and great flexibility; the way is not to exhaust either the play or the students, but to break off when what is being returned is less than the time and labor being spent.

We may point out also that the very *lack* of speed with which teacher and class move through the text of a great work is—far from being a fault—a positive virtue of this method. Though none can reasonably question that there is value in being able to read printed pages at high speed—even. to a maximum of entire volumes gulped down in ten or fifteen minutes, as some individuals are reputedly capable of doing after intensive training—yet there is also value in learning to go slow. Few college professors of English have ever been heard to complain that their students *read Shakespeare too slowly*. The universal complaint of college professors is that their students, freshmen in particular, expect to rush through a play, or a rich poem, as fast as the eye can sweep the page. Most freshmen are simply astonished to find that a passage of ten lines is considered worthy of a whole hour's hard concentration, and if there may be said to be a continuing, semester-long struggle between a college instructor and his class, it centers on his insistence that they learn the necessity of slowing down. At either the high school or the college level, reading Shakespeare line by line with students is the best method of demonstrating this necessity.

Finally, though this method is admittedly not speedy—indeed, the lesson it teaches is "go slow"—it is not in fact *as* slow as its opponents would have us think. By comparison with its chief rival method—independent reading followed by discussion—it may even turn out to be faster. If the teacher makes advance assignments of reading to be done either in class or at home and in either small units, such as scenes, or large ones, such as acts, and if study of the play is to be thorough enough to warrant undertaking the play at all, it goes without saying that intensive follow-up discussion of what has been read will be necessary. In conducting this discussion, the teacher has a choice of two methods: to move through the scene or act systematically from first to last, or to ask questions and invite questions from students that may eventually "cover" the entire scene or act though not systematically.

No matter which way the teacher chooses, it is certain that any appropriately thorough discussion will make it necessary to read out virtually every line in the scene before the hour is over. To have profitable discussion, students need the text immediately before their eyes; a "closed-book" discussion of Shakespeare, based on students' recollection of what they read haltingly and only half understood a day or a week before, is not only time-consuming but wasteful and frustrating. Thus no time is actually saved by having students first read through a scene and thereafter discuss it; as often as not, the discussion will take longer than if teacher and students had read and discussed together in the first place. And if it is a random, hit-or-miss discussion, it will regularly prove both lengthy and inadequate. The method of reading and discussing with students is not really "slow," comparatively, because it is an orderly *combined operation*. It is, at the same time, for reasons that will appear, far more satisfactory and satisfying than the rival method.

2. *Invites inattention, shirking of individual responsibility.* Confirmed disbelievers in the method of teaching Shakespeare by reading with students have sometimes drawn unflattering pictures of the method in operation: teacher reading, pausing sometimes to labor a point and sometimes to exhort students to pay attention and behave themselves; students looking out of windows, sitting with eyes closed, half asleep, passing notes, giggling, staring vacantly at ceiling or floor, reading something "more interesting" hidden behind the propped-up Shakespeare textbook, yawning, holding wrist watches to their ears in disbelief; indifferent, rudely inattentive, and most certainly completely *uninvolved* in the fate of Brutus or Macbeth.

It would be pleasant to assert that the description is purely imaginary, that no classroom ever really looked so hopeless—or at least not while Shakespeare was being taught. Unfortunately, such debacles do happen. But they do not always happen, and the fact of failure cannot be laid to the method itself. In contrast to this portrait of an uninvolved class is that of a class in which every mind is intent on the text and the questions that rise from it, in which every face expresses absorption, in which external distractions of sight and sound have literally ceased to exist. This is no imaginary or rare portrait, either, but a real one that teachers who have mastered the art of simultaneously reading and discussing Shakespeare with their classes have learned to take for granted.

Two reasons for failure with this method suggest themselves at once: first, the teacher is—for one or another reason—inept; second, the students, accustomed from past experience to every kind of activity *except* that of sustained attention to the text of a work of literature, have yet to adjust themselves to their role in the procedure. If the teacher is inept, the remedy is not easy; it requires, first, deliberate and continuous personal study of Shakespeare, and, second, steady and intelligent practice in using the method. Chapters that follow here present general suggestions that may be helpful—but there is no real substitute for better acquaintance with Shakespeare, or for intelligent practice until one learns to "play by ear." If the students, on the other hand, are at fault because their previous experience has taught them to expect some less exacting procedure than that of steady application to text, experience and an apt teacher will get them into the habit sooner than might be imagined.

3. *Piecemeal approach fragmentizes the play.* In the theater, one of Shakespeare's plays takes from two to four hours, depending on the length of the play and the kind of stage. Silent reading without pausing to ruminate takes about the same amount of time, two to four hours, depending on reader and play; painfully slow readers obviously require much longer and even so may emerge at last with little sense even of "what happened." A studio recording of a full play runs a little shorter than production on a "fast" stage.

In contrast, reading a play aloud and adequately discussing, at the same time, words, lines, passages, scenes, and acts requires on the average, say, twenty-five class hours—which, of course, must be spread over a period of five or six weeks. This is a long time to keep interest alive, a long, annoying delay for those who are impatient to find how everything "comes out." Even more importantly, it is a long time to keep in mind all that has gone before, *a long time to hold on to a sense of the whole*, which stands every chance of being overwhelmed and lost in the daily discussion of details.

Further, one vitally important part of the artistic experience of a play is the effect of "compressed time." In many plays, and particularly in some that are most appropriate for reading in high school, like *Julius Caesar*, *Macbeth*, and *Romeo and Juliet*, Shakespeare *shrinks* time to give the illusion of swiftly consecutive incidents. By a kind of dramatic magic, an audience is made to feel that the seventeen years of Macbeth's reign are contained within three hours. In *Romeo and Juliet*, the lovers first meet on Sunday night and are dead together in the tomb on Thursday night. The swift rush of action not only contributes to the tragic effect that the spectator should feel, but is itself a contributing cause of the catastrophe. Can a class stretch out the reading of a play over five weeks without sacrificing some of the indispensables of its artistic force—the very reason for reading the play? Is there a way, or are there ways, by which these losses can be prevented, or at least minimized? If not, surely this method must be found unsatisfactory and dismissed from further consideration. That the method will defeat some of the very reasons for using it, unless the teacher takes care, there can be no doubt. But how take care?

Devices that teachers have used to prevent losses like those named above include telling or reading the story of the play through quickly in advance of line-by-line study; playing an abbreviated recording that can be heard within an hour; first reading the play aloud—the teacher alone reading, as rapidly as possible—perhaps in three class meetings; assigning the class to skim through the play in one evening or over a week end. All these devices represent efforts toward the same goal—that of somehow planting *a sense of the whole* in students' minds that can, hopefully, remain during the weeks of study that follow. They express an intuitive recognition that such a sense is precious.

We may agree that, ultimately, having a sense of the whole is a *sine qua non* of artistic appreciation. But to say so much is not to say that this sense must be fixed in the mind *before* the intensive study of the play is begun. On the contrary, a driving purpose of the long intensive study is to *build* a sense of the whole, and such a sense is not to be confused with superficial and quickly gained knowledge of "who gets killed" or "how it all comes out." The "organic unity" of Shakespeare's plays that Coleridge's great insight detected is a phenomenon that must be discovered by working from the inside out, just as it grew from the inside out.

The problem is, thus, not one of "sustaining" or "holding on to" a sense of the whole while study of the details is progressing week by week, but one of actively *building* it week by week. Reading a play well means maintaining a steady awareness of all that is relevant, from the first scene forward, to understanding of the particular moment of action that is immediately under study. Teaching students to read Shakespeare means, in large part, teaching them the awareness that an experienced reader maintains and brings to focus upon any givén point in the action. In all of Shakespeare's major works, including those that we have found best suited for study in high school, there is, quite literally, a steady necessity to refer to lines, scenes, passages that have gone before—to maintain, one may truly say, a constant vision of the whole past up to the current moment.

It is quite false to assume that line-by-line study of Shakespeare means concentration on the meaning of individual lines in isolation—hence certain loss of what went before and what comes after. Managed by an able teacher, it means more nearly the direct opposite—an incessant reciprocative action going on in the mind, relating part and whole, with each illuminating the other. A peculiar virtue of the line-by-line method, well managed, then, is that, far from causing the student to lose sense of the whole, it demands that he constantly build, hold, and use this sense. Shakespeare's way of developing a plot—with its complex of actions, situations, characters—is, in direct terms, a matter of filling the mind with cumulative awarenesses: what has góne before bears heavily upon—indeed, determines—what now is and what will follow. The primary task of the teacher who proceeds line by line is to help students keep this growing bundle of awarenesses intact.

The need, then, to supply students with a "view of the whole" before intensive study is begun is not actually as important as we may have supposed, and certainly it is not crucial, as it has seemed to teachers who make an unfailing point of telling or reading the story, playing a recording, or otherwise "fixing" the main outline beforehand. Even so, perhaps it is reasonable to suggest here that teachers should try both ways—with and without preliminary overviews. They may conclude that, in the last analysis, neither the overview nor the absence of it makes a really significant difference. Some will find that the line-by-line study "goes a little better" because the briefing has alerted students to particular characters and moments of action and thus motivated their serious assault on the text. But others, just as surely, will find that some students, or many, will mistakenly suppose that, having already heard the story, they have really nothing more to learn about the play—"Why don't we just go on to another one?" In the latter case, the teacher will find that there is more to overcome than before.

We still must deal with the problem of saving the sense of swift, continuous action that is a vital part of the dramatic experience and that is surely lost in a line-by-line study that takes weeks. This is not an easy problem to solve, but neither is it an impossible one. *The time to solve it is not before the intensive study begins, but after it is finished.* One way is to have students hear a full recording—an effective way except that unless some extraordinary arrangement is made it will be necessary to extend the experience over three or four class hours—which is to say, three or four days; thus, almost if not quite, the sense of swift action is again lost. Another way is to play a greatly abbreviated recording that can be heard in one class period; this may catch the sweep of action, but its disadvantages are obvious: successive high spots do not make a whole play. A filmed version of the play, if one is available, presents the same problems in even more severe form: if the film is full, it will take several class hours; if it is cut to the length of a class period, it is worthless for the specific purpose. Often teachers in metropolitan areas have the good fortune (or manage their timing adroitly) to finish studying the play just in time to take the class to a theater where the filmed or live production is showing; this is no doubt the happiest solution of all—but also the least assured.

All else failing, the teacher can do what many college teachers do after they have spent several weeks with freshmen over the text of, say, *Hamlet* or *King Lear*—namely, instruct students to set aside three hours, isolate themselves, get comfortable, *and read every word from beginning to end of the play without getting up from the chair.* If the student has a full recording, he can of course hear that straight through while he follows in the text.

Further consideration is given to recordings, films, and such aids in a later chapter.

4. *Holds students to the same pace.* English teachers have long been advised that in ideal circumstances students should be allowed to read at their own speed. This point of view is the basis

for programs of individual reading, in which students work independently, reading selections at their own level, of their own
choosing (within limits), and at their own pace. In a month's
time, thus, one student may manage half a dozen novels, for
example, of fairly "hard" character, whereas another in the same
class may get through only one or two relatively easy ones.

It is not our purpose at this time to dispute the claims of those
who advocate or practice this procedure or any variation of it.
But it is necessary to contradict any notion that this is the *one*
appropriate kind of procedure to use in all English classes throughout the year with all literary works. Though it may be entirely
right to have students read freely during some part of each year
in novels, short stories, and various nonfiction works, it is certainly entirely wrong to have them proceed so at all times and
never to study certain texts closely with the teacher and one
another. Poems that are worth reading intensively must unquestionably be treated in the latter way, and so must the plays of
Shakespeare. We might continue here by insisting that at least
one absolutely first-rate novel should be taught in this way each
year, some essays, and even certain first-rate stories. But it is with
Shakespeare only that we are immediately concerned.

It is, of course, a fact that when the teacher reads aloud with
students following silently, all must keep not only approximately
but exactly together; the slow must move along faster than they
normally read, and the fast must restrain their impulses to hurry.
But it is also a fact that when the method is working smoothly
neither the slow nor the fast student is even *aware* that he is
reading faster or more slowly than usual. He does not think anything about the rate at all, because his attention is claimed by
the profusion of elements that are unfolding in line and passage
in scene after scene.

No doubt much that is read in high school English classes is
preferably read by students on their own, at their own speeds.
The student who can sweep whole lines at a glance should be
encouraged to do so, and the slower reader should often be free
to work at texts that will give him the best opportunity to increase his speed. If a teacher were to take such texts as are appropriate for this purpose, and to attack them with the same
drastic method that we recommend for Shakespeare—reading line

by line and compelling fast and slow students alike to hold to the common pace—surely the practice would deserve to be called vicious. To read, say, *Treasure Island* or *Little Britches* line by line with an "average" ninth- or tenth-grade class would simply be wasteful; the method would be excessive; it would be more exacting than the text demands. But a Shakespeare text has depth enough to keep the mind of the fastest reader at least as fully occupied as that of the slowest reader. The principle is to give the particular work the particular treatment that it requires.

One additional point also renders invalid the charge that reading Shakespeare with students is "bad" because it holds all students to the same speed. The point is simply that the teacher does not merely *read straight along*—when rate of reading might truly be an issue—but pauses to comment and to question as frequently as word, line, and passage require. No doubt it is because of this fact that neither slow nor fast student is aware that his normal reading rate is being inconvenienced.

5. *"Spoon feeding" does not teach students to read Shakespeare independently.* There seems no choice here but to take vigorous and unqualified exception to the argument that this method prevents students from learning to read Shakespeare on their own. Though we should not go so far as to insist that this is the only right method for any teacher to use with any and all high school classes, we shall insist that this is the best, if not the only, way of teaching classes to read Shakespeare independently. Our claim is thus diametrically opposed to the objection.

The purpose in reading with students is not, in fact, merely to get a particular play of Shakespeare's "read." It is to develop students' own power to read masterpieces of literature. The ultimate aim is to equip them to "get" as much from a great work unaided as they get when teacher and class read and discuss line by line. We do not exaggerate when we insist that the only way to accomplish this purpose (except with one student in hundreds) is by steady demonstration—which is what this method basically is. In reading, commenting, questioning, awakening a multitude of relevant awarenesses, the teacher is teaching the art of reading a masterpiece by doing just what the able reader has learned to do for himself. The able reader reads a masterpiece with his mind fairly buzzing with activity; it is this buzzing activity that the teacher's demonstration aims both to stimulate and to simulate. Reading with students is not itself independent reading; but it is the way to it.

The charge of "spoon feeding" might better be brought against either of two other teaching practices: First, that in which the materials being read are of a kind that students could handle easily enough on their own, but which the teacher treats as though they required line-by-line study by teacher and class; second, that in which, given richly complex texts such as Shakespeare's, the teacher merely reads *to* the students and literally *tells* them everything. But the charge does not apply to our method of reading *with* students, which steadily involves teacher and students in close collaboration on a text that is constantly before them. Except that students are younger and the textual probing somewhat less deep, this method does not differ essentially from that used by professors in Shakespeare seminars. Because of the constant alertness and mental activity that it demands, the method is more nearly the direct antithesis of "spoon feeding."

Now that we have, hopefully, exonerated this method from a gross libel, perhaps we should take one moment more in which to say a charitable word *even* for "spoon feeding," that practice which has been so long reviled as possibly the very worst sin that an English teacher can commit. We may begin with the following statement: that though it is certainly not necessary to "spoon feed" Shakespeare to high school classes, if for some incredible reason students could get no Shakespeare except through spoon feeding, we should insist that spoon-fed Shakespeare is preferable to no Shakespeare. *If it were necessary to spoon feed Shakespeare at the rate of twenty lines per day, like translating Virgil, we should insist on the practice.* The worst sin that an English teacher can commit is not that of spoon feeding students with first-rate works that they cannot read on their own; the worst sin that an English teacher can commit is that of using worthless reading materials and justifying their use on the grounds that students can read them on their own.

6. *Reduces or eliminates group activities.* From about 1935 to 1955, the "ideal" portrait of an English class represented bustling

activity, with students in clusters of four or six around tables, talking animatedly, drawing freely on diverse materials—magazines, newspapers, books, and one another's remarks. Such groups, always described as "dynamic," had chairmen and secretaries, undertook projects, discussed topics, reached conclusions (often by voting), and ultimately shared their "findings" with the whole class by panel presentation or elected spokesman. All aspects of "language arts" thus came into play, students gained practice in democratic processes, shy and reluctant individuals "grew" through vital participation, and teachers "managed workshops" rather than "taught."

The values of these procedures are not in question here. Much that should be accomplished in high school classrooms can probably be done best by just such means. But this is not the way to study Shakespeare, or any literary masterpiece that requires the close collaboration of a teacher whose familiarity with the work and greater maturity can be of inestimable aid to young students.

The assumption that reading with students eliminates active student participation is entirely false; this method *demands* student participation. We have earlier characterized the line-by-line study of the text as a joint enterprise of teacher and all members of the class. The teacher provides the reading voice, makes pointed comments, asks questions, and controls discussion. But the members of the class participate actively with eyes, ears, voices, and minds. At its best, this method produces "dynamic group activity" of the very highest order, and it yields results more satisfying than those that can otherwise be gained. The entire class becomes an active group, united in the single task of finding "what is there" in the text of a masterpiece. At the best moments, the teacher becomes a referee in an exciting pursuit of truth.

As for related activities, involving individuals or small groups, these do not form part of the actual presentation. Their place will be considered in a following chapter.

7. *Denies students the experience of reading aloud.* As we have so far described it, this method of initial presentation calls for the teacher alone to read the text aloud. Regularly, students will reread lines or passages aloud in the course of the discussion that

accompanies presentation. But it is quite true that only the teacher does the initial reading.

The time for students to read aloud, we must continue to insist, is not initially, but afterwards. Every student should be permitted—even required—to read, or speak, as many lines of Shakespeare aloud in class as time permits. The study of the play should not be considered finished, as we have said before, until all students have had their chance to try out their own voices on the sounds of Shakespeare's verse. But this, too, is a subject for a later chapter.

8. *Presumes an ability not possessed by all teachers, that of reading Shakespeare well aloud.* At the base of objections that many teachers have made to this method of presenting Shakespeare is to be found one that is not so much an objection as it is a kind of fear: "But I can't read Shakespeare well enough!" It is interesting to note how often other objections vanish when this one has been removed.

That all English teachers should be able to read well aloud, every English teacher knows. Reading well is a kind of career insurance like no other that a teacher can own. The ability can be acquired, or it can be enormously improved, by practice. The beginning teacher could do much worse, before beginning the first year, than to spend the summer reading aloud—not only Shakespeare, but anything and everything, from newspaper columns to Milton. The inept reader of poetry is simply not a teacher of poetry; indeed, one might as well say, not a teacher of English. To announce that one "Cannot read well enough," as though that ended the matter, and therewith to justify dependence on student reading and recordings, and films, or else to abolish the *sounds* of literature from the classroom, is to shirk a responsibility that is not peripheral but central. For an English teacher, the obligation to read well aloud is not optional; it is mandatory.

These emphatic admonishments would seem to offer scant encouragement to the insecure, especially to those who are already only too well aware of their vocal limitations—who know that they lack and can never really develop Shakespearean actors' voices, however hard they may try. Would it not be better, after all, to let the recorded voices of professional actors guide students even through the initial reading of the play? Or would it not be better to distribute parts for the initial reading among boys and girls in the class, so that there will be at least a variety of voices and physical statures?

The answer, still, is *No.* The teacher is the one who knows the play and should do the first reading.

We should ask, at this point, what is meant by "reading well aloud" in this context. Reading well aloud on the stage, at a public performance, is one thing; reading well aloud in a classroom *as a means of laying the text of a work of literature open for study* is quite another. Many teachers, particularly those just beginning, are unnecessarily worried because they suppose that "reading well aloud" in the classroom means giving a dramatic performance—so that when the hour ends and students are leaving they will say to one another "Doesn't she read magnificently! What a voice!" or "What feeling! He should go on the stage!"

We shall exaggerate only a little if we suggest that, on hearing such comments as these bubbling from students after spending an hour on the text of Shakespeare, a teacher would do well to wonder whether, despite the compliments, he or she may not have misspent the hour. For the purposes of initial presentation and the accompanying study of text, "reading Shakespeare well aloud" does not mean displaying teacher's vocal and histrionic arts. It means reading so unobtrusively, with the teacher's personal talents so submerged, that students actually tend to forget that the teacher *is* reading. It means reading so unostentatiously that, though indeed the teacher is furnishing the voice, it will seem to the students—following in their texts silently—that they themselves are doing the reading. It means reading so that students are conscious of the text and not of the teacher.

In one respect, at least, this sense of what "reading well aloud" means can bring comfort to teachers who, distrusting their histrionic talents, fear their inability to give a striking performance: they need not and *must* not give a performance. But on the other hand "reading well aloud," though it does not mean giving a performance, does not mean "reading badly aloud," either. It does not mean sing-song, or stumbling, or misreading, or reading as though one did not know what the words mean. It means honest, unpretentious revelation of text, getting the lines "out and up" before students so that they can be discussed; it means *rendering meanings audible*—but doing so inconspicuously, without flourish, so that *all* the attention of students is attracted to the text, and none to the teacher. Learning to read in this way takes at least as much preparation as learning to "perform," but preparation of a different sort: faithful study of the text, sound understanding of the whole play as a work of art, and, then, much practice with or without an actual class until the manner is natural.

Finally, why is it better to read in this way than to "perform"? One main reason has already been implied: a "performance" emphasizes the teacher rather than the text. Another, even more important, is that whereas interruption of a "performance" for comment, question, and discussion of word and line is awkward, unnatural, grating, and intolerable—it may even seem unthinkable—such interruption of "non-performance" reading does not seem like interruption at all, but like a normal part of a complete process. In short, "non-performance" reading in the classroom admits *discussion* as its equal partner in the total process of study. A third, and immensely practical, reason for preferring "non-performance" reading is named below.

9. *Too demanding on teacher's voice and energy.* Akin to teachers' fears that they "cannot read well enough" to carry the initial presentation alone, without the aid of recordings or other means, is the fear that voice and general strength will not hold out through five hours a day through several weeks of steady reading. Obviously, teachers should not be expected to read steadily through the day, day after day, taking all the parts in the play and projecting the voice so that the whole class will be held in a state of dramatic agitation. But in "non-performance" reading, the teacher neither reads nor talks steadily. In an average hour, at least half, perhaps two-thirds of the time will be taken up by students' discussion. Neither does reading need to be *louder* than the teacher's normal teaching voice; if it *is* louder, the method is probably being abused. So long as the teacher remembers that the situation is that of teacher and class, and not that of performer and audience, the teaching day with Shakespeare should be no more exhausting than any other day that is well spent in the English classroom.

10. *Forces teacher's own interpretation on students*. Earlier, we raised the objection that seeing a filmed or staged performance in the place of initial presentation by study of the text forces a ready-made interpretation of the play upon students that is likely to become their permanent image. To the student who sees Olivier's filmed *Hamlet* before reading the play, Olivier *is* Hamlet—or, rather, Hamlet is Olivier; all the while study of the text progresses, the image of the actor intrudes between eyes and text—and it is the harder to brush aside because the student knows no real need to brush it aside.

Try as he might, the teacher in the classroom could never impose on students' minds any such vivid and indelible impression. What is dictated about Hamlet by the most dogmatic teacher can be, after all, only words; but the actors on a stage are physically *real*: the details of image are entirely filled out, complete with hair, height, shape, complexion, clothes, facial features and expressions, voice, and all else that "real" as opposed to imagined beings have.

Even so, by any method of teaching, the teacher can exert a powerful influence on students' interpretation of a play or any other work of literature. That the teacher *should* exert a very strong influence is no doubt true; otherwise why should teachers be valued who have mastered a work beforehand and perhaps lived with it and pondered it for many years? The ripened judgments of teachers are clearly invaluable guides for students who are working their way through a Shakespearean play for the first time. But teachers of ripened judgments will no doubt be least inclined to force "absolute" interpretations upon students; they will best know that many interpretations are possible, and that the most fruitful study of Shakespeare is that which explores them all.

The plain fact is that line-by-line study with students is the best way to explore them all, and, rightly used, best guarantees that the teacher will *not* merely dictate "right" interpretations. By this method, teacher and students engage in a continuous discussion, *with the text immediately before the eyes of all*. Lines and passages are pondered as soon as they have been read aloud; they can be debated, reread in various ways, debated again.

When a teacher *lectures* on a play either before or after the students have read it on their own, the books are normally closed, the textual evidence hidden; in that case, interpretations are much more likely to be merely "received" than jointly explored. Similarly, when students have been assigned to read through on their own, and then, the next day or the next week, are put through a discussion of whole scenes or acts—often in the manner of question and answer, with books closed—the likelihood is much greater that the teacher's "right answers" will readily be accepted by students who have already half forgotten the details of text; and for what was obscure to them in their preliminary reading, they will passively accept whatever ready-made explanation the teacher gives them. It is always quite possible, of course, that this ready-made explanation is also the *best* one; but the objectionable feature is that it was given rather than discovered by a universal putting-together of heads.

One way that is used by experienced teachers who are aware of the danger of dictating interpretations is to say at the beginning of study—and repeatedly thereafter—"I shall often try deliberately to 'sell' you on my own view. When I do, resist with all the evidence the text offers." Truths are sometimes discovered even by students whose main purpose is only to prove the teacher wrong.

It appears that what has been called a dangerous fault in the method of line-by-line study is in fact one of its best virtues. Far from increasing the likelihood that teachers will foist arbitrary interpretations upon students, it most nearly guarantees that students and teachers will jointly build interpretations on the evidence of the text that is constantly before their eyes. That is what the good reader always does, what the good critic always does; and if that is what students learn from line-by-line reading and discussion, what more can be wished?

CHAPTER 7

Just How Does It Work?

WE HAVE NOW SURVEYED THE POSSIBLE WAYS OF PRESENTING A Shakespeare play in a high school classroom, discussed their strengths and limitations, and finally fixed upon a "best" method. Because this way has been out of fashion—running as it does exactly counter to the philosophies that have prevailed in English programs for many years—we were obliged to discuss it in reverse, first clearing away the strong objections that have been responsible for its unpopularity. Ordinarily, we should have proceeded by first discussing details of managing the method and thereafter dealing with objections and with any abuses to which it might lend itself too easily. But in this case, the general disapprobation has been so long standing that it seemed necessary to clear away erroneous assumptions and false charges in order to assure the method of an honest hearing.

But as a matter of fact, in the course of dealing with the major objections we have also named some positive virtues and treated many questions of managing line-by-line study. For example, we have considered such questions as the *speed* at which teacher and class should move, the maintenance of *a sense of the whole* while examining parts, the manner of the teacher's *oral reading,* and the care for students' *active participation* in the search for meanings and the building of interpretations. A very few questions have been left for amplification, and a few new questions, both large and small, remain to be introduced. It is with these that we are next concerned.

More precisely, though the questions appear to be multiple, and almost infinite in number, all converge upon a single one: *exactly how does this method work?* They press for intimate details of the operation: How large a "block" does the teacher read before stopping—a line, a passage, a scene, a whole act? How does the teacher know *when* to stop for comments or questions? Or should the teacher let students signify when clarification is needed, and thus determine the stopping points? What *kinds* of matters should the teacher stop to discuss—meanings of words, images, verse patterns and variations, dramatic techniques, motives of characters, relation of immediate line or passage to what lies behind or ahead? How *long* should the class stop to deal with one question before reading on? Should each class hour begin with a résumé? Should the reading of each larger unit—scene or act—conclude with a résumé and discussion of that unit as a whole? How can one avoid going too fast or too slow, too deep or not deep enough? Should the teacher *always* wait until the class has found the "right" answer to questions, or sometimes save time by supplying it? Should the teacher, or a student, reread lines when questions of interpretation can be illuminated by trying various inflections? It will be noted that all these questions have something in common: they concern "stopping and starting."

These are among the many questions that are always asked by teachers new to the method and unsure of it; they are also questions that experienced teachers are almost always asking themselves, though they rarely ask other persons. Those who ask them often appear to suppose that there are, or ought to be, rigidly "right" answers which, when possessed, will solve all problems of using the method, for once and all. The method might commend itself more readily to many teachers if that were so; but of course it is not so. Most of the questions need to be answered anew with each play and each class—indeed with each line. A teacher who works through the same scenes of, say, *Macbeth* with five successive classes in a single day will be unlikely to "stop and start" at exactly the same places in any two classes, and will be almost certain not to remain stopped for discussion the same length of time in any two classes. Further, if a teacher *did* deliberately stop and start on a fixed and unchanging schedule in successive classes, the best feature of this method—its free-wheeling flexibility—would be sacrificed.

Does the teacher stop on a word in the middle of a line? Indeed he may, and either instantly offer a familiar equivalent or invite a quick one from the class. Does he stop at the end of a line? Indeed he may, either to give or get a quick paraphrase. Does he stop at the end of a full speech of some length? Indeed he may, and then go back to pick up the words, phrases, or lines that need clarification so that the meaning of the speech, and its spirit, can be caught. Does he read through an entire scene before stopping even to clarify one word? Indeed he may, when the dramatic force depends more on the scene's being heard unbroken and less on the immediate explanation of particular words and knotty lines. Thus, for example, the teacher may want, above all else, to keep the experience—which is like an experience of music—of the first balcony scene in *Romeo and Juliet* intact, and therefore might read through without stopping—but it is not inconceivable that the same teacher, meeting the second-period class, might stop half a dozen times to inject clarifying comments or questions, and, during the third-period class, might stop at quite different places, or again might not stop at all.

The experienced teacher knows better than to seek inflexible answers in advance to these various questions. What has been said earlier may perhaps now be repeated with clearer meaning—that line-by-line study of Shakespeare must be mainly "played by ear." So managed, it is not only the most fruitful method, but the easiest and most natural, the most satisfying to teachers and students alike. Ease, naturalness, informality, flexibility, unpretentiousness, honesty are at once its normal characteristics and its best graces.

If there are, then, no set rules that can be learned in advance and followed in the classroom, what *do* teachers need to know, and what can they be advised to learn before they use this method? The answer is the same as that which has been asserted often enough in this book to be taken for its main theme: *they need to know Shakespeare*, not only the particular plays they will teach, but Shakespeare generally. When line-by-line study is managed well, it appears to an observer that the teacher, like the class, is proceeding through the play for the first time—making discoveries, coming upon surprises, groping to relate new developments to old situations, striving to get the "feel" of emerging characters. But appearances are deceiving: the operation will be managed well only when the teacher knows every inch of the ground. "Playing by ear" is the easiest of methods, but only when the text is completely familiar. Its effectiveness depends much on the teacher's sensitivity to the class, on the teacher's ability to keep the "feel" of the total situation during each shifting, changing moment while class and text are engaged face to face. It is this "feel" that tells the teacher when to "stop and start," when to go deep and when to skirt the quagmire. The "feel" itself can be acquired rather quickly; it does not take years of practice—but it depends ultimately on *knowing the text*, and that does take time and close study; there is no shortcut to it, and no substitute. Only when the teacher is at home with the text being studied can the all-important "feel" be trusted to guide the hour.

Before leaving the general question of line-by-line study, we should deal briefly with another aspect of it: should this method *always* be used, throughout every play, at every high school level, with every kind of class, without variation of any kind?

To insist that there is only one "right" way to do anything is to risk being absurd. What we have maintained to this point is that line-by-line study is an effective, efficient, and satisfying way of proceeding with Shakespeare in high school classes at all levels. We have argued what is nothing other than fact—that when this method is *not* used, Shakespeare is reserved for "college prep" or similar classes and is represented by only two plays in four years. Even worse, he is likely to be represented by bastard versions of the plays—"adapted" or rewritten texts in which what makes Shakespeare Shakespeare has been crudely transformed. We have insisted that the restoration of Shakespeare to widely successful use depends upon universal return to a method by which teachers and students examine the text together—read, question, reread, discuss, decide, and move on.

Is this the same as insisting that only this method ought ever to be used? May no high school classes *ever* be trusted to proceed more nearly on their own? Is it not conceivable, for example, that after teacher and students have gone through four plays line-by-line in the ninth and tenth grades, they might, in the eleventh and twelfth grades, be assigned to read ahead in a play, or to the end of it, and thereafter discuss what they have read? If, for example, they have worked line-by-line through *Julius Caesar, The Mer-*

chant of Venice, As You Like It, and *Romeo and Juliet,* may they not be put more on their own in the next two years with *Macbeth* and *Hamlet?*

This is not an easy question, and no one should ever think it is. The purpose of line-by-line study with a teacher, we have said, is not merely to get a particular play read and understood, but also to advance students toward the day that, without a teacher, they can get as much from the play as they can with a teacher. The question is not whether students on their own can get *something* out of *Macbeth* and *Hamlet*—as of course they can, having studied the other four plays thoroughly—but whether they can get *as much* out of them unaided as they could with a teacher. Further, if the teacher is a good one, who knows Shakespeare generally and is especially primed in advance for *Macbeth* and *Hamlet,* the plain certainty is that they will *not* come as near to seeing all that is to be seen in these plays unaided as they would with the teacher. The question therefore answers itself: they should read with the teacher.

But, now, when is this process of reading with the teacher to come to an end? Are students *never* to reach the point at which the teacher will simply say, "Go to it"? When do they stand on their own feet?

The logic of the question nevertheless remains unchanged: in school, teachers *are* available, and because students *do* see more of what is in Shakespeare when they read the plays with the teacher, they should continue to read them with the teacher. It is improbable that any high school students—even those who are especially gifted but are nonetheless relatively inexperienced—can get to, or can be brought to, the point at which, proceeding on their own, they will see as much of "what is there" as they will see under line-by-line study with an able teacher. Indeed, it is highly unlikely that any college students reach the point at which they, proceeding alone, see as much as they do in the close company of an able teacher.

But in spite of this line of logic, there is unquestionably a great purpose to be served by gradually increasing students' responsibility for independent reading. In the view of some people, this purpose is so important that it must be served at any cost. What is here finally suggested, then, is that teachers should find and use means of assigning increasing responsibility to students. But how can they do so, while the basic method remains that of reading line by line under the teacher's direction? Two ways are suggested below.

First, let us suppose that in the ninth grade two plays are to be studied in class, one directly after the other. They are, let us say, *Julius Caesar* and *The Merchant of Venice.* The teacher will certainly read and discuss the first play line by line with the class, with no assignments of independent reading in advance of the class reading and discussion. But with the second play the teacher may wish to experiment, not once but repeatedly. The first two acts, perhaps, can be read and discussed as usual, and then, for overnight reading, the first scene of Act III can be assigned. On the following day, one problem for both teacher and students as they discuss that scene, is to determine (1) the difference (if any) between what individual members of the class were able to see for themselves and what they are now able to see with the teacher's guidance, and (2) the difference between their enjoyment of this scene, read independently, and their enjoyment of earlier scenes read in class.

After discussion, followed by reading and discussion of the next scene during the same hour, teacher and class together can decide whether to repeat the experiment at once or wait until later in the play. Again, in the years that follow, presumably teacher and class will work their way together through the first play read in each year; but increasingly, especially in the junior and senior years, responsibility for independent reading of scenes and acts of the second play should be placed on the class. The object of this kind of progressive assumption of responsibility is obvious: it is, gradually, to narrow the gap between what students can see on their own and what they can see when the teacher is at their elbows. Ideally, they would eventually reach a day on which the teacher could add nothing to what they were able to see for themselves. That day should be an occasion for high festivities.

CHAPTER 8

What Activities—
During and After?

PRECEDING CHAPTERS SHOULD HAVE MADE IT CLEAR THAT THE BASIC activity during the weeks of reading a Shakespearean play in class is precisely that—*reading the play*.

Of the activities that accompany reading or follow it, one is so intimately related and so important that we have necessarily dealt with it while dealing with reading. This activity is the *discussion* that accompanies the reading of the text as closely as a spotlight accompanies a performer. It follows the reading of a word, or a line, a passage, a scene, an act, and ultimately the finished play. It is virtually inseparable from the reading itself; the movement of students and teacher through the play is one operation, with reading and discussion the components of the single activity. We need say no more of it here, but illustrative emphasis on discussion is included in the following chapter on specific plays.

But though discussion is the one activity that should be constantly associated with reading, it is not the only important one. Several others are appropriate and useful; some are even indispensable. The business of this chapter is to survey these, to consider some specific ways and means of managing them, and to suggest a system of priorities among them. Specifically, the activities to be discussed are (1) writing, (2) outside reading, (3) dramatic reading or acting out, (4) memorization, (5) films, recordings, etc., (6) testing, (7) miscellaneous.

1. WRITING

Increasingly now, it is as unthinkable to many teachers that students should study a Shakespearean play without writing in connection with it as that they should study it without discussing it. With this point of view it would be hard to find any reasonable basis for disagreement.

If we accept the view that has regained favor during the past few years, namely, that most writing in high school should be done in direct connection with the literary works read, we are even more likely to identify writing as the activity that should hold second place only to discussion during and after the reading of a Shakespearean play.

Probably no literary works in the curriculum lend themselves better than Shakespeare's plays to a great variety of writing experiences. How many writing assignments the teacher makes during the four to six weeks given to a play will of course be determined mainly by the purely physical facts of the situation —which is to say, the number of students and the number of classes that must be served. If the teacher has, say, thirty-five students in each of five classes and the five classes are simultaneously studying Shakespeare, mere practical necessity will dictate frugality in writing assignments. If on the other hand the teacher has, say, twenty-five students in each class and only one or two classes are engaged with a play, composition assignments could reasonably be more lavish during this particular period. The point, in any event, is that the number of writing assignments will be limited only by external, practical considerations and not by the plays themselves, which offer literally boundless opportunities for writing of every kind. One of the mysteries of the past thirty years is why so many teachers and textbook writers have set students to work on sterile topics such as "My Favorite Uncle" and "My Summer Vacation" when all works of literature, and especially Shakespeare's plays, offer rich and varied abundance of inspiration, idea, and subject matter for serious composition.

In limited space we can do no more than roughly classify broad "kinds" of writing experiences that the plays make possible and to identify some representative forms, topics, and ideas. In the chapters that follow, where particular plays are treated, some specific suggestions are presented.

Perhaps we should begin by asking *when* students, should, or might, write in relation to the actual reading of the play. The possible answers are three: *before, during,* and *after.* If teachers took advantage of all three, students would presumably be writing regularly from the time they began preparing to read the play until they are ready to move on to the next work. No week would go by without some writing. Students might write once "before," repeatedly "during," and once "after." It is proposed here that—if the teacher's circumstances can be made to accommodate the amount of correction necessary—students will write from ten to twelve times during the four to six weeks; their compositions will represent a variety of forms, approaches, and lengths. We should now consider the range of possibilities, and for the sake of convenience let us follow the "before," "during," and "after" order.

What kinds of writing might students do *before* they begin the actual reading of a Shakespearean play? Traditionally, they have often written some form of report based on investigation. They have sought information on one or another aspect of background: the life and works of Shakespeare, the Renaissance, the Elizabethan stage, and so forth. Clearly, the possibilities here, including subdivisions of large topics, are nearly unlimited, and at the same time, in a sense all represent valid undertakings because they contribute to the general fund of knowledge that students will have to draw upon as they study the play itself, which is a document of the times. Teachers sometimes have students complete their reports and present them (often orally as well as in written form) before the reading of the play is begun; others have made the assignments as work to be carried on outside while reading of the text continues in class.

But what we have earlier said about the approach to a play is obviously at odds with prior writing assignments of this kind. In considering approach, we have insisted that the place to begin the study of any Shakespearean play is with the opening scene of the play and have recommended that relevant information on background be introduced at appropriate times during the reading of the play, whenever it *becomes* relevant. This view we now reassert. "Outside" investigations of background would better serve if they were assigned and undertaken not before the reading of the text is begun, but during the reading. Need for specific information often arises as early as the opening scene; additional occasions occur in scene after scene thereafter.

In the opening scene of *Julius Caesar*, for example, excellent purpose would be served if a student, or several students, were assigned to make a brief special report, supplementing the immediate information supplied by the teacher, on the rivalries and wars of Caesar and the Pompeys. The force of such information is no doubt best appreciated *when the text itself has created a need for it.*

In the case of *Julius Caesar*, the method would work as follows. During the reading of the opening scene, the question of Caesar and the Pompeys would arise. The teacher would quickly supply information essential to understanding of the allusions made in that scene. But the teacher would simultaneously show the desirability of gaining a fuller understanding of the complex situation, and would ask for volunteers or directly assign certain students to prepare a report. The report would not be a lengthy term-paper project, but a *brief, relevant* account designed to serve the immediate, definite, and obvious purpose of informing the class. The report would be in writing—a single full paragraph would serve—and would be read to the class at the beginning of the next meeting, after which it would be turned in to the teacher. The reading of the play would continue as soon as any questions were cleared up by the student or students responsible for the report.

In the course of reading the entire play, many occasions for such written reports will inevitably arise; the same holds true for all plays used in all high school years. Shakespeare's plays are studded with allusions, for example, to classical mythology. Good editions of the plays supply footnotes which identify Jason, Hecuba, Janus, Niobe, Hippolyta as their names occur in the text; but they do so usually in a sentence or a phrase, thus:

> Dido: queen of Carthage, who killed herself when Aeneas abandoned her.

Almost invariably, behind each classical (or Biblical) allusion is a famous, memorable tale which a footnote can only glance at. Obviously a teacher cannot assign students to look up and report on every such allusion in the course of reading the play, for the allusions are innumerable and even three-minute reports, with discussion, would take so much time from each class hour that reading would not move along as it must. But the abundance of opportunity illustrates the point to be made here: the text of

Shakespeare furnishes gold mines of opportunity for learning, practice in investigating, practice in writing, practice in quick oral reports. Allusions represent only one example of such abundance.

Certainly, then, the familiar "background" kind of investigation and writing will serve better "during" than in its traditional position "before." So used, it plays a vital role in the activity going forward day by day, that of reading-discussing-writing. Is there, then, no form of writing assignment that would be more appropriate before the class begins the reading? One alternative to the approach earlier recommended—namely, that of simply beginning the reading of the text without any kind of overture—is as follows.

Let us suppose, again, that *Julius Caesar* is the play to be read. Without mentioning this play, and indeed without even mentioning that it will next be read, the teacher can generate a class discussion on a question that is at once a central concern of the play and a familiar problem in the experience of living. The question, let us say, concerns a conflict between personal loyalty and social, or public, responsibility. Class discussion of this perennial issue in human affairs might begin with the most immediately local applications. For example, the loyalties of brother and sister in conflict with parents and the "good" of the family or the relations of friend to friend in the classroom or the school in conflict with the teacher, the student body, or the administration. The discussion might continue outward through widening circles: a community's loyalties and interests in conflict with those of state or country; national interests in conflict with international ones.

Once the essential *idea* of this conflict has been made clear through a discussion that involves real and hypothetical cases, local and remote situations, individuals near at hand and great statesmen on the world scene, the teacher can propose that each student commit himself on the subject by expressing his views in writing. So long as it illuminates the central issue, the student's composition can be personal or general, wholly expository or mainly narrative, based on real incidents and details or created of hypothetical ones. In trying their hands at the subject, students are as yet quite unaware, preferably, of what is to follow: a play in which Shakespeare tries his hand at it. The moral dilemma of Brutus, with his

> I know no personal cause to spurn at him,
> But for the general . . .

And his

> Not that I loved Caesar less, but that I loved
> Rome more . . .

is one that they will find more familiar, more human, more moving, more "real," when they meet it in the text, because their own minds, as best they could, will already have grappled with it.

Similar preliminary wrestlings with a subject, theme, or issue can be arranged—if this way seems desirable—for every play that a class is to study. The subject chosen for discussion need not always be "the" subject or theme of the play; as a matter of fact, "the" theme of any one of Shakespeare's plays is not easy to isolate, and perhaps in many cases there is no such thing. But it should be an issue of basic importance in both the play and life. Using this way, teachers find no great need to waste words in lectures on "the universality of great literature."

Unquestionably the greatest number of compositions will and should be written *during* the reading of the play. We have already identified and described one appropriate kind—the written report on specifically relevant information, which has more often been assigned "before," but which we found preferable to use when need arises in the course of reading. But, indeed, the possibilities of writing "during" are so numerous that we shall need a way of classifying broad kinds. In general, these kinds may be characterized as follows:

1. Some form of reproduction of the original line, passage, scene.
2. Some form of analysis, writing about an aspect of the work.
3. Some form of original writing, using the work, or a particular point in it, as a springboard.

We shall consider these in order.

One of the most widely used ways of "reproducing" the original is *paraphrase*. This form calls for close, literal rendering of the substance of line or (usually) passage. Of all the forms of writing, it is most like translation. Poetry is made into clear, modern, direct prose; modern equivalents replace obsolete, rarely used, or "poetic" words and phrases. Imagery is made literal statement. In paraphrasing, one makes no comment on the passage, but aims only to reproduce faithfully what is said, neither adding, distorting, nor omitting. A very great deal of what teacher and class do orally in studying the play together is, in fact, paraphrasing. Thus in assigning a written paraphrase, the teacher introduces nothing new and strange, but merely asks students to do individually and more formally what they regularly do together as they read and discuss meanings.

Paraphrasing is excellent exercise in both exact understanding and exact expression. It gives also a certain amount of practice in organization, since though it follows very closely the general outline of a passage, it also often involves reordering of words and lines to make the clearest prose statement. Like every other kind of writing assignment, paraphrasing can be abused by being used to excess. When the class groans at the sight of each new passage that looks like an obvious choice for another exercise in paraphrasing, it may be a sign that this form of writing is being overused and that the enjoyment of the play is being impaired by it. But the services of exercises in paraphrasing to both reading and writing are not to be denied. The exercise is rarely inspiring, admits little creativity and no originality—but it demands objectivity, honesty, precision. It is thus a valuable counterbalance for most other writing that students do.

Probably in the course of reading a play, students should paraphrase as many as five or six passages. Ordinarily these passages would be of key significance, so that their very importance will argue for special attention given them. Paraphrasing is fairly obviously an exercise to perform in class rather than out of class. It can be conveniently handled in at least two ways. First, in the course of reading the play, the teacher reaches a passage of special importance, and reads it carefully aloud, as usual, but then, instead of probing its meaning orally, with all the class joining in, assigns ten minutes for individual written paraphrase. Or, second, when assignments to read ahead independently are given, as described in the preceding chapter, the teacher can begin the next hour by asking for a written paraphrase of an appropriate passage. Next, the class proceeds to discuss all that has been read independently, and when the discussion reaches the passage just paraphrased, students read out their versions.

Finally, two special remarks on paraphrasing may be appropriate here. First, it will be noted that with both methods of assigning paraphrase as sketched above, the students' individual efforts will be closely related to the general discussion of the scene that contains the passage paraphrased; thus the student gets an immediate and useful check on his own progress—more specifically, on the double ability that is required in paraphrasing: comprehension and expression. Second, both methods actively serve the need that we have acknowledged for experience in individual, independent reading, since in each case the student is put on his own in extracting the detailed meanings of passages. Paraphrasing, in short, is an admirable means of bringing together the distinct virtues of the two basic methods of presenting Shakespeare—line-by-line reading and discussion by teacher and students together, and individual, independent reading.

A second form of writing that involves, essentially, reproduction of the original is the *précis*. This form, used in connection not only with drama but with essays, poems, stories, novels, has long been a favorite of many teachers. The same caution needs to be used with it as with paraphrase: overuse is abuse, and the device can become a deadly instrument that kills the joy of reading works of literature. Most students, at some time in their careers, encounter teachers who are, so to speak, addicted to some single form of writing assignment; the assignment of précis can easily become a habit, and it has often become a bad one.

Précis differs from paraphrase in that whereas the aim of the latter is to reproduce full detail faithfully, the aim of the former is to reveal the gist. In paraphrasing a passage of Shakespeare's packed blank verse, one must often use three or four times as many words as Shakespeare used; in making a précis, one strives to distill the original, reducing it to one fourth the length, or less.

Probably paraphrase, deservedly, is more frequently used than précis with Shakespearean passages. As a test of the ability to read closely, to comprehend all the details of a passage, it has no equal; at the same time, it places a powerful demand on ability to express meanings precisely. Précis requires the student, as reader, to grasp the *essential thought* of a passage, and, as writer, to express this thought succinctly. No doubt the two forms complement each other well as exercises because of the contrasting demands they make, and for that reason one might almost say that *both* should be used if either is. It is a fact, startling as it may seem, that students will often paraphrase a passage of twenty lines with admirable clarity and precision—and then be quite unable to say what the passage means *as a whole*; they may actually lose sight of the general sense because of their enforced preoccupation with details. On the other hand, students can often catch the general "drift" of a passage even though particular words and lines defy them. Used alternately, or approximately so, both forms serve valid purposes and each is a specific corrective for the fault of the other. In general, passages selected for paraphrasing are likely to be somewhat shorter than those chosen for précis writing; but also the same passages can be used for both.

A final form of writing that involves reproduction of the original is *narrative summary*. Characteristically, the assignment runs thus: "Tell in your own words the events of Scene 3"; or "Tell in your own words what happened to Hamlet from the time he sailed for England until his return." What the assignment asks is, in fact, no more than a retelling in narrative form of action presented by Shakespeare in dramatic form. Obviously, this kind of writing deals in larger units than does paraphrase or précis. Where those forms concentrate on passages of twenty lines (or much less) and yield anywhere from a single page down to only a few lines of student writing, narrative summary normally requires recapitulation of an entire scene or act, or even more, and may yield several pages of narrative. Because it is an easy, highly convenient way of getting students to write a considerable amount of prose, and because it does consolidate their recollection of the details and incidents that make up dramatic action, this form of writing no doubt serves worthy purposes.

It is nevertheless suggested that its values are inferior to those of paraphrase or précis, and inferior to those of other kinds of writing that are yet to be named. Yet for younger and less able students this kind of writing may be worthier than for others; and perhaps in some cases it is about the only kind that students can be expected to do fairly well. Unquestionably a ninth-grade class of average or lower ability that can recapitulate in story form the events that befall, say, Helena, Hermia, Lysander, and Demetrius during their wild night in the woods outside Athens has gained something from reading and something more from retelling in written form what they have read. But for abler and more mature classes it is suggested that narrative recapitulations be taken care of quickly and orally and that writing assignments be of kinds that, in general, will demand smaller quantities of more potent prose.

The second general class of writing "during" the course of reading a play is that which we have identified as *analysis* or writing "about" some aspect of the text. In contrast to the first general class, which merely reproduces the original in the student's own words, the second kind always involves *comment upon* the original. Because this comment comes out of the student's own mind, it is inevitably more original and, at least so far as individual thought is concerned, more demanding than paraphrase, précis, or summary. There the student had only to understand, rephrase, and repeat; here he must, in effect, create. Very probably, of all the writing that is assigned between beginning and completing the reading of a Shakespearean play, much the greater part will and should fall somewhere into this wide general class.

So very wide is this class that before we attempt to suggest the variety of composition assignments possible within its range, we should offer two statements of principle that are applicable to all such assignments. First, these compositions will be brief and numerous rather than lengthy and infrequent. Most, it is suggested, should be written in class, and the most useful, as well as practicable, form for the purpose is the paragraph. If students take ten to fifteen minutes every third or fourth day to develop a single good paragraph, they will gain an impressive amount of experience with composition without seriously impeding the reading and discussion of the play; moreover, single paragraphs can be read and marked quickly.

Second, in virtually all cases the actual writing assignment *will grow out of discussion*. Teachers can deliberately shape and direct the course of discussion toward a specific proposition that, in the final fifteen minutes of the class period, they present as a writing assignment, either to be finished at the end of the hour or to be returned at the beginning of the next meeting. Adroitly managed, discussion and composition will tend to nourish and supply each other: discussion motivates, leads to, and clarifies the subject for composition; and composition, from examples read aloud, feeds back into the stream and renews discussion. When the system is working well, the teacher is the happy manager of a virtual perpetual motion machine.

Preferably, then, the subjects assigned for brief composition during the course of reading the play are essentially the same as those that are continually discussed during the reading of the play. Indeed, if these subjects are notably different in kind from each other, it is time to suspect that something has, somehow, gone wrong.

Many teachers tend to think of subjects for writing as being "different" from subjects for discussion. Most people, including teachers, have a tendency to write much less naturally than they speak. It is evidently some twist of this sort that accounts for the usual difference between discussion and composition subjects. No doubt the best cure for this particular ill is not to "think up" subjects for composition at all, but to let them arise as naturally as do the subjects for discussion. It is suggested that if students can be assigned to *write* about the same subjects that they discuss, they may in time come to write more naturally, too.

It is true, of course, that not every topic talked about while the play is being read will make a suitable subject for composition. Obviously, much of the continuing discussion consists merely of seeking and substituting a familiar word for a less familiar one, a familiar phrase for an obsolete one, a direct statement for an image, a clarifying sentence for a knotty line. Though these might serve the purpose of written paraphrase, they do not lend themselves to the kinds of composition with which we are concerned just now.

Most of the other matters that take discussion time, however, adapt themselves as well to composition as to discussion. These include all questions of the dramatist's poetic and dramatic art; aspects of individual character, motives of characters, "growth" of characters, relations of characters with one another and with plot; meanings and implications of words and actions both within and beyond what is directly stated or exhibited; relation of scene to scene, of atmosphere and mood to action, of decision to consequence. Indeed, not merely the questions but the very categories are endless. We shall deal more specifically with many of them in the following chapters on particular plays. For the present, perhaps a random illustration or two will suffice.

An inescapable subject for discussion in connection with reading the opening scene of *The Merchant of Venice* is surely the place occupied by Antonio among his friends. Shakespeare takes the first two-thirds of the scene to exhibit and establish as a key dramatic fact the *centrality* of the merchant as an object of warm affection, both given and received; the remaining third of the scene marks the true start of the action, which has its inception in this very fact of Antonio's capacity for friendship. Brief discussion that runs concurrently with the reading of the scene will amply prepare the way for a single paragraph written when the scene is done. The question for the paragraph might ask for no more than a pulling together—a "composition"—of items randomly discussed during the reading: "What place does Antonio hold in the regard of his acquaintances?" It might go farther, to represent a preliminary assault on the mysteries of dramatic techniques: "*By what means* does Shakespeare communicate to us a sense of Antonio's place in the hearts of his friends?" It might ask students to *project* the present situation imaginatively into the future: "As a mature dramatist, Shakespeare did not waste the beginnings of his plays. Imagining what may lie ahead, why do you think he placed such emphasis, in this scene, on Antonio's love for his friends and theirs for him?" There exists even the possibility of inciting students to a mild debate through their paragraphs: "The play opens with three of Antonio's acquaintances, in succession, 'ribbing' him unmercifully. Are they *really* friends, or is their 'friendship' colored by jealousy, envy, malice?"

These questions are, of course, not the only ones that might serve as writing assignments based on this one scene; but perhaps they will serve for the present to illustrate the range of possibilities and, more importantly, to underscore the suggestion that writing assignments *should grow out of discussion* and should use either subjects that have been discussed in passing or subjects that are similar in kind to those that have been discussed. If it can be shown that sometimes people *talk* about questions and sometimes *write* about the same questions—rather than about drastically different kinds of questions—a truly fundamental truth has been demonstrated.

It will be noted that all the examples of writing assignments given above are in the form of questions. The main advantage of putting assignments in this form is obvious: it provides the student with an immediate focus, gives him something to write "to." The student has, in fact, only to develop an answer in terms of the evidence the text supplies, and his paragraph is virtually assured of unity, if nothing else. For this reason the question form of assignment is far superior to the statement of a topic, thus: "Discuss the place held by Antonio among his friends as shown in Scene 1." An invitation merely to "discuss" is an invitation to produce random comment—mere "writing" as opposed to "composition."

A second way of presenting a writing assignment that can provide the same guide toward unity that a question provides is to present the class with a sharply focused topic sentence. Thus, instead of asking the question "What place does Antonio hold in the regard of his friends?" ask the class to write on this statement: "A conspicuous function of the first scene is to show that Antonio occupies a place of warmest affection in the hearts of his friends." In developing the paragraph from this topic sentence, students might in effect merely select and arrange, i.e., "compose," points that were randomly made in the course of earlier oral discussion. In later assignments, and particularly in later high school years, questions and topic sentences can readily be made increasingly sophisticated and can be based on matters not specifically discussed previously, but merely *opened* by discussion.

The third general class of writing during the course of reading the play we have distinguished as that which uses the text as a "springboard." This kind of writing does not involve analysis or criticism of any aspect of the play, but rather "takes off" from a line, an idea, a problem, a situation, or, indeed, any convenient starting point offered by the play. The material of the composition itself comes out of the students' own background of experience, knowledge, attitude. The very simplest device to prompt this kind of writing is a single line that offers a "developable idea." For example, from the same scene in *The Merchant of Venice* that we have been drawing on, take Gratiano's "Let me play the fool:/With mirth and laughter let old wrinkles come." The problem is not to "comment on" the line, but to use it as the first sentence of a paragraph and to go on from there, building a case, presumably, for living a merry life. Shakespeare is so rich in these "developable ideas" expressed in a line or two that almost any scene will provide a superfluity. The only problem for the teacher is to select those that will best stimulate the imagination of students.

One objection to this kind of writing is that, if it is abused, it may compel a student to accept, or seem to accept, and to advocate a philosophy in which he does not believe—which may, in fact, be thoroughly distasteful to him. Suppose, to take the example just named, that one soberly ambitious member of the class heartily resents Gratiano's gleeful assertion that the carefree life is the good life. Should he be required to wrack his brain to supply material for a paragraph endorsing it? One might argue that it would "do him good" to adopt, temporarily, a point of view contrary to his own and to try to apprehend what attractions others find in it. The argument is tempting.

On the other hand, to force him to write what he does not truly believe is to give him a bad lesson in writing. Good writing is honest, not dishonest or artificial; students should learn to set down what they really see, believe, find true. For the student who cannot honestly espouse Gratiano's view of life—or whatever view is affirmed by a particular "springboard" line—there should always be an alternative assignment: let him write his paragraph in contradiction of this view; or if he thinks Gratiano is "half right," let him develop an argument for moderation.

If this kind of writing, in which a student "rounds out" an idea or attitude taken from the text in terms of his own life, environment, experience, and thought, is easily subject to such abuse as that mentioned above, so is it also, when it works well, an admirable way of establishing a functioning bridge between literature and life. It actively relates the experience of other times, other worlds, other persons to the student's own time, world, life. It helps to break down the notion that literature is something outside, separate from the reader, to be looked at, examined as an object apart, of no immediate relevance to one's own life; it provides, in short, a means of assimilating others' experience and thereby expanding one's own.

So far we have illustrated only the simplest "springboard" device —the line that supplies a "developable idea." But, of course, springboards abound not only in lines, but in passages, scenes, acts; in characters, their faults and virtues, attitudes, decisions, actions; in situations, incidents, even settings. The devotion of Hotspur, Brutus, or Hamlet to ideals of honor may, after discussion, spark an essay on honor in general, on honor in some particular walk of modern life, or changing concepts of honor. The opportunism of Henry IV, Edmund, or Cassius may touch off paragraphs or essays in which students explore the topic in its contemporary applications—local and otherwise. Edgar's description of looking down from a terrifying height may furnish model or inspiration for a student's account of a comparable experience. Duncan's persistent failure to distinguish appearance from reality in the features of Macbeth and Lady Macbeth and in their seemingly peaceful castle can open for discussion and composition the general topic of appearance and reality, with its myriad applications and manifestations. Creative-minded students can go even farther in "taking off" from a passage, situation, scene, or character: they can invent a new character to place in a crucial situation from *Macbeth*; or they can place Macbeth in a modern situation of their own invention. They can keep the essentials of a plot and furnish a contemporary setting: if they are extremely successful, they may create another *West Side Story*.

That there are dangers in writing assignments that use the play, or some point in it, as springboard for "original" composition, every teacher knows who has ever tried them. At worst, having nothing to say, some students "make up" any kind of wild nonsense that will fill space. Especially those who are essentially noncreative will tend to do so when they are confronted with the more imaginative assignments suggested at the end of the preceding paragraph. For this reason such assignments ought ordinarily to be elective and students who have no real interest discouraged from choosing them.

One great advantage, however, has already been named: that these assignments provide a direct way of getting students to relate literature to their own lives. Another advantage is that they allow respite and change of direction from what is undoubtedly the great staple of a writing program based on reading—namely, writing *about* literature. That major way of writing requires students to look *into* works, to analyze and evaluate techniques, characters, plots, and other aspects of form and content. But presumably English teachers do not want students only to look into works and write literary criticism. Presumably we want students also, having looked into the works, to look out again at their own lives and the world around them. *It is precisely this purpose that this latter kind of writing assignment eminently serves.* And with Shakespeare, whose lines teem with ideas, whose characters represent all kinds of values, the opportunities to use it are abundant to superfluity.

We have now explored some major ways of writing before and during the reading of a play. We have next to consider possible writing assignments *after* the play has been read and discussed.

At the outset, a few general principles for such assignments will help in organizing our consideration. (1) We can perhaps assume that compositions written "after" will tend to be longer and fuller than those written "before" or "during." (2) Usually, though not invariably, preparation for the actual writing will be underway before the reading of the play is finished. (3) As with writing assignments described under "during," subjects for composition will normally grow out of discussion during the reading of the play. (4) Any of the three general classes of writing assignments that we have distinguished—"reproduction of the original," "critical analysis," and "springboard"—would be possible, but the first of these will obviously be least applicable. (5) Probably for the first time since work with the play began, extensive writing based wholly or in part on outside reading will be appropriate. Let us look briefly at each of these points.

As to the *length* of assignments, it has seemed reasonable to suppose that all or virtually all of the compositions written before completion of the reading will be short—paraphrases of brief passages, précis or summaries of scenes or longer passages, paragraphs developing specific ideas arising from the text, occasional brief essay treatments of character or technique, occasional brief creative efforts using situations, characters, or ideas as "springboards." Indeed, far the most practicable unit of composition to use during the whole course of reading the play is undoubtedly the paragraph. The reasons for brevity are obvious: longer compositions would interrupt the running continuity and seriously impede the flow of daily reading-discussion, and they would overwhelm the teacher with more written work than could be read and kept closely related to the continuing study of the play. On the other hand, when the reading-discussion phase has been finished, writing of more substantial essays, which might range from 500 to 2000 words, depending on subjects chosen and the maturity of students, can appropriately take over as the principal activity during the final week on the play.

This "final week on the play" may prove too short, of course, unless at least the preliminary preparations for writing—choosing a subject and beginning the collection of substance for its development—*are underway or even completed* by the time the week begins. Psychologically, too, it is preferable to have students committed to their larger writing assignment before the play is finished. For a major project involving considerable serious work, if it is announced after the last scene of the play has been read, can seem a burden indeed—like confronting the guests with a sinkful of dirty dishes after the party is over. But if, individually, students have begun assembling the details needed, the actual writing of the paper can seem like the consummation that, in fact, it is.

Preparation for the final writing can more readily be started or even finished while the play is being read if the subject, like the subjects for brief papers written during the reading, has emerged from class discussion. A special obligation of students individually, while the play is being read, is to be alert for potential subjects that especially attract them and that might become the subject for the final essay. Correspondingly, a special obligation for the teacher—and one that can be carried out easily and naturally in the ordinary course of directing discussion—is to point out or lay open an abundance of potential subjects while reading continues. It is, as a matter of fact, not uncommon for some students to become especially interested in a particular aspect of the play before the end of the first act, and once they have identified a possible subject they can keep one eye out for it, so to speak, throughout the period of reading and discussing the rest of the play. When the play is finished, the far-sighted few will already have collected the substance for their essays and will have only to organize and write. The finished essay, for these, will be the product not of a single, hurried week, but of five or six weeks of noting, collecting, and thinking. Their "Shakespeare essay" can become the big writing event of the year, and for seniors the climax of four years.

One general cautionary remark is in order at this point. Though the advantages of getting students to watch for and fix on a subject for composition early in the reading are obvious, for the good of the eventual essay, yet the teacher will need to resist temptation to place *too* much and *too* steady emphasis on this aspect of the continuing threefold activity of reading-discussing-writing. It is unfortunately very easy—in fact, it is all too easy—to give students the gravely wrong impression that the play itself is being read and discussed mainly in order to write the final big essay about it. This impression, if it were held throughout the reading, would do fatal damage to the experience of the play as a work of art. Because the reading experience is the one thing that, above all, must *not* be damaged, most teachers will no doubt agree that it would be better to give *no* attention to writing than to risk damaging it —drastic as that omission would be.

Further, if students do succeed early in identifying a writing subject, the danger exists that from that point on *they* will have eyes and ears only for those elements of the play that furnish grist for the mill of their eventual essay. For example, Hamlet and his problems can be let slip by without any notice—for *they* have fixed on a study of Claudius and the effects of his conscience upon his actions. Obviously, the study of any work of art can be distorted ruinously by single-minded scrutiny of any one aspect in preparation for writing a paper. The moral of all this is plain: it is the teacher who must manage to maintain a balance of emphasis in the reading-discussing-writing operation that protects the whole play at any cost, and yet prepares students to have something ready to write at last.

Of the three major kinds of writing that we have described on page 124, it is likely that the second, which involves either critical analysis or some other mode of writing "about" the play, will be the choice of most students for the final paper; certainly this kind can most easily be motivated during the reading and discussion. As for the first kind—some form of "reproduction" of the original

—it is better suited to short assignments in passing than to the final paper. Because it necessarily involves some manner of retelling, without comment by the writer, this kind is more useful as a check on accuracy of reading and retention of detail than as a major writing experience. Though it may be quite in order, on occasion to ask students to retell in their own words the events of a single scene, or even an act, it would not seem particularly desirable, when the play is finished, to ask students to "retell in your own words the story of the play." In dealing with a narrative form, such as short story or novel, teachers sometimes have students convert whole or part to dramatic form. If it is carried out with serious effort, this kind of assignment has merit and can be a major writing project. But there seems much less merit in converting a dramatic work to narrative form.

As for the third mode, that of writing creatively "out of" the play, using some part of it as a "springboard," this can afford ample scope for the final paper if it is undertaken seriously by those with real interest and possibly some talent. Here the possibilities are of almost infinite variety. Students have been known to provide an Act VI for *Hamlet*, to write a short story with Mercutio as the main character, an imaginary conversation of Lady Macbeth and the Witches, a happy Act V for *Romeo and Juliet*, a version of the Orlando-Rosalind wooing scene in contemporary setting and idiom, and so on.

Less creative students, having read *Macbeth*, have written an essay on superstition in modern life; having read *Julius Caesar*, an essay on demagoguery in America today; having read *King Lear*, an essay on contemporary causes of strife between parents and children; having read *The Merchant of Venice*, an essay on racial prejudice in their own city; having read *A Midsummer Night's Dream*, an essay on the more "practical" difficulties in boy-girl relationships; having read *As You Like It*, an essay debating the virtues of city life and country life.

All these, it will be noted once again, *turn out from* the play itself—which may, indeed, never even be mentioned in the essay. It would be dishonest to pretend that all efforts in this kind, or the more "creative" kind exemplified above, have been successful in the past or will be so in the future; probably this kind of writing offers the greatest danger of going completely wrong and coming out with nothing. But at best, when ability and genuine interest together drive the writer on, the results can be satisfying to the student and heartwarming to the teacher.

Nevertheless, the favored subjects for writing after the play has been finished will no doubt continue to be those that do not turn away from but turn back into the work and that emerge as subjects from the normal discussion that follows reading. After the opening two scenes of *Macbeth*, one student may seize on the idea of studying Shakespeare's use of paradox ("Fair is foul and foul is fair") in all its aspects throughout the play. Another student, observing how the dramatist shifts back and forth between blank verse and prose in the opening scenes of *The Merchant of Venice*, may undertake to solve the problem of the "why" of these changes. More will be said on the possibilities of such subjects in the chapter that follows.

Finally, the period after the play is finished is an appropriate time for writing on *outside reading*, either with or without direct connection with the particular play just studied. It is here suggested that the outside reading used as the basis of writing can conveniently be either of two sorts: (1) "background" reading about Shakespeare, his other plays, his age, his theater, his contemporaries, his sources, his genres (i.e., a study of "tragedy," etc.); or (2) independent reading of another Shakespearean play. Since the latter possibility is necessarily discussed in Chapter 11, we shall confine our remarks here to writing in connection with "background" reading.

Teachers will doubtless agree that most students in the junior and senior years, and particularly those who intend going on to college, should have experience in independent, investigative reading and in writing what is variously called the "term paper," the "research theme," and the "investigative report." A Shakespearean play provides obvious occasion and opportunity for this kind of experience. Whether this is also the *best* kind of writing to do after reading a Shakespearean play is, however, at least a debatable question.

What we have suggested earlier is that in the course of reading the play, the class will often encounter a need for special, pertinent information, and that on these occasions certain students, volunteers or appointees, might be assigned to find the salient facts and report them briefly. These brief sorties into reference books would not be dignified by such grand titles as "research projects," but would be treated more humbly as quick and practical hunts for information to be directly applied to the place where it is needed. When, for example, at the end of a scene, someone on stage makes a point of removing the body of another killed during the scene, the class will be receptive to information as suddenly as it can be brought in, on the Elizabethan stage and its lack of a front curtain. When, as has been suggested earlier, Caesar's past triumphs over Pompey bear upon a present situation, the time is ripe for a businesslike account of the historical facts. When Shylock threatens the city of Venice with loss of its charter for failing to enforce the law, there is immediate need for a short, clear explanation of "city states," "charters," and the like. When the "plague" is mentioned—as frequently it is in Shakespeare—a student or a committee of students can assemble pertinent details on medieval and Renaissance plagues. When in *Hamlet*, Rosencrantz and Guildenstern, with Hamlet, make fun of the juvenile actors who are at war with the "common stage," a quick report is in order.

It is supposed that all such reports will be brief and to the point; what is essential can often be set down in a page or less and reported in two or three minutes. Such reports represent research undertaken for a demonstrable, immediate purpose—application to an actual problem. Perhaps these reports make clearer to students the *reason* for "library work" than do most larger projects carried out under a more ambitious title and with many more trimmings, but without evident purpose except that of gaining the experience itself, and completing an assignment.

It is nevertheless not the intent here to suggest that students who, after finishing the play, wish to prepare a "background" kind of paper rather than a critical one should be denied the privilege. If they prefer to do the reading necessary for such a paper because they truly want more knowledge of the subject, their preference surely should be indulged. They will thus get experience in using the library, will unquestionably learn many facts, and finally, will gain one useful and special kind of writing experience. The total experience is valuable, perhaps even indispensable as an exercise in techniques; *but it should not be confused with the experience that comes with writing a paper on a subject that permits the student to say something "on his own."* The latter is creative; the other is not.

What is most important, perhaps, is that students themselves should not confuse the two kinds of experience. The student who has conscientiously investigated twenty sources of information about Elizabethan staging, taken notes in his own language, and finally presented his findings in an orderly fashion has completed a legitimate undertaking and deserves praise for his work. The student who has conscientiously examined the imagery in *Macbeth*, pondered all the evidence of the text, come to a definite conclusion about it, and finally written an essay demonstrating that—let us say—the key function of this imagery is in creating and sustaining an effect of horror has also completed a legitimate undertaking and deserves praise for his work.

We need not here pass judgment on the relative merits of the two kinds of experience, but teachers and students should be clear that the two kinds differ. The one student dealt with a subject about which he could not reasonably be expected, in a brief time, to have anything to say on his own; he could only assemble and report. The other student dealt with a subject about which he could make an assertion. The possibility is strong that the first student's paper will "look" somewhat the better of the two; it may be orderly and obviously substantial, even impressive in its accumulation of information. The second student's paper may be less orderly, have defects in relating evidence to conclusion, be unconvincing; it is even possible that its main assertion—that the key function of imagery in *Macbeth* is in creating and sustaining an effect of horror—is either wrong or less than the whole truth. But the paper represents an effort at creating, at least to the extent that development of a student's *own ideas about evidence* represents creating, whereas the other paper involves only accumulation, organization, and presentation of data.

Students very easily gain the erroneous impression that if they have faithfully accumulated, organized, and presented information without plagiarizing another writer's *words*, they have done all that is to be expected of them; and, indeed, with the "backgrounds" kind of paper they are often quite right. Experience with the critical paper, which demands that the writer take a definite point of view toward the materials and shape his essay to develop some specific assertion—his own "idea"—about them, provides a needed correction for this mistaken conception of what writing involves.

2. OUTSIDE READING

We have so far argued that during the weeks of reading through the text of a Shakespearean play, the whole of time in class will best be spent in reading, discussing, and writing, with only occasional assignments of overnight reading or writing. Obviously, then, so far as the particular play that is being studied is concerned, students will have almost nothing to do outside of class. Now and then, we have said, especially in the eleventh and twelfth grades, they will be asked to read scenes in advance and prepare to discuss them, and now and then they may be asked to prepare brief reports or write paragraphs outside; but the main responsibility for the text will be carried by teacher and class together during class time. Does this mean, then, that students should be virtually free of home assignments in English during the weeks spent on the play?

The idea is not without merit; it could help to make the weeks given to Shakespeare the most popular of the year—as, indeed, they should be.

On the other hand, these weeks of freedom from the duty of preparation for daily classwork give students a rare opportunity for independent reading. What should they read? They may, of course, be left as free to choose as students normally are for outside reading—as free, that is, as they usually are in preparing to make book reports. They can read novels, plays, poems, stories, biographies of any period or country. If every work has literary merit and is not beyond the individual student's powers, this method of wide-ranging choice will serve admirable purposes. Its freedom will provide a welcome contrast to the tightly controlled, rigorous reading experience going forward in class. It will result in the reading of good books that students might otherwise never read. It will promote healthy competition among students in terms of both number and quality of books read. It will furnish a stimulus for pride of personal achievement. All told, it can have such merit that some teachers may not wish to forego it for any reasons;

and certainly they should not forego it unless they are genuinely convinced that some other way is better.

One way that some teachers prefer—and that is here recommended as preferable—is the use of a much more restricted range of "outside reading" works. Choices are limited to works *that have some kind of connection with the play that is being studied intensively in class.* The range of choice will depend on the strictness with which one defines "connection." What is here suggested is that the word be liberally construed, so that acceptable outside reading would include works as diverse as, say, a life of Sir Philip Sidney, Scott's *Kenilworth*, a play by Ben Jonson, the plays *Elizabeth the Queen* and *Mary, Queen of Scots* by Maxwell Anderson, Bacon's *Essays*, Marchette Chute's *Shakespeare of London*, a collection of Elizabethan lyrics, one of Shakespeare's own plays, Spenser's *Faerie Queene*, Tillyard's *The Elizabethan World Picture*, a volume or volumes of *Hakluyt's Voyages*. Thus works chosen might be novels, plays, poems, histories, biographies, critical studies; they might be either of the period or about it; they might pertain to Shakespeare, his plays, his contemporaries, or the period; they might be imaginative or factual. The range should be wide, but all works would somehow relate to the study going on in class; they should be substantial and excellent in their own right; and they should be read not as research for "report" purposes, but for themselves and the *general* illumination they offer.

The advantage of this system is not so much that it equips students with useful pieces of information to be brought forward and applied when occasion arises during study of the play in class, but that it keeps the reading in class and the reading out of class within a single frame and maintains a healthy harmony between them that is beneficial to both. The Age of Elizabeth is peculiarly rich both in what it produced and in what it has inspired. Excitement engendered by the play read in class can carry over to whatever works of or about the period are read outside, and similarly that engendered outside can bring added vitality to the particular play being studied by the whole class. Thus the "inside" and "outside" activities complement each other.

Within the range of related works for outside reading, should certain works, or kinds of works, be encouraged more than others? While *As You Like It* is being studied in class, is it better to induce a given student to read a play by Jonson than a life of Sidney? Would it be better still to press him to read Lodge's *Rosalynde*, the long prose romance that was Shakespeare's source? Or better still to recommend *Kenilworth?* Or best of all to "push" another of Shakespeare's plays that will not be studied in class —*The Merchant of Venice*, or *Romeo and Juliet?* Are there differences between the kinds of works that should be "pushed" for ninth and tenth grades and those that should be urged for eleventh and twelfth grades? Should the former, for example, include more novels and simple biographies, and the latter more critical studies and histories? Is the choice of another play by Shakespeare as appropriate for a ninth-grade student as for a twelfth-grade student? Should a second play by Shakespeare form one part of a student's independent outside reading at *each* level from nine to twelve?

These are questions to which answers will vary from teacher to teacher and class to class; they will not be answered arbitrarily or categorically here. What is suggested is that teachers lay out for each grade, to keep company with each play that is to be studied intensively, a wide range of good books from and about the age, taking into account, of course, the relative difficulties of genres and works. Obviously the *Faerie Queene* or *King Lear* would be an absurd choice for a ninth grader's independent reading while teacher and class are diligently pooling their wits to understand *Julius Caesar* during the class hour. Similarly *Master Skylark* would make a silly choice for a twelfth grader whose class and teacher are engaged with *The Tempest*. But *Kenilworth* might go in any year, and so might *Elizabeth the Queen*.

Finally, we have only to mention the relation of such outside reading to the program of composition discussed earlier. Presumably students will be expected to present evidence of their reading in some definite form, and their compositions, critical or otherwise, will naturally become part of their total collection of papers written "before, during, and after" study of the play. For many students, the composition based on the outside reading can serve as the major work written "after."

At worst, this composition will be no worse than the papers on "research" topics described earlier, where students have read, accumulated, organized, and presented data in their own words but without any further personal contribution. But at best, it will take an attitude toward and develop an assertion about the work or works read. The composition may or may not directly relate the outside reading to the play studied in class. If there *is* a natural connection to be established and developed, that way offers admirable opportunity for integration of "outside-inside" work.

Let us say that the play studied is *Hamlet* and that one student's "outside" book is a life of Sidney. Here opportunities for comparison in terms of Renaissance ideas and ideals abound; the student may even want to draw a parallel of Sidney and Hamlet as portraits of the Renaissance "great man." Or let us suppose that the play studied is *Henry IV, Part 1*, and that a student has read Bacon's *Essays*. Here opportunities abound for pursuing lines of similarity in political philosophy and for discussing numerous characters (Henry, Prince Hal, Worcester) in terms of Baconian thought. Henry, for example, relates rather obviously to "Of Simulation and Dissimulation"—as, indeed, do Hal and Worcester. "Of Wisdom for a Man's Self," however, relates even better to Worcester, and "Of Great Place" has meaning for the portrait of Hal. In any event, it seems reasonable to suggest that where natural points of relation exist between outside reading and the play studied, students should be encouraged as much as possible to explore them.

We should finally mention that a favorite way of many teachers, at both high school and college levels, is actually to *assign* a second play by Shakespeare to be read independently while one play is being studied in class. At least two advantages of this method are apparent: first, it enables students to put into practice immediately, in their independent study, what they learn about reading Shakespeare from the day-to-day demonstration in class; second, it virtually guarantees that every student can find an essay subject that relates the outside reading to the class play. These advantages are great and obvious, and no doubt they help to explain the popularity of this method. And because it is popular, we should raise and try to answer some basic questions about it.

First, is it appropriate for all high school grades? It would seem reasonable to suppose that it will in any event be *more* appropriate in grades eleven and twelve than in grades nine and ten. It may very well be that young students should have read at least two plays in line-by-line study under a teacher's direction before they tackle *any* Shakespearean play on their own. It is quite clear that abilities of classes will vary, but this principle seems generally applicable. Underlying all that we have said in these chapters is the desire to avoid turning students sour on Shakespeare by putting them on their own too early, confronting them with what they cannot, by themselves, read with genuine pleasure. We might, then, agree to some such policy as this: that for the most part assignment of an "outside" play by Shakespeare should be reserved for the eleventh and twelfth grades, but that if two plays have been read intensively in class in the ninth grade, an "outside" play might be tried in the tenth grade. At the same time, the principle should be understood as flexible, to allow for differences in classes and individuals.

Second, should there be any particular relationship of the "outside" to the "inside" play? For example, if the class play is a comedy, should the other be a comedy also? And, much more importantly, what should be the relative difficulty of the two plays? As for the first question, it seems likely that the carry-over of class instruction in reading a play will be greater if the outside play is of the same genre; but perhaps the necessity is less strong in the upper grades, by which time classes should have read both comedy and tragedy. It should be pointed out, too, that identifying an appropriate "outside" play in the same genre can sometimes be difficult. Suppose, for example, that *Julius Caesar* is being read in grade ten. What other tragedy would make a reasonable outside assignment? *Romeo and Juliet?* Obviously not, because the language of that play makes it more difficult than *Julius Caesar*. In this case, then, it would be preferable to assign, say *As You Like It* or *The Merchant of Venice*, though these are comedies.

We are brought up against the second question, what should be the relative difficulty of the "outside" and the "inside" plays? Though the question looks deceptively easy, we shall find it not at all easy. We have implied an answer already in suggesting that *Romeo and Juliet* would be an inappropriate play to read "outside" while *Julius Caesar* is being read in class. It would seem similarly perverse to study *The Merchant of Venice* or *As*

You Like It intensively and to assign *Twelfth Night* or *The Tempest* for independent reading. We can agree that, ideally, the play to be read outside should be less complex, less subtle, more openly exciting in its action than the play chosen for line-by-line study. All this is obvious enough. The trouble is that it is not always possible to maintain the ideal relationship; it will be necessary to settle for approximately equal difficulty.

Among Shakespeare's plays, there is surely no such thing as determination of subtle shades of difference in difficulty, as has been pointed out much earlier. But a reader long conversant with all the plays or a teacher of long experience gains a definite sense of plays that are more and less demanding, and this sense should be sufficient to decide which play should be "in" and which "out."

3. DRAMATIC READING OR ACTING OUT

We have earlier insisted that, although reading aloud by students should normally have no part in the initial presentation—except as need arises to read and reread lines during discussion—the study of a play should not be considered complete until each student has had the experience of speaking Shakespeare's lines aloud in class. Possibly this experience becomes less essential in the eleventh and twelfth grades; even so, we reassert the principle as applicable to all four grades.

The formidable obstacle is familiar enough to all experienced teachers: *time*. Even the least pretentious method of dramatic reading or acting-out of parts takes much time merely to do. More elaborate projects take time for organizing, preparing, and performing.

Let us begin by considering the two extremes—the simplest workable device for getting students to read substantial portions aloud, and the most elaborate classroom "production." But first let us reiterate a basic condition of any undertaking of this kind: we are assuming that the entire play *has already been read and discussed*. Thus our dramatic reading by students is to serve neither as a means of "initial presentation" nor as an "accompanying activity," but always as a "following activity."

Surely the simplest device, and the least time-consuming, is that of reading aloud from the beginning either the whole play or selected scenes, with students remaining in their seats, reading parts assigned on the spot by the teacher, and yielding frequently to new "cast" members. By this method there are no props, no costumes, no gestures, no "business," no delays, but only fast reading with such expression as students can manage. Even this method, happily uninterrupted by anything extraneous, will take about four class meetings for most plays. Advantages are obvious: a full review of the play, substantial oral experience for every student, a "putting together" of action that had been fragmented by earlier, slower reading and discussion. Some disadvantages are inescapable also: boredom induced by slow, bungling, or inaudible readers; distractions caused by insecure readers who "cover up" by showing off; consumption of much time in spite of efforts to move rapidly. A modified plan, by which students do not read the whole play, but only consecutive major scenes, saves time and retains some of the advantages.

At the opposite extreme is a full-scale classroom "production" of the play, with makeshift props either found in the room or quickly assembled, some suggestions of costume, impromptu stage settings, appropriate gestures and movements, exits and entrances, and some improvised devices (placards, announcements) for marking scene changes. Advantages here are impressive: the thrill of participating in an exciting enterprise, the opportunity to apply imagination to the physical realization of parts, the discovery of new dimensions of meaning in the play that were left unrevealed by the most careful line-by-line study. Disadvantages are inescapable also, but only one of these is so formidable as to discourage most teachers: the enormous amount of time required for organizing, preparing, and doing. Though the time can be much reduced by having *no* preparation, but merely calling students forward to the "stage," the files of readers going to and from their seats and the awkward attempts at action by unprepared performers can make such a shambles of the entire undertaking that more harm than good may come of it. A total fiasco at this point will lose some devotees previously won by the line-by-line study.

A better solution than either extreme is the acting out of

selected scenes by various groups of students. At the most, students may learn the lines of their parts and perform without books, using a member from another group or the teacher as prompter; at the least, they should study their respective parts thoroughly, rehearse as a group two or three times, and stage their performance with a real sense of lines and stage business.

One great advantage of the "selected scene" method is its unlimited flexibility. Every play of Shakespeare's that we have considered especially appropriate for study in high school lends itself admirably, for each offers at least six and as many as twenty scenes that are eminently adapted to performance by small groups. The groups, too, can vary widely in size: two girls can elect to work up the discussion of Portia's suitors in Act I, Scene 2 of *The Merchant of Venice*; eight or ten students can prepare the entire courtroom scene from the same play. From *Julius Caesar* a boy and a girl can undertake the Brutus-Portia scene (II,1) after the conspirators have left the house; another pair can follow with the Caesar-Calpurnia scene (II,2); from ten to a dozen boys can enact the assassination of Caesar; two boys can do the quarrel of Brutus and Cassius (IV,2). Climactic scenes, comic scenes, moments of intense conflict, moments of meeting and parting, incidents of exciting action, or incidents of crucial decision: not one of the plays will fail to accommodate the tastes and composition of diverse groups within a given class.

The teacher's function during these activities is as vital as during line-by-line study. An obvious necessity is to see that no student is left out; tact and diplomacy in aiding the formation of acting groups, without domination, can result in clusters of students working happily together. Neglect of supervision will almost certainly result in over-exposure for clique leaders and in misery for isolated individuals. The teacher must somehow find the point of compromise between forthright appointment of members to acting groups and free election of members. Groups cannot well be formed before scenes to be acted are chosen, since the number in the group will obviously limit the choice of scene: a group that consists of three boys and three girls who have paired off for essentially non-Shakespearean reasons will likely feel constrained to hunt up a scene that includes parts for three boys and three girls—even though that scene may not particularly attract any of the six. It is simply a fact that this kind of arbitrary make-up of groups, in advance of choosing scenes, leads to difficulties and dissatisfaction.

On the other hand, if scenes are to be chosen before the acting groups are made up, who is to choose them? If the teacher alone chooses them, some of the spirit of the enterprise is lost at the outset. Some teachers—remembering, no doubt, disasters of an earlier year—do make all arrangements arbitrarily. They decide in advance which scenes are to be acted, announce them, and assign the actors for each. The advantages are that time is saved, every student is used according to the teacher's sense of the individual abilities and interests, and no one is left out or otherwise hurt by the machinations of clique leaders. Very truly—as teachers come to realize soon enough—high school classes exist in which this drastic method of assignment seems the only fair way of proceeding. But the damage to the general morale that may follow arbitrary assignment to casts is such that it should be avoided if there is another way.

Another and no doubt better way is to have the class as a whole, under the teacher's direction, first draw up a list of the scenes that offer the most attractive possibilities, without regard to casting, and then to proceed to fill most parts with volunteers —subject to the teacher's veto when necessary—and the others by assignment. Acting groups can thus be formed *impersonally*, by teacher and class together, rather than by choice of members already in command of particular groups. Obviously, variations of this general plan are possible, and perhaps no two classes would ever need to proceed in exactly the same way to the final disposition of roles.

Two points, in this connection, should be made in passing. First, because Shakespeare's plays usually have more good parts for boys than for girls, a certain amount of juggling to compensate for the disproportion is unavoidable. One solution—not very satisfactory from any point of view—is to have girls play men's parts. A better solution is to select some scenes in which only girls appear or in which they predominate—the Nerissa-Portia scenes earlier mentioned, the Rosalind-Celia and Rosalind-Phebe scenes from *As You Like It*, the great Viola-Olivia scenes (I,5; III,1) from *Twelfth Night;* the Juliet-Nurse scenes from *Romeo and Juliet*, the witch scenes from *Macbeth*. Second, and especially because of this same imbalance of boys' and girls' parts, there seems no good reason why different casts should not compete in performing the very same scenes; many girls can be employed when three different pairs do the Portia-Nerissa, Juliet-Nurse, or Rosalind-Phebe scenes. Competition among such groups is inevitable, as well as healthy, and the whole class can benefit from the rival interpretations.

Out of such classroom experiments with selected scenes have come, in many schools, portions of assembly programs, and occasionally out of such beginnings have emerged full-scale public performances of *Twelfth Night*, *Macbeth*, or *As You Like It*, executed by the senior class or by the student body. Whether they lead often or only occasionally to such major productions, or whether they stop with the classroom, devices that induce students to read Shakespeare aloud or to act out parts are surely more than merely valuable; they are indispensable.

4. MEMORIZATION

So much has been spoken and written in the past thirty years against assigning "memory work" that we might conveniently consider the practice as standing condemned and let it pass without discussion. On the other hand, so much of what was spoken and written during those years about *all* aspects of teaching English in high school has come under suspicion in recent years that we are justified in suspecting the attitude toward memorization as well.

Although the objections to memorization have been expressed in various terms, the basis of them is not hard to isolate. Heavy "social" emphasis has pervaded English programs during the past thirty years, directing the selection of materials, the choice of methods, and the very purpose itself. "Free" reading in wide-ranging materials, literary or non-literary, and an extraordinary preference for "dynamic group activities" have combined to make the essentially lonely task of memorizing poems or passages from Shakespeare seem quaint and contrary. To a prevailing philosophy that cared less for quality than for quantity, the very notion that any particular lines could be of such special worth as to deserve the concentrated effort that is required in memorizing smacked of discrimination.

Traditionally, memorization stood as a standard and respected fixture in the English program of experiences. Few studied *Julius Caesar* without getting Antony's funeral oration "without book," *As You Like It* without memorizing Jaques' great analogy of life and the stage, *Macbeth* without the "dagger speech," *Hamlet* without "To be or not to be," *The Merchant of Venice* without Portia's disquisition on the nature of mercy, *A Midsummer Night's Dream* without Oberon's "I know a place where the wild thyme blows" or Theseus' "The lunatic, the lover, and the poet"—or both.

During the thirty-year moratorium on memorization imposed by an unsympathetic educational philosophy, however, by no means every English teacher conformed to the pattern. Older teachers, in particular, affirm that they "never stopped." Questioning of successive college freshman classes over a period of roughly the past twenty years reveals that—among students who studied at least two plays in high school—between one third and one half were either required to memorize passages from Shakespeare or allowed to do so as an option. What is more significant is the fact that in more recent years the proportion has markedly increased.

In view of the latter evidence, it appears that we will not, after all, be out of order in giving the question of memorization at least a brief airing here; nor will we find ourselves without valued allies even if we take the drastic step of expressing an unequivocal endorsement of memorization as an appropriate activity.

Though "memory work" was truly out of harmony with generally advocated English methods and purposes between, say, 1930 and 1960, it will already have become evident that it is quite *in* harmony with the study of Shakespeare as we have described it in preceding chapters, and quite in harmony with other activities so far named as appropriate in this chapter. Studied and discussed line by line, used as a basis for such writing exercises as paraphrase and précis, reexamined as key pieces of evidence of longer compositions, and, finally, read aloud once more in the scenes "acted out" by student casts, many passages in a play will inevitably be all but memorized in the normal course of events. The teacher who wishes can let matters stand at that, or can go one step farther and advise that key passages in the acted scenes be deliberately committed to memory even though books may be used when scenes are presented. Genuinely involved students will find that in learning to read the lines aloud well enough to reveal the meaning—that is, in coming to a clear understanding of them in their own minds—they have in effect memorized them.

What has just been suggested is possibly the most efficient, least irksome way to deal with memorization. This way is in harmony with all other recommendations for the study of Shakespeare that we have made; more even than "in harmony," it is actually a result of them.

But this solution will still leave many questions unanswered or only equivocally answered, because it does not cover all situations. Does it imply that the teacher should never require "proof," oral or written, that passages have been memorized, but should only assume that passages read well aloud have actually been memorized? Does it mean that the teacher should never formally assign passages for memorizing? What about students who take very minor roles in the acted scenes—servants, messengers, with only such lines as "Yes, madam," and "Madam, I go with all convenient speed"? What if, for lack of time, scenes are not acted, but only read aloud from the seats, with no special preparation?

We may agree that an imposed assignment to memorize, with rigid requirements of "proof," is the least desirable way to manage this activity. On the other hand, if we genuinely believe that memorizing extraordinary passages from Shakespeare's plays is a basically valuable experience—as valuable as anything that students might be doing instead—we may also agree that this drastic way is better than no way at all. If there is no other way, it may still be worth imposing the assignment despite a chorus of groans. But surely there is little need for matters to reach that extremity.

We have elsewhere insited that questions for discussion and subjects for writing should grow out of the daily study of the play. If every student understands from the outset that in the course of reading the play he is to choose a longer passage, or two or three shorter passages, to commit to memory, the proverbial groans can be stifled in advance. Further, many teachers have learned that groans, on such occasions, do not always signify real protest, but are a kind of game that students play; there are good-humored groans that actually disguise a high morale. And, finally —and this on the testimonies of teachers and students alike—it is a rare student who, having successfully committed a great passage to memory, fails to experience a thrill of satisfaction and pride; in the halls and classrooms of schools, in the conversations of students, it is a common thing to hear lines that were memorized in October breaking out in May; it is also common to hear them spoken many years later.

The question of obtaining "proof" beyond that given when students participate extensively in acted scenes is not an easy one, and again the basic problem is that of time. Traditionally, students who were formally required to memorize, say, "Friends, Romans, countrymen," proved their mastery by reciting the passage before the class; shyer students were permitted to stand at their own desks to recite; and those for whom the ordeal was painful to the point of being impossible were allowed to write out the passage. But at best, with a class of thirty to forty students, the operation is time-consuming and the cumulative effects of repetition become intolerable. Students who have already had their turn grow weary of it all long before the thirtieth speaker has been heard—and this last speaker, if he is a nervous one, has had to suffer longer than anyone should. The experience, in this case, is bad for the speaker, his audience, and Shakespeare.

One solution is to begin taking volunteers just as soon as they are ready. At the rate of two or three a day, during a period of several weeks, all students can be heard by an audience not yet exhausted with listening. When students have not all been required to memorize the same passage, but have been encouraged to choose during the several weeks of reading the play, this method works even more smoothly. Some students will identify passages early, during the reading of the first scenes, and will be ready on the next day to volunteer. Thus by the end of the reading, students will have heard notable passages spoken almost daily, without monotony, and the very repetition of passages will help to review scenes read yesterday or the day before.

To save time, teachers sometimes break up the class into groups of five or six students each, and members take turns speaking their chosen passage to the rest of the group. If five students have chosen, say, "To be or not to be," they make up one group;

others, who have chosen "How all occasions do inform against me," make up another, and so on. But there is obvious merit, too, in grouping students together who have chosen different passages; then, while one speaks his particular passage, others follow in their books; there is thus much review, without tedium.

Again, teachers sometimes make a rather "big thing" out of memorizing by having students record their speeches on tape; or the "winner" from each group is rewarded by having his speech recorded and played back for the whole class. Once more, the chief problem is time: recording takes much time and playing back takes nearly as much; in a class of thirty or forty students the problem of getting around to everybody *twice* is formidable. One obvious way to solve it is to spread the individual recordings out over the whole period of reading the play, with students coming in before school, during the noon hour, whenever they have their passages ready, to record in private; then, when the play is finished and every student has taped his speech, the whole class hears the playback—which, with its various passages and interpretations, is likely to be filled with enough surprises to offset tedium. Students have been known to keep their passage secret until the day of the playback; from this laudable practice grows suspense that lends excitement to the occasion.

Managed in one of these ways—or in other and possibly better ways, for the possibilities are many—memorization need not be the irksome task, inflicted like punishment by ogrelike teachers, that its opponents of the past thirty years have suggested. It can be an integral and exciting part of the study of the play, taking its place of importance beside discussion and writing as a major activity. Much earlier, we insisted that the study of a play should not be considered finished until every student has spoken significant amounts aloud; we shall be in accord with that view in now insisting that the study of a play should not be considered finished until every student has memorized a significant number of lines and, if possible, has heard his own recorded voice speaking them to his classmates.

5. FILMS, RECORDINGS

Most of what might be said at this point about the use of films and recordings in connection with the study of Shakespeare has in fact been directly stated or implied earlier (notably in the discussions of "approach" and "presentation"); it is therefore possible to deal summarily with these matters here.

The first necessity is to repeat a principle earlier stated emphatically: that if films (of a play, of Shakespeare's life, of England's "Shakespeare country," etc.) and professional recordings of plays are to be used, they should be used not before or during but *after* the text of a play has been studied by teacher and class together. They are neither a substitute for textual study nor a crutch to support the reading.

We may now, finally, use the same form of assertion as that with which we concluded our consideration of reading aloud and memorization—namely, that the study of a play should not be regarded as complete until students have heard the whole play or significant portions of it interpreted by the voices of professional actors. Filmstrips "about" the play, the stage, the author, the age, etc., no doubt have value, but in the very fact that they are "about" the work, their claim on the precious time allowable for the total study of the play would appear less valid than that of perhaps *any* activity that deals with the work itself. They can be useful, not indispensable. It is likely that a fifteen-minute filmstrip dealing with Shakespeare's stage is preferable to an hour's lecture on the same subject, if for no reason than that it takes less time; but quick, passing references to a good drawing of the stage—even to a sketch drawn on the blackboard—can take still less time and yet be adequate.

For students who can see live productions of the plays, the use of filmed Shakespeare is surely less urgent than for those who will possibly never see one of the plays except on film. For these latter, the experience of seeing actors give physical dimension to the images they have formed in the mind's eye will be worth whatever effort the teacher must undergo in order to provide a film and a showing. Even so, one reservation may be appropriate here. Bad Shakespeare, on film as on the stage, can be worse than no Shakespeare; it can diminish rather than enhance the view of Shakespeare that has been gained by careful study of a play. Badly done Shakespeare disappoints the expectations. Illustrative "scenes" from the plays filmed expressly for schools, accompanied by lecture, take time that might better be spent in reading a second play or in hearing students themselves recite.

Similarly, older professional films may actually be detrimental to the study of a play. It is an unfortunate fact that, until recently, efforts to adapt Shakespeare's plays to the motion picture medium have produced results that are neither good Shakespeare nor good cinema. Inevitably, and especially with young students accustomed to seeing movies that are at least technically well-done, badly filmed Shakespeare suffers terribly by comparison and tends to discredit the plays themselves. Teachers must use care to see that the appreciation of Shakespeare they have built through careful study is not undermined by a filmed spectacle of rolling eyeballs, shuddering gestures, and creaking camera techniques. It is absurd but it is true that to the minds of young students whose expectations have been heightened, Shakespeare himself seems the cause of the disappointment. In its time (the mid-1930's) the Reinhardt *Midsummer Night's Dream* was a film to take students to see, for it was approximately as well done as other movies of its time; but, seen today, it is a crude, laughable curiosity which by association damages the play itself. Possibly the earliest film that a teacher should risk showing—and that with some misgivings—is the production of *Romeo and Juliet* with Norma Shearer, Leslie Howard, and John Barrymore. Thereafter, the Charlton Heston *Julius Caesar*, the James Mason-Marlon Brando *Julius Caesar*, Laurence Olivier's productions of *Henry V* and *Hamlet*, and the Maurice Evans-Judith Anderson *Macbeth* are assets rather than liabilities. The Laurence Harvey *Romeo and Juliet* and the Orson Welles *Macbeth* are films that the teacher should see before showing.

Nothing of the risk that accompanies the selection of filmed Shakespeare need accompany the selection of recorded Shakespeare. In the past few years, many recordings of extraordinary quality have been made available by leading, highly reputable companies, with the finest actors in the world playing roles in all the plays. That all schools should have a wide selection of these recordings *on hand for regular use* by English classes there can surely be no question. Besides the fact that these provide splendid readings of the plays and that they are readily accessible and easily manageable in the classroom, a great advantage of hearing recordings (in contrast to seeing a film) is that students can follow, line by line, in their own books. In this way, they gain not only an all important aesthetic experience, but also *a lesson in reading* that is very possibly beyond any other that they have ever had or will have.

6. TESTING

Ideally, as probably most teachers of literature would agree, there should be no formal testing when students have finished studying a Shakespearean play. Practically, and especially because the full study of a play may take up as much as an entire grading period, some kind of testing seems unavoidable if marks from A to F are to be distributed with justice and reasonable precision.

On the other hand, the method of dealing with the play that we have outlined in the preceding pages has the additional virtue of making formal testing much less necessary than it is with any other method we could name. The "initial presentations," for example, with teacher and students reading and discussing line by line, ensures that students will have covered the entire text minutely. When, instead, students first read the play on their own, it is necessary to test to find whether they *have* in fact read the assignment. Teachers who use the "on-their-own" form of presentation, making daily assignments of a scene or two, often give a brief "quiz" merely to check on the reading. A virtue of this procedure is that the test questions can serve as focal centers for discussion. If the test questions get at basic matters, they can direct discussion that might otherwise be random and aimless. But an obvious fault that perhaps outbalances this virtue is that students may get into the habit of reading scenes in order to pass the expected test at the next meeting. They may learn mainly to look out for things that are likely to be asked about. Instead of being moved—as one wishes they might be—by the power of lines like—

> . . . the isle is full of noises,
> Sounds and sweet airs that give delight and hurt not.
> Sometimes a thousand twangling instruments
> Will hum about mine ears, and sometimes voices
> That, if I then had waked after long sleep,
> Will make me sleep again; and then, in dreaming,
> The clouds methought would open and show riches
> Ready to drop upon me, that, when I waked,
> I cried to dream again . . .

—they may react only with the shrewd observation, "This looks like something that will be on tomorrow's quiz. I'll underline it and remember who said it."

The "practical" attitudes forced on students by the read-test pattern tend inevitably to thwart the artistic impact that is, surely, the supreme reason for reading Shakespeare or any other literature of moving power. But if the teacher reads line by line with students, there is no necessity to test merely to find whether they have read—for the teacher *knows* they have read.

Further, reading through a play in this fashion is accompanied by steady discussion of great things and small, and such discussion, day after day, provides "gradable" evidence in abundance. Also, as has been suggested earlier, reading and discussion will provide many subjects for writing: there will be paraphrases, paragraphs, other brief pieces—at least a dozen in all during the weeks of study, all of which are eminently gradable. Finally, the oral or written account of outside reading done during this period, the longer paper based on the play, and the participation in whatever activities of memorizing, oral reading, or acting are used to complete the study of the play will all add significantly to the mass of evidence needed to determine the individual student's mark. Surely, all together, these contributions of students during the entire period of work with the play will furnish ample evidence for a just evaluation without the necessity of any formal test.

But, it may be protested, these sorts of evidence gained piece-meal over a long period are not an adequate substitute for a final, conclusive examination to discover what each student actually "knows"—what he has "retained." Does he know the principal facts of Shakespeare's life and dramatic career? Does he know the important characteristics of the Elizabethan Age? Does he know about comedy, or tragedy, or history as a dramatic genre? Does he know the features of the Elizabethan stage, Elizabethan acting, dramatic verse? And, of course, does he remember details from the play itself?

At this point it may be worth reasserting that from the beginning of our consideration of teaching Shakespeare, we have insisted that the experience of the play itself is the thing most to be valued. Accordingly, we have resisted any kind of "approach" that would make it appear that knowledge of the age, author, and genre were the main thing to be learned, with the play itself diminished to the role of specimen or example. Similarly, we have argued for that form of "initial presentation" which would best reveal "what is there," in the play, and would thus most nearly ensure that students would have the experience of the play. Finally, we resisted such "accompanying and following activities" as are clearly peripheral, more concerned with what is outside than inside the play, and warmly recommended activities that keep the play itself central and are designed to deepen and consolidate the experience of it. It would surely be absurd, at last, to repudiate the consistent emphasis that has run through approach, presentation, and activities by confronting students with a test covering historical and related knowledge. To end with such a test would be, in effect, to announce: "We have pretended until now that the experience of the play is the main thing; but now the game is over: what have you *learned* about age, author, and genre?"

But again, it can be pointed out that knowledge of the age, author, and genre will necessarily be absorbed in the course of studying the play, especially during the actual presentation, when what is relevant to the full experience of the play will be introduced at the moment it is needed. Also, it is not at all unlikely that, when facts of age, author, and genre are introduced at the precise moment they are relevant to the experience of the play, students will both acquire and retain *more* facts than if the acquisition of these had been the guiding purpose. They will have acquired them incidentally, but meaningfully.

Teachers raise another kind of argument that we cannot ignore. The gist of it is simply that when students know, from the beginning of study, that they are to have a comprehensive test on the play when it is finished, they maintain a keener interest in all proceedings than when no such test is promised. Because of their interest, the argument continues, they are more likely to learn "what is there," in the play, in all its aspects, than they would otherwise do; and since the all-important "experience of the play" cannot possibly take place at all unless students do at least know "what is there"—i.e., unless they have paid steady attention throughout the reading of the play—it follows that the promise of a test designed to discover whether they know "what is there" has a salutary effect.

One reply to this argument is that a Shakespearean play has, potentially, a great deal of interest and that, if the teacher teaches well enough from day to day, students will remain involved without the promise (threat) of a comprehensive test at the end. In theory, this answer should be sufficient to dispose of the argument. But the argument is advanced by many teachers, not only by the weak or inexperienced, but by first-rate ones of long experience. These know that countless affairs in the lives of high school students compete fiercely for their attention and that, powerful as is a Shakespearean play's potential claim upon their interest, the chances are at best no better than even that this claim will prevail. If, therefore, the odds in its favor can be raised by adding the colder-blooded incentive of passing a test, then the test is justified. Anything, says the practical teacher, is justified if it helps to get the job done; and when "the job" is to induce students to have the experience of a work of literature, we can but agree.

By experimenting, teachers can find whether they *need* a test. If they find that they do, it is here suggested that, at least, the test emphasize the play itself, to determine how well students know "what is there." Such a test need not be unpleasant; it can even be fun. It can, for example, be given orally, the teacher reading out perhaps twenty lines or short passages to be identified by speaker, immediate situation, and any special significance; five names of relatively minor persons whose function is to be identified; five or ten unusually significant and well known lines or short passages with a key word or two omitted, to be supplied by students; and additional items of kinds appropriate to the particular play. Some teachers include, finally, an essay question that calls for some sort of synthesis; but if writing assignments have been made throughout the study of the play, further "essay" evidence should be unnecessary.

7. *MISCELLANEOUS*

All of the preceding activities center on the play itself, and, besides having intrinsic values, also contribute in some degree to achieving the primary end, which is experience of the play as a work of art. Though any one of these activities, if it were badly managed, could conceivably damage this experience, each is, in its best form, an entirely worthy part of the total study and needs no apologies.

Not so much can be said, however, for an enormous number of additional "related activities" that are sometimes used in connection with the reading of a Shakespearean play. What is most objectionable in such activities is that they are time-consuming and at best peripheral to the essential purpose of the entire undertaking. They mislead the minds of students about what is important. The fact is that a Shakespearean play has attractions enough in itself; it does not need to be "helped out" by dressing and gimmicks. The inventiveness of the teacher can be a tremendous asset in the teaching of a play; but this inventiveness is best directed toward ways of revealing what is in the play than toward devising tricky peripheral activities. It has been shrewdly remarked by more than one observer that teachers who devise peripheral "aids" in teaching Shakespeare do so because they do not *really* trust the dramatist himself. Probably the best advice of all is to trust him utterly, to leave as much of the job to him as possible. If teachers succeed in showing "what is there," Shakespeare needs no sideshow attractions.

Dismissing thus abruptly a veritable host of peripheral activities that at best contribute nothing significant to study of the text and at worst detract from it, we have finally to deal with one more form of activity which, though it is intended to facilitate close study of the text, we are nevertheless obliged to reject.

Rejection will seem the more paradoxical because throughout this book we have insisted that close study of text is basic to everything else and have tended to favor whatever methods seemed most likely to promote it. But this final activity, *the use of "study questions" that are to be answered in writing,* we find it necessary both to reject and to denounce as emphatically as words permit.

Study questions are used almost universally by teachers who assign students to read Shakespeare on their own. The reason for their enormous popularity is clear enough: experienced teachers know that most students flounder "on their own" in Shakespeare, and therefore they provide classes with "guides" in the form of detailed questions, scene by scene, to be answered, usually in writing. Teachers' motives here are clearly commendable; they *do* want students to study the text closely and to understand "what is there." They want students to find meanings first, but they want them also to note puns, recognize figures of speech, perceive devices of characterization, appreciate dramatic techniques of all kinds. All these are purposes also of teachers who read and discuss plays line by line with students.

Editions of plays prepared for classroom use generally include scene-by-scene study questions. But many teachers prefer to work out their own, and among the most-prized possessions of countless experienced teachers are the elaborately detailed study guides they have personally developed through the years for use with *Julius Caesar, Macbeth, A Midsummer Night's Dream, As You Like It*. These guides run to as many as fifty typewritten sheets that are mimeographed or "dittoed" for distribution to classes. Individual scenes, especially major ones, are given as many as forty questions, and there are often more general questions covering whole acts and yet more general ones covering the play as a whole. Directions for answering are typically specific: "Answer the following questions on Act II, Scene 1. *Write complete sentences.* Give full answers, with supporting evidence."

Fully detailed, personally prepared, such guides no doubt indicate better than anything else what sorts of things teachers think important and want students to "get" from a particular play. It is needless here to catalogue varieties of information asked for, but typical questions or instructions run as follows: (1) This scene is filled with *puns*; identify at least five, explaining the "point" of each. (2) Two notable examples of *dramatic irony* occur in this scene. Point them out and explain the irony in each instance. (3) Write a *paraphrase* of lines 26–28. (4) What predominant *trait of character* does Brutus reveal in this scene? Quote the lines that express it most clearly.

If there is anything wrong with these questions, or with the hundreds like them that make up a complete study guide, it would be difficult to say what it is. They represent hours of conscientious work by individual teachers who prepared them, and they bear witness to the zeal of these teachers for close study and understanding of great texts. In all respects, they are purely commendable. On what grounds, then, do we reject them?

We do not, in fact, reject them. What we reject is the practice of distributing them to students *with instructions to write out the answers* as "aids" to initial, independent reading. We should reject them also, though slightly less emphatically, if instructions were to "prepare answers for oral discussion tomorrow."

Anyone who has watched a student—or a great many students —"do" assignments of this kind will see the reason for our objection. The student opens his book to the scene that he has been assigned to read, and then does one of two things: (1) reads quickly through the scene and then immediately begins searching the text for the "answers" to be written out; or (2) opens the study guide, reads the first question, searches for the "answer" in the scene (his finger running down the text line by line), writes out the answer, and turns back to the guide for the next question. Even an author as great as Shakespeare cannot survive this kind of study; the all-important "experience of the play as a work of art" simply cannot come through this treatment. Fingers running down passages in a cold-blooded search for the "answers"— whether puns, examples of irony, or whatever—are strictly non-conductors of the literary experience.

"Discussion questions," we have maintained throughout, should arise from the text in the course of line-by-line reading and discussion by teacher and students. Prepared in advance, either by the teacher or by the editor of a text, they can stimulate, supplement, expedite discussion, call attention to important matters that might otherwise be overlooked. But their place is clearly as accompaniment of discussion and not as guide to the initial reading. Reading the text of Shakespeare in search of answers to study questions is not the same as reading Shakespeare and discussing the questions that emerge from the text.

CHAPTER 9

Notes on Teaching Particular Plays

THE COMMENTS THAT FOLLOW ARE NOT INTENDED AS EITHER complete or in any sense prescriptive. They supplement, or perhaps implement, with specific reference to individual plays, the general attitudes toward teaching Shakespeare that have been expressed in preceding chapters. Thus, it is supposed, what has been said generally about the purposes and problems of teaching Shakespeare is relevant to any one play, and the particularities of application can be worked out by the teacher: what has been said of "approach" in general applies as well to *Julius Caesar* in the ninth or tenth grade as to *The Tempest* in the twelfth; what has been said of "presentation" applies as well to *A Midsummer Night's Dream* in the ninth or tenth grade as to *Macbeth* in the eleventh or twelfth; what has been said of "accompanying and following activities" applies as well to *The Merchant of Venice* in the ninth or tenth grade as to *King Lear* in the twelfth. In short, the preceding chapters have been intended to furnish a *rationale*; the following are intended as illustrative applications. Though, it is assumed, the ways of "going at" Shakespeare will be generally the same from play to play throughout the high school years, particular plays also raise particular problems. Thus, while all can be treated in the same general way, each must be treated differently in detail, because every play is different in its detail. The necessity, always, ake his cue for specific emphases from the

Caesar (Grade 9 or 10)

insisted earlier that no one is likely to make
a better "app... to a Shakespearean play than Shakespeare
himself makes. The opening scene of *Julius Caesar* is a case in
point; Shakespeare takes care of literally everything. The place to
begin, therefore, is with it, and nothing is needed that will not be
"cued" by close reading of the lines themselves. Words and lines
themselves, that is to say, should prompt the teacher to offer
immediate, always brief explanation. Caesar, Pompey, Capitol,
tribunes, senators: these call for quick, passing comment on the
reputation of Caesar in the history of the world, the wars of
Caesar and the Pompeys that preceded this triumphal return, the
governmental "situation" of Rome at this date. By reading Plutarch, the teacher can know what, essentially, Shakespeare himself
knew of these matters; and *in the course of reading the first scene
with students* can establish what "background" is relevant—and,
preferably, no more.

The point, as we have insisted earlier, is that the introduction of
Julius Caesar should not serve as an excuse either for hours of
"research" by students into the history, government, customs, and
costumes of Rome in Caesar's time or for hours of lecturing by
the teacher on the same. To teach *Julius Caesar* in order to "learn
about Rome" is to make information about Rome primary and
the play itself secondary, to make Rome the end and Shakespeare
the means. To avoid this regrettable but common reversal is not
difficult, but certainly a crucial point of danger occurs during the
"approach," when overdoing "background" will establish a false
perspective for the entire study of the play. We do not need
Shakespeare to learn about Rome; if we want to learn about
Rome, we read history.

Some teachers, it is true, use a different kind of approach.
Before beginning to read the first scene—and at first without making any connection with *Julius Caesar*—they involve students in
discussion of debatable issues that they will later find important in

Julius Caesar: the question of personal loyalty *vs.* public duty, of bringing about a great "right" by doing a "wrong," of leaders and common citizens, of state and individual, of dictatorship and democracy. Some teachers even manage to focus discussion on such questions to the degree that, at the end of an hour, a clear question has been defined on which students can be directed to express their thoughts in a well-developed paragraph or short essay. It is often an exciting moment when, later, they discover that Shakespeare, too, treated the same issue.

That this kind of approach is preferable to either an approach through a study of Roman times or an approach through a study of Shakespeare and Elizabethan times, the whole of this book insists. Whether it is preferable also to plunging directly into what Shakespeare wrote in the first scene and letting whatever "issues" it contains boil out as they will in the course of reading, is a question that teachers will presumably decide for themselves by trying both ways. There is merit in each.

Emphases in Presentation and Discussion. As with all other Shakespearean plays, it is assumed that *Julius Caesar* will first be read aloud by the teacher and discussed continually by teacher and students.

Because *Julius Caesar* is likely to be (and almost certainly should be) the first Shakespearean tragedy read by high school students, a greater emphasis on *form*—that is, the form of tragedy—than will ordinarily be necessary is very possibly appropriate. More importantly, this play itself particularly invites special attention to the tragic genre because it is the play in which Shakespeare first worked out a pattern for what we generally think of as "Shakespearean tragedy." It is possibly because he was very deliberately seeking out his way that the stages or steps in the tragic action are marked so clearly (some critics, indeed, would suggest that they are too obviously marked). In any event, as it stands, *Julius Caesar* lends itself peculiarly well to provide a "lesson" in Shakespearean tragedy. Perhaps, even, it lends itself *too* well, so that unless a teacher is careful it will seem to be no more than that. Most teachers would presumably agree that it would be as faulty to use *Julius Caesar* primarily to illustrate "Shakespearean tragedy" as it would be to use it primarily to teach about life in Rome.

Nevertheless, the dramatist's own emphases in working out his pattern give clear direction for much of the teacher's emphasis in presentation. "Steps" in the tragic action could even be listed and numbered as they occur, so clearly were they marked by Shakespeare as he worked out the way. "This," he seems to say, "is how to write a tragic play":

1. Establish the enveloping situation, the "environment" or "world" in which the action will take place. (Shakespeare demonstrates in the first scene the fickleness of the people, the abiding, dangerous element in this environment.)

2. Establish the specific situation. (Caesar returns in triumph, but is greeted by violently divided reactions.)

3. Introduce the hero (tragic protagonist) and boldly exhibit the qualities of his character that will ultimately destroy him. (Brutus says:

> If it be aught toward the general good,
> Set honor in one eye and death i' the other,
> And I will look on both indifferently.
> For let the gods so speed me as I love
> The name of honor more than I fear death.)

4. Show the temptation of the hero. (Shrewdly, Cassius works on precisely that in Brutus which can be best worked on—his devotion to "the general good.")

5. Show the hero in self-debate which ends in self-commitment. (Brutus says:

> O Rome, I make thee promise;
> If redress will follow, thou receivest
> Thy full petition at the hand of Brutus.)

6. Show the fatal act itself. (In this case, it is the assassination, surrounded by supernatural manifestations and prophecies.)

7. Represent the hero in a succession of "fatal decisions" made in accord with his previously established character. (Actually, these begin prior to the assassination itself: the decision to kill Caesar, the refusal to kill Antony also, the insistence that Antony speak at the funeral, etc.)

8. Mark the climax or turning point. (In this play, it is the

shift of public opinion expressed by the citizens directly after the first section of Antony's oration.)

9. Represent the "falling action," the worsening of the hero's position which runs straight on to his destruction and the defeat of all his hopes.

10. Provide a final "lift." (Brutus dies honorably and is eulogized by Antony; even Octavius speaks well of him.)

No later tragedy follows precisely the tragic pattern here first worked out, and certainly no later tragedy so conspicuously exhibits its "steps." But those that followed were built upon this groundwork.

Of course, the tragic pattern of *Julius Caesar* is only one of an enormous number of elements that will be discovered and discussed as teacher and students move through the play in a common effort to see "what is there." The sharply delineated character portraits of Brutus, Antony, Caesar, Cassius, Octavius, Casca, all developed with a boldness similar to that with which the steps in the tragic pattern are displayed, will emerge in the course of alert, close study. The style of speech of each major character, sharply differentiated, closely fitted to the nature of the man, will become apparent almost at once: the haranguing style of Marullus, based on a vocabulary that breathes contempt; the blunt, churlish speech of Casca, the most "Anglo-Saxon" Roman of them all; the open, almost naive manner of Brutus' speech, which exposes his heart too directly to both enemies and allies; the eloquent irony of Antony, veiled by shrewdly chosen words and emphases; the pompous, windy, vain utterances of Caesar; the coldly arrogant tones of Octavius ("I do not cross you; but I will do so"). The character portraits of *Julius Caesar* stand out as obvious points of emphasis, and they offer the broadest, easiest of all access routes into the mysteries of Shakespearean drama.

The consideration of characters and their speech leads naturally into discussion of blank verse and prose, the differences between these, and the "principle" of their distribution throughout the play. Indeed, the alternation of verse and prose in the opening scene, where the tribunes speak verse and the citizens prose, establishes a pattern that will stand throughout the play. But, of course, much more is to be said than pertains merely to the basic principle of apportionment: the special qualities that fit both verse and prose to character and occasion are virtually palpable features of Shakespeare's art. Thus, at the opening of Act I, Scene 2, when great Caesar makes his first entrance, the blank verse taps out the cadence of soldiers on parade, marching or marking time:

CAESAR.   Calpurnia!
CASCA.   Peace, ho! Caesar speaks.
CAESAR.   Calpurnia!
CALPURNIA. Here, my lord.

How should the most famous warrior in all history enter if not in syllables that are like marching steps? The precise appropriateness of the verse quality to the occasion is not always as boldly apparent as it is here, or as it is, for example, in Antony's oration at Caesar's funeral. However, it is regularly an artistic feature that is worthy of note.

The orderly progress of teacher and students through the five acts will thus quite naturally turn up points, both major and minor, for discussion and clarification. No doubt the main necessity is to keep students aware of the total situation at each moment. The breaks between scenes and acts are the obvious places to hold brief reviews, make brief recapitulations, predict what action is likely to follow, and to what end, by projecting what has gone before. Proceeding so, teacher and class will deal with the many and varied aspects of the play at the moments they *need* to be dealt with: verse and prose, character and characterization, relation of character to action, functions of particular characters and scenes, dramatic devices and effects, rising and falling action, climax, catastrophe.

A chief virtue of this orderly yet flexible method is that it keeps all aspects of the play in perspective and avoids the distortion that inevitably occurs when emphases of discussion are predetermined. But though teacher and students should move inductively and empirically, intent on seeing "all that is there," this does not mean that the teacher should not know "what is there" in advance. The final effectiveness of the whole presentation depends upon the teacher's knowing very well what is in the play and as much as possible of what is around and about it; otherwise the orderly inductive process, even with an open play like *Julius Caesar*, can become a guideless, haphazard misadventure in strange woods.

Accompanying and Following Activities. Obviously the foremost activity that accompanies the presentation of *Julius Caesar* is discussion, which, as we have suggested, grows directly out of the reading of the lines. Next after discussion comes writing, and it is to this that we now turn.

We have earlier maintained that writing should grow directly out of discussion, just as discussion should grow out of reading. To begin the play with a prearranged list of subjects on which students will be required to write at intervals during the next four to six weeks, and to follow this list like a schedule, would be to impose directions in advance on both discussion and writing and thus destroy the spontaneity and freedom that should characterize the whole enterprise. An experienced teacher, certainly, can predict what discussion will grow out of certain specific passages and scenes, and may also be able to predict, in some instances, just which subjects of discussion will "shape up" as subjects for composition. But it is simply a fact that no two classes ever take exactly the same degree of interest at *all* the same points in *Julius Caesar*, or any other great work. A given passage may inspire excited debate in one class, and this debate may spark an ambition in each student to have his say on the question in writing; but in the class that is taught during the next hour, the same passage may inspire no more than perfunctory discussion out of which would come, at best, only perfunctory writing. The second class, like the first, should have its opportunity to find what excites it. When all the "points" have been predetermined by the teacher —or by the editor of the textbook—the odds favor a listless series of compositions.

If we would be consistent, therefore, we should suggest here, *for purposes of illustration only*, a few points at which discussion may produce subjects for composition. Probably Act I, Scene 2, to take a first example, can be counted on, in one passage or another, to furnish a springboard for a paragraph. In this scene, the tempter Cassius sounds out Brutus rather remotely at first, and then abruptly goes to work to rouse him to action against Caesar. Even as their conversation continues, the drama onstage is height-

ened by the drama offstage, marked by a "general shout" thrice
repeated; and thereafter Cassius urgently renews his campaign.
How does Cassius use the circumstance offstage to aid his wooing
of Brutus? Is Cassius most driven by envy and spite, by personal
ambition, by honest regard for Rome, or by what? Cassius is a
cunning man, and couches his arguments in the terms that he
thinks will be most persuasive. But if Brutus is uncompromisingly
noble, should we expect him to find everything that Cassius says
persuasive? Does he truly suppose that the motives of Cassius are
as honorable as his own? or can he recognize that Cassius is less
honorable than himself and *still* be moved by Cassius' arguments?
At the end of the scene, Cassius remarks that Brutus' "honorable
metal may be wrought/From that it is disposed"—which is to say
that it can be twisted to serve Cassius' purposes. But does Cassius
mean that Brutus can be made to be knowingly dishonorable? If
so, is he mistaken? Or does he mean that Brutus can be made to
do what is dishonorable by being made to *suppose* that what he
does is honorable?

A second scene—it could as well be any other substantial scene,
for purposes of illustration—which should easily yield subjects for
composition is Act II, Scene 1. Here Brutus engages in self-debate,
meets and plans with fellow conspirators, converses tenderly with
Portia, and, finally, sets off with Ligarius to keep his fatal appointment at the Capitol. At the end of about sixty lines, reasoning in
the pattern that his own nature dictates, Brutus has fully resolved
his problem: he will assassinate Caesar. "Since Cassius first did
whet me against Caesar," he says, "I have not slept." Does this
mean that he would never have moved if Cassius had not
"whetted" him? Though the final decision is Brutus' own, evidently Cassius had a share in making up his mind. How much?
If Cassius had a great deal of influence on his decision, is Brutus'
own responsibility for the assassination that follows—and for his
own ultimate downfall—thereby lessened? Or is the responsibility
his alone, whether Cassius had much or little influence on his
final decision?

The conspirators enter Brutus' house with hats pulled down and
cloaks pulled up to hide their faces. They want to swear an oath
of fidelity to the general conspiracy. Next they want to kill Antony
as well as Caesar. Brutus is shocked and revolted by each of these

incidents. Why? Another kind of man, similarly shocked, might well have washed his hands of the conspiracy at once; but Brutus, because he *is* Brutus, dedicated to what he conceives to be a noble purpose, keeps on. Is Brutus "right" or "wrong" in his reactions? Should conspirators engaged in so dark an enterprise hide their faces? Should they bind themselves together by oath? Should they kill Antony with Caesar? Should Brutus retain the leadership of an enterprise the ugly realities of which are revolting to him? Will the enterprise be more or less likely to succeed under his leadership?

Portia, proud that she has strength to bear all griefs that afflict her husband, begs to be informed of their cause. Given such a wife, is Brutus nobler or less noble for refusing to share his worries with her? How does the incident serve the play as a whole?

To this point we have been concerned with writing assignments that grow—though this very "spontaneity" is teacher-planned—spontaneously out of specific areas of discussion. The argument of the foregoing discussion is simply this: the teacher should be ready to seize upon *whatever* subject of discussion takes fire and promises more than perfunctory performance as a writing assignment. Such a subject might be, or be very much like, one of those suggested in the foregoing paragraphs; or it might be something very different and quite unexpected. The teacher should always be ready to abandon the predetermined in favor of the unexpected when the unexpected looks more promising. Managing writing assignments is as much "playing by ear"—or should seem to be—as are presentation and discussion.

But in addition to spontaneously generated writing assignments are others that can be determined in advance. The principal example of this kind is paraphrase. In all the plays, certain passages lend themselves better to paraphrase than do others. Passages chosen for written paraphrasing should normally be significant or even key passages; they should make a real demand on both interpretation and expression; and they should be brief enough for students to do them in ten or fifteen minutes.

Such passages in *Julius Caesar* include the following: Act I, Scene 2: (1) Brutus, beginning "Cassius,/Be not deceived" to "Forgets the shows of love to other men." (2) Brutus, beginning "I would not, Cassius," to "more than I fear death." (3) Brutus, beginning "That you do love me," to "Is like to lay upon us." (4) Cassius, beginning "Well, Brutus, thou art honorable," to "worse days endure." *Act I, Scene 3:* (1) Cassius, beginning "Cassius from bondage will deliver Cassius" to "shake off at pleasure." (2) Cassius, beginning "Poor man!" to "And dangers are to me indifferent." *Act II, Scene 1:* (1) Brutus, beginning "It must be by his death" to "And kill him in the shell." (2) Brutus, beginning "No, not an oath" to "Of any promise that hath pass'd from him." (3) Portia, beginning "Is Brutus sick?" to "Even from darkness." *Act III, Scene 1:* (1) Caesar, beginning "If I could pray to move" to "Unshaked of motion." (2) Antony, beginning "O mighty Caesar!" to "master spirits of the age." (3) Antony, beginning "O pardon me" to "groaning for burial." *Act IV, Scene 1:* (1) Antony, beginning "So is my horse" to "And open perils surest answered." (2) Octavius, beginning "Let us do so" to "Millions of mischief." *Act IV, Scene 3:* (1) Brutus, beginning "You must note beside" to "Or lose our ventures." *Act V, Scene 1:* (1) Brutus, beginning "No, Cassius, no" to "this parting was well made." *Act V, Scene 4:* (1) Brutus, beginning "Countrymen" to "That have but labored to attain this hour."

From these the teacher might select half the passages—but more or fewer depending on the alacrity with which a given class acquires skill in giving Shakespeare's blank verse clear meaning in modern prose. Paraphrasing assignments, therefore, might be heavy in the opening scenes of the play and light or even non-existent toward the end. In this, too, the teacher should "play by ear."

Finally, we have very briefly to consider what kind of long paper —or in any event longer than the paragraphs and paraphrases so far mentioned—can appropriately be undertaken when the presentation of *Julius Caesar* has been finished. We have earlier suggested that, ideally, subjects for this longer paper would grow rather naturally out of the presentation and discussion and that, again ideally, all students would "find" their subjects, and actually begin preparations for writing, before the reading of the play has come to an end.

We have earlier suggested also that these final papers should normally differ from the brief ones written while reading is in progress by being concerned with the play as a whole or with some significant aspect of it. One subject that will assuredly come up for oral discussion, as the play progresses, is that of the title of the play. Did Shakespeare title it appropriately, or not? It is impossible to predict at what precise point the class will naturally raise the question, but it is fairly certain that it will have been raised by the time of the assassination. (Obviously, if the class never thinks of raising the question, it is the teacher's business to see that the class *does* think of it.) In any event, oral discussion will never "settle" the question and, in fact, *should* never settle the question until the class has finished reading the play. Discussion, in short, raises a question to which students are to be alert throughout the rest of the reading—and some students may commit themselves to special alertness by marking this out as their subject for the final essay.

Oral discussion will have brought out the main problem, that though the play is named for Caesar, its hero, with whose fate the dramatist asks the audience to become most involved, is Brutus. An essay, based on all the evidence of the play, could present both sides of the question as honestly and fully as possible, and could conclude by favoring one side or the other. Or, if students are inclined to debate the question fiercely in oral discussion, they could continue the debate in writing, taking the side they prefer and making an honest effort to persuade others.

What has just been said, by way of example, about the question of title as a subject for the final essay is equally applicable to other questions. While the play is being read, questions will arise from the text and will be discussed. Many can be answered there and then—questions of meanings of words, interpretation of lines, questions of fact. Other questions which also pertain to individual lines, passages, or scenes will be "answered" in paragraphs or other short compositions. But still others, like that of the appropriateness of the title, pertain to the play as a whole and should not be "answered" until all the evidence of the play is in and considered in perspective. It is from this latter group that most subjects for final papers can be shaped.

The "rightness" or "wrongness" of Brutus' act is another such question, which needs to be developed in terms of all the evidence of the play: if Caesar truly was, as Brutus stated, dangerous to the future of Rome, was Brutus justified in joining the conspiracy and killing him? Other questions will arise that pertain to other persons in the play, individually and comparatively. Generally speaking, a "character sketch" is too slight an undertaking for the final paper and ought rather to be used as the basis of a paragraph whenever specific occasions occur. But a character question that relates one man to another, or to the play as a whole, can turn into something larger and more significant than a mere "character sketch." Thus Brutus' character studied throughout the play in relation to the decisions he makes and to the ultimate outcome makes an entirely adequate and sufficiently demanding undertaking.

A study of Shakespeare's techniques of characterization can also serve admirably when students understand clearly that "characterization" and "character" are not the same thing. If students will examine closely the means by which Shakespeare *reveals*, say, Caesar, Brutus, Cassius, and Antony, they should discover some interesting differences—for example, that with Caesar and Brutus Shakespeare makes greater use of unconscious self-revelation. When Caesar boasts, as he regularly does, does the audience gain exactly the sense of him that he has of himself and that he supposes his hearers will gain? On the other hand, does Antony ever unconsciously reveal himself, or reveal something of himself that he does not intend to reveal? Does Cassius? Obviously, before subjects in this area are finally "fixed" for writing, oral discussion should be used to clarify the problems and to define at least a tentative focus. Subjects of this kind that at first seem too complex for high school students, especially ninth- and tenth-grade students, to write on are, in fact, "hard" only if oral discussion has not been allowed to suggest the possibilities of development.

Much harder, and indeed impossible, are those subjects that turn "out and away from" the play itself and leave students floundering in abstractions like "justice," "personal and public duty," "democracy and dictatorship." Where students talk about these matters, they should do so *in direct connection with the play*, in relation to specific actions and decisions and consequences. Students can be relatively sophisticated with such matters so long as they keep to the body of the play and aim to show how these concepts operate *there*. The teacher's task, in helping each student to define his subject, is to see to it that the subject clearly requires discussion of any such abstractions in terms of the body of evidence that is the play, and that the student's definition of his subject does *not* point outward, away from the play, toward justice in general or duty in general. That is to say, the teacher should take such care unless he wishes to invite floundering.

Much more might be said about writing in connection with *Julius Caesar*, and a countless number of specific subjects might be suggested. But we repeat that the naming of specific subjects is not our purpose here. We have insisted that specific subjects should be allowed to "boil up," so to speak, out of discussion that has itself boiled up out of the reading of the play. With this point clear, perhaps the foregoing suggestions will be taken precisely for what they are, not subjects to be assigned, but examples of subjects that might be used for writing *if* discussion pushes them up and excites students' imaginations.

We turn now, and briefly, to two remaining activities—"acting out" and memorization of lines.

In *Julius Caesar* there are literally no scenes (excepting the brief, choppy later ones where the war is in progress and much is confusion) that will not serve well for students in groups of two, three, four, and more to act out, or at least to read before the class with a reasonable show of action. The first scene of tribunes and citizens is splendid and involves several persons in strong leading parts and others in minor but active roles. The entrance of Caesar with his train, leading on to the first, crucial conversation of Brutus and Cassius, is similarly excellent. The parallel scenes of Brutus with Portia and Caesar with Calpurnia might well be performed one after the other—or even performed two or three times each, with different members of the class in the husband-wife roles.

Then there is the famous funeral scene. Here the class can serve dramatically as the citizens as Brutus and then Antony speak. There are many other possibilities, and the teacher should have no difficulty in finding scenes in *Julius Caesar* that are perfectly adapted to short performances in class.

Passages in *Julius Caesar* that are eminently suitable for memorization are well marked and by no means as numerous as might be first supposed. Actually, passages that students have traditionally been required to memorize include not more than half a dozen, some of which are very brief: Caesar's "Cowards die many times before their deaths," Antony's "Friends, Romans, country-men," Brutus' "There is a tide in the affairs of men," Antony's "This was the noblest Roman of them all." But, indeed, the memorization of Antony's funeral oration has been so nearly universal in the experience of generations of high school students that no other speech in all Shakespeare compares with it in point of wide familiarity. Its closest competitors in other plays would be Jaques' "All the world's a stage" (but only a very few high school students even read *As You Like It* in comparison to the great numbers that read *Julius Caesar*); Macbeth's two soliloquies, "If it were done when 'tis done" and "Is this a dagger"; and Hamlet's "To be or not to be"—again not a close competitor because far fewer students have read *Hamlet* than have read *Julius Caesar* and *Macbeth*.

There seems no sound reason to oppose the continued use of Antony's oration as an exercise in memorizing and speaking; if students are to be assigned to memorize a single speech from this play, the choice is obvious. But we may here reassert what has earlier been said: namely, that the most effective way to handle memorization is to have students either memorize wholly or commit virtually to memory the lines and passages that occur in the scenes acted out by individual groups. If this method has a disadvantage, it is that students who take leading parts in the acted scenes will draw significant, "juicy" passages, whereas actors in minor roles will often be limited to lines like "Why, sir, a carpenter." But teachers can easily devise means of equalizing the privilege and burden of memorizing: students can appear in one scene in minor roles with few lines, and in a second scene in major roles with significant passages; or students who appear only in minor roles can be assigned the additional responsibility of memorizing some larger passage elsewhere in the play.

2. Macbeth (Grade 11 or 12)

In all probability, *Macbeth* stands second only to *Julius Caesar* as the most teachable, most readable of Shakespeare's plays. That juniors or seniors will "get more out of it" than will freshmen or sophomores is entirely likely—but the same argument can be made also for *Julius Caesar* or for any other first-rate work of literature. In recommending it for grade eleven or twelve, we are possibly bowing to tradition more than we ought to be willing to confess. Like *Julius Caesar*, *Macbeth* is easier to teach than any Shakespearean comedy, even the "easiest" ones, *The Merchant of Venice* and *As You Like It*, which are plays that we have recommended for the ninth or tenth grade and which are, in fact, most often taught in those grades. On the surface, it does not look like very good sense to follow tradition in recommending that *Macbeth* be taught in the upper years and these comedies in the lower years.

But there is an argument that may prove persuasive if it can be made clear. The point is that while *Macbeth* is, for reasons that will shortly be stated, an eminently teachable play at any high school level, it is also a relatively "deep" play. It is "deeper" than either *The Merchant of Venice* or *As You Like It*, even though these, being comedies, are "harder" to teach. These latter plays, if they were saved for the junior or senior year, would allow students to go somewhat deeper than freshmen or sophomores will likely go, but *Macbeth* will allow juniors or seniors to go a great deal deeper because there is potentially much greater depth to be plumbed. It is for this reason that we shall treat it here as a play for the upper years.

Approach. If our general principle is sound, namely, that Shakespeare himself provided the best possible "approach" for a reader or viewer of his plays, it is surely so in the case of *Macbeth*. To "get ready" for this play by lecturing on Shakespeare's age, stage, and life, or on blank verse, Shakespeare's language, and the nature of tragedy, or on the history of Scotland is surely to diminish the likelihood that the play will come through to students as an exciting and memorable experience. The place to begin *Macbeth* is just where Shakespeare began it, on the blasted heath with the Witches.

But a second choice, similar in kind to that which was suggested for *Julius Caesar*, is to involve the class in preliminary discussion of a subject that will emerge soon after the reading of *Macbeth* is begun and should remain as one of the lasting "ponderables" after the reading is finished. This is the question of fate and free will. In the junior or senior year of high school,

.the question should not be an entirely new one for students. They should have ideas about it which they have gained from previous reading and from their private thoughts. The teacher's problem —supposing that this kind of approach is used—is to provoke an hour's serious discussion of it before the pages of *Macbeth* are opened, and, indeed, before *Macbeth* is even mentioned. If students have read, for example, a Hardy novel, a Greek tragedy, *Romeo and Juliet* or *The Bridge of San Luis Rey*, they will have a starting point for discussion. For that matter, Cassius' argument that "The fault, dear Brutus, is not in our stars,/But in ourselves," which they will certainly have pondered a year or two earlier, will serve as the springboard to discussion.

But if the teacher distrusts this question as being too abstract to serve the immediate task of "getting into" *Macbeth*, either of two others that are closer to home may serve. One has to do with ambition: Do all people have it in some degree? Is it possible to have an excess of it? Can it be a vice rather than a virtue?

Another question has to do with conscience: What is it? Where do we get our ideas of "right and wrong"? Is conscience in reality anything more than fear of punishment? One way to start discussion of ambition is to read Bacon's "Of Ambition." One way to start discussion of conscience is to read Poe's "The Tell-Tale Heart." But obviously such subjects as these—resting as they do on common human experience—can be opened for discussion without reference to any literary work; the very words alone will start debate.

Emphases in Presentation and Discussion. As with *Julius Caesar*, our assumption is that *Macbeth* will be read line by line by the teacher and steadily discussed in class, and that the cues for discussion will be provided by the text itself. The teacher should therefore avoid preparing in advance the specific subjects to be discussed in class. This is not to say that the teacher should have no ideas, no sense of direction, in advance. The class will come upon subjects in a spirit of true discovery, and this spirit the teacher's method should encourage beyond all else. But the teacher can best encourage it by knowing in advance as much as possible of "what is there."

Some of the central matters have already been suggested: the question of fate and free will; of ambition; of conscience. All of these, as is evident enough, relate especially to the protagonist —as, indeed, do all the major questions of the play. It is therefore appropriate that our consideration of a few subjects that are sure to come up for discussion should concern Macbeth.

What kind of man is he? The question is basic to consideration of any tragedy in which the hero's own nature largely determines the ultimate outcome of action. The question should normally first come up for discussion at the end of the second scene, after the Sergeant has extravagantly praised Macbeth's martial valor and both Duncan and Ross have added admiring touches to the portrait. It should remain a constant question throughout the third scene, where both Macbeth and Banquo hear the Witches' promises and react to them in characteristic ways that reveal their contrasting natures. But clearly the most significant single scene in the play for its probing to the very soul of Macbeth's being is Act I, Scene 7.

The key passage of this scene is Macbeth's famous and much-memorized soliloquy that begins "If it were done when 'tis done." In this soliloquy Macbeth, like Hamlet in his "To be or not to be," most completely bares the quality of his soul; but whereas Hamlet is concerned to know what is the noblest possible action that a man can take, and does not even stoop to question whether one ought to take that action once he knows what it is, Macbeth is concerned only with knowing whether, if he kills Duncan, he can get away with it.

He reasons, in short, like a brute that knows no reason not to kill except that punishment is likely to follow killing. Nor is his a religious fear of punishment after death: "If I could do it and escape the consequences here on this earth," he says, "I'd ignore whatever might happen in the life to come." He is after earthly gain, and fears only earthly consequences. He decides, as he proceeds to expose the best moral reasoning of which he is capable, that he should not kill Duncan because Duncan is a guest, a kinsman, and a *good* king—and for just an instant it looks as though he *could* be partly swayed by nobler considerations than mere fear of consequences. But then he reasons on, and the ugly truth comes out: it is, as he sees it, worse to kill a guest, kinsman, and good man *because then the public will become especially angry and the danger of retaliation will be increased.*

It is on just these grounds that Macbeth talks himself out of murdering Duncan: "We will proceed no further in this business," he tells his wife—and adds a completely hypocritical reason for his decision—"He has honored me of late," etc.

The rightness of this unflattering view of a brute nature is confirmed by the rest of the scene. Lady Macbeth, knowing her husband well, wastes no words in assuring him that killing a king is not such a bad thing, after all; rather, she goes straight to the only point that, she knows, really matters: *she shows him how they can do it and get away with it.* When she has done so, Macbeth agrees instantly, because the sole objection that his "moral" nature had been able to put up against the deed has been put down:

> Will it not be received,
> When we have marked with blood those sleepy two
> Of his own chamber and used their very daggers,
> That they have done it?

Allied to the question of Macbeth's nature is the question of change in it, and this, of course, is one that will recur as a subject for discussion not once but repeatedly between the moment of Duncan's murder and the end of the play. Scene follows scene, in which Macbeth commits additional murders and is represented as a steadily worsening tyrant, maddened by simultaneous false hopes and desperation. But does the nature of the man actually grow worse? Do successive wicked acts really do any more than bear out what was potential in this nature to begin with, what was implied by the soliloquy "If it were done"?

On the other hand, does his nature change for the better? While in the very act of murder, he learns that Heaven cannot be set aside so cavalierly as he had earlier assumed it could:

> But wherefore could not I pronounce "Amen"?
> I had most need of blessing, and "Amen"
> Stuck in my throat.

Shaken by his experience, he thinks that all the oceans will never wash the blood from his hands, and already he wishes the deed undone. Thus, when the Porter knocks, he says: "Wake Duncan with thy knocking! I would thou could'st."

But do these experiences make him a "better" man in the sense of being able to repent the moral wrongness of his act? Throughout the play, Macbeth is alternately shaken and cheered by events and prophecies. He becomes "wiser" in that he learns more of what can and cannot be trusted and of what one can and cannot get away with in life. But, morally, is he ever changed by his experience, for either better or worse?

If Macbeth is truly as morally empty as he appears to be at the beginning, incapable of understanding right and wrong except in terms of "getting caught" and not "getting caught," and if he is morally unchanged at the end, how then can it be that we become personally involved with him as a tragic hero and can sympathize with him? This question of *how* Shakespeare manages to gain a measure of sympathy for his protagonist after first showing him to such grave disadvantage, is one of the truly great subjects for discussion. Macbeth quickly becomes, of course, an "underdog" as we see him, despite the fact that he is king and tyrant, for he is at the same time a plaything of Fate and we know him to be doomed. Further, the loss of his wife, his frantic efforts to hang on to what he has gained, and to win out against impossible odds—all make forceful demands upon human sympathies. Besides, the physical courage—whatever his moral condition—that he displays throughout even to the final "Lay on, Macduff!" forces a degree of admiration that helps make sympathy possible.

But Shakespeare makes his strongest dramatic bid for sympathy on behalf of his protagonist by making Macbeth a *poet*, and one whose poetic powers markedly increase as he gets into deeper and deeper trouble and as his awareness of this trouble grows. The splendid poetry is, of course, one of the most famous attributes of the play, and as such deserves close attention.

Since most of the best poetry is spoken by the protagonist himself, classroom discussion—instead of floundering among random images and flights of fancy—should center on the development of Macbeth's poetic powers, and on the service of these powers to the tragedy as a whole. Sharp contrast can be made, for example, between the "phony" poetry invented by Macbeth as he describes his sight of Duncan lying murdered in bed, and the later great utterances such as "Tomorrow and tomorrow and tomorrow." But, of course, the gift of poetic imagination shows in all Macbeth's speeches, from his first encounter with the witches to his last violent gasp; the two famous soliloquies ("If it were done" and "Is this a dagger") are packed with the signs of a poetic habit of thought and expression. That so bloody a tyrant should be so rarely gifted is a paradox of the play—and "paradox" now suggests another basic subject for steady attention and discussion.

It is needless here to catalogue the examples of paradoxical statements that run throughout the play and are most conspicuous in the opening acts, playing variations on the theme of "Fair is foul and foul is fair" and "Nothing is but what is not." "Look like the innocent flower," Lady Macbeth tells her husband, "But be the serpent under't." How do these paradoxes—and greater, deeper ones than these varbal expressions, such as the paradox of Macbeth's own nature—bear on the play itself? Are they merely devices of poetic and dramatic expression, used to decorate the drama? What is their relevance, their appropriateness to the tragic theme?

The subject of paradoxes brings us inevitably to the kindred subject of irony—verbal irony, dramatic irony, irony of fate. For example: "There's no art," says Duncan, speaking of the former Thane of Cawdor who had proved a traitor, "To find the mind's construction in the face"—but he says this just as Macbeth enters, who as we know is even now entertaining the thought of murdering the king; and as Macbeth leaves, Duncan adds, "It is a peerless kinsman"!

Macbeth, with a plan to kill Banquo already set, enjoins him to "Fail not our feast," obviously enjoying the joke; but Banquo replies "My lord, I will not"—and indeed he does not fail, though it is as a bloody apparition that he puts in his appearance. To consolidate his wickedly won position, Macbeth had Banquo killed—yet it is the frightful aspect of the apparition at the banquet that violently upsets him and makes his crown more insecure than it was before. So also his slaying of Macduff's family redoubles Macduff's determination to overthrow the tyrant. And enveloping all the passing incidents of verbal and dramatic irony is the whole, veritable ocean of irony in which Macbeth struggles with complete futility against Fate, against the dictum of what will be, regardless. Irony, then, is a swiftly deepening current in the play. In discussion, it should first come up when the first ironic lines are spoken. Thereafter, the progress of the current and its deepening should be treated as occasion suits. But of course discussion should not only mark the separate instances of irony, as a catalogue of isolated items, but should ultimately aim to assess its force and function as an element in the total work.

Accompanying and Following Activities. Once again, as with *Julius Caesar*, writing should presumably stand next to discussion as the activity most emphasized during the course of the initial reading, and after that has been completed.

Written paraphrase would be appropriate as early as the Sergeant's and Ross's speeches in the opening scene; and thereafter no scene of any significant length fails to provide at least one passage that a teacher could select. Because of the highly figurative manner of Macbeth's speech, every passage spoken by him that runs to more than five lines offers students a challenging exercise in first interpreting meaning and next in expressing it in clear, direct prose. A special virtue of paraphrasing as an exercise is the heightened appreciation of the original that it encourages. Students do not always see what is so "great" about poetry until they have the experience of trying seriously to express its meanings in their own prose. This point is made just now because it is especially applicable to the case of rendering the uncommonly poetic utterances of Macbeth in "plain" English. The exuberant abundance of Macbeth's images—which come pouring from his mind in moods of joy, grief, anger, and joviality, and always with such a startling "rightness" for the occasion—will always offer a hard challenge to the paraphraser. But the struggle to transpose this rich and pithy poetry to direct prose statement will surely teach students a healthy respect for poetry's power to say what cannot be wholly said in any other way.

Though any of Macbeth's speeches of five or more lines in length will serve admirably for paraphrasing, certain of them have rather obvious claims. There is point in assigning key passages that have basic significance for the character of Macbeth and for the action that grows from his character. An added purpose in assigning these is that they are also likely to be the ones chosen for memorization—and a passage that has been carefully paraphrased and heavily discussed will be half memorized already.

It is surely appropriate to use key passages to serve the multiple purposes of discussion, writing, and memorization. The most obvious passages we have already mentioned. They are the two soliloquies, "If it were done" and "Is this a dagger." Beyond these, among others, are the following: Act I, Scene 3: "Two truths are told." Act III, Scene 1: "To be thus is nothing." Act III, Scene 2: "We have scotch'd the snake," and "Be innocent of the knowledge, dearest chuck." Act IV, Scene 1: "Time, thou anticipat'st my dread exploits." Act V, Scene 5: "She should have died hereafter," and "If thou speakst false."

Aside from Macbeth's speeches are certain others of which perhaps those exceptionally suitable for paraphrasing are the following: Lady Macbeth in Act I, Scene 5: "Glamis thou art," and "The raven himself is hoarse"; in Act I, Scene 7: "We fail." Lennox (for his fine irony) in Act III, Scene 6: "My former speeches have but hit your thoughts"; and Malcolm in Act IV, Scene 3, "Macduff, this noble passion."

We should now turn away from paraphrase to consider other sorts of writing assignments in connection with *Macbeth*. Let us first consider assignments for short compositions, especially paragraphs.

As with *Julius Caesar*, we must begin by reasserting a basic principle, namely, that subjects for short compositions are not different in kind from subjects for oral discussion and should, in fact, consistently grow out of discussion. In suggesting specific points in the text at which compositions might be assigned, therefore, we are in a sense going contrary to this principle. Normally, we have maintained, subjects for composition should not be assigned unless discussion has made them look fruitful; and since we cannot be sure in advance of just which subjects of discussion will engender excitement and truly involve the minds of students, we cannot logically identify *any* specific subjects on which students should be assigned to write.

With this understanding, then, we shall again suggest some

specific subjects only for the purpose of illustrating *kinds*. Some points in the text at which discussion may kindle composition are the following: First, the encounter of Macbeth and Banquo with the Witches (Act I, Scene 3) should spark discussion at many points from beginning to end. A possibility for writing is provided by the contrasting reactions of the two men to the Witches themselves and to the prophecies they utter. A paragraph on this subject, once the scene has been read and discussed, would provide an experience in organizing a comparison-contrast development and in use of close supporting detail from the text. Further, the subject is one of obvious importance because it forces attention to certain qualities of Macbeth's character that look straight toward his subsequent actions and their consequences.

Act I, Scene 5, provides an opportunity for a second comparison-contrast paragraph, this time setting Lady Macbeth's reactions to her husband's word of the Witches' prophecies against Macbeth's own reactions. The question of the relationship of this couple is, of course, a central consideration of the tragedy. Our first view of this relationship is provided in this scene. Possibly the first impetus to oral discussion that may lead to composition is given by the richly and variously interpretable initial exchange between the pair:

MACBETH.   My dearest love,
          Duncan comes here tonight.
LADY M.   And when goes hence?
MACBETH. Tomorrow, as he purposes.
LADY M.   O, never
          Shall sun that morrow see!

Who makes the first "move," by an intonation of voice, giving a first glimpse of secret thoughts to the other? Is Lady Macbeth's "And when goes hence?" only a request for information? Is Macbeth's "Tomorrow, as he purposes" a simple answer to the question? Or is the voice of each—or of one or the other—loaded with import, giving a subtle cue that the other can pick up if he chooses? When the couple exchange these lines, we have already had an opportunity to form some opinion of the character of each. Students draw on all the evidence available in order to argue one side or the other of the question, "Who makes the first 'move'?" This is a chance for a persuasive paragraph that probes the essential qualities of the two principal characters in the play.

The importance of Act I, Scene 7, we have already touched in connection with oral discussion and paraphrase. Where, now, is the likeliest spot in the scene to spark a paragraph or other short paper? The possibilities are numerous.

A relatively direct problem for composition is to trace the reasoning by which, first, Macbeth talks himself out of doing the murder, and, next, Lady Macbeth talks him back into doing it. Perhaps a more sophisticated approach, and one that in effect encompasses the other, is to try to focus, in a paragraph, all the evidence here given on the question, "Who better understands the other—Macbeth or Lady Macbeth?" Yet another point of departure for discussion and eventual composition is the statement made by Macbeth in defense of his decision against the murder: "I dare do all that may become a man;/Who dares do more is none." This statement is not in accord with the actual reasoning of his "If it were done" soliloquy, nor is it this objection that Lady Macbeth chooses to eliminate in order to persuade him to do the murder: she rather goes at once to his *real* objection, which is that their enterprise might fail, and overcomes that. Macbeth appears to have attempted to appease his wife by mouthing a high-minded reason against killing Duncan. Evidently, however, she perceives that the reason is not sincere, and by raging at her husband fairly forces him to blurt out the true one: "If we should fail?" Does Macbeth so poorly understand how completely his wife understands him as to think he could deceive her with a "reason" that is alien to his nature?

It should be noted that, all three of these suggested starting points would require discussion of the same basic points: the husband-wife relationship, the real and the feigned objections to murder, the subtler inner qualities motivating the actions of the two principal characters.

Like those used for short papers, the subjects for longer compositions that conclude the study of the play should normally grow out of discussion. In the course of identifying, earlier, some major centers of discussion, we have also, presumably, identified the areas out of which essay subjects will take shape. In addition, some of the subjects suggested for short papers—especially those that involve the relationship of Macbeth and Lady Macbeth—can be expected to grow into subjects for longer ones. Often, the short paper can serve as the tentative exploration of a major subject; thus, for example, a short paper discussing the reactions of Macbeth and Banquo to the Witches, limited in its scope to the evidence of the single scene just then being studied, can provide the entering wedge for a full-scale essay on Macbeth and Banquo as their relationship to each other and to Fate is developed by the entire tragedy. The relationship, of course, is not concluded with Banquo's death—indeed, its main significance for the tragedy may be said to begin at that point. Similarly, the short paper on the characters of Macbeth and Lady Macbeth based on the evidence of a single scene can serve as starting point for an essay on the two characters throughout the play: their comparative strengths and weaknesses at first, their relative strengths during and immediately after the murder, the later effects of their guilt on their characters and their relationship.

Other possible subjects for essays based on the evidence of the whole play include the instances and functions of paradox, imagery, or irony, the dramatic functions of minor characters with respect to the tragedy as a whole, the comparative responsibilities of character and Fate for the fatal outcome, the "conscience" of Macbeth, and Macbeth as a poet. These, and other such subjects, are alike in that all require study and restudy of the play itself, and all should grow out of discussion.

Though we have consistently recommended these subjects as preferable, we should not move on without at least mentioning others of a very different sort that some teachers (and even some students) prefer. These are subjects that involve historical research, or reading in materials other than the play itself.

In connection with *Macbeth*, a likely subject is demonology and witchcraft. A way to focus such a paper so that it will be more than mere summary of secondary documents, is to ask and seek to answer the question, "How would Shakespeare's own audiences, in the age of James, have regarded the Witches?" This kind of subject, it is here suggested, is superior to more typical

research projects because it uses reading in outside materials
to throw light upon what is in the play. Similarly, a study of
Shakespeare's source for *Macbeth* (in Holinshed) could be focused
in such a way as to relate the reading in outside materials intimately to the play itself. Again, the essay will no doubt be more
successful if, instead of attempting to compare Holinshed's account and Shakespeare's treatment in general, the student finds,
or is directed to, a focal point. Thus, a paper comparing the place
of supernatural elements in the two versions, or a paper comparing
the apparent attitudes of Holinshed and Shakespeare towards
Macbeth, will allow the student to develop a thesis rather than
merely assemble data without point.

That much valuable experience can be gained in writing essays
that use reading in secondary materials for the purpose of illuminating the primary work, we have never questioned. Our objection has been, and is, to the more typical kind of research
paper that neither originates in the text of the play nor uses its
information to illuminate an aspect of the play, but is content to
survey an historical topic without making specific application to
the play. Thus "Political Conditions in the Reign of King James"
or "Theatrical Companies under James I" would seem inferior, in
kind, to others that have been suggested by way of example.

We must here turn from writing as an activity to consider two
remaining activities, oral reading or "acting out" and memorization.

Macbeth is the shortest of the great tragedies, and one way to
treat it after it has been carefully read and discussed is to read it
all again, rapidly, without interruptions during class hours, with
students taking turns at a mere nod from the teacher; so managed,
it can be read in three class periods. The advantages are obvious:
everyone gets many chances to read, the whole play is reviewed,
and at least some sense of the play's swift rush of action is con-
veyed. Very possibly, for juniors or seniors, this fast collective
reading of the play is a more appropriate activity, being more
sophisticated, than acting out scenes at the front of the classroom.

On the other hand, *Macbeth* is so rich in scenes that are
eminently suited to acting out either impromptu or with a minimum of rehearsal that this activity is difficult to resist. If *Macbeth* were used in the tenth grade (as it might well be), the

informal acting out of these scenes might appropriately be the dominant activity as soon as initial reading has been finished. The Witch scenes obviously lend themselves well, both those parts that involve the Witches alone and those that involve Macbeth or Macbeth and Banquo as well. Although students rarely act them out in quite the same macabre spirit that Shakespeare presumably intended, no great harm is done if students have a degree of fun with them, especially if the class hears a recording in which professionals effectively project the dark and ominous tones of the text.

The Banquet scene is particularly excellent for acting out, both because it can use many students—the whole class can make up the guests at table—and because it is intensely dramatic. The scenes of Macbeth's famous soliloquies, of the murder of Duncan, and of its discovery are obvious choices that need no recommendation. Budding actresses can undertake Lady Macbeth's sleepwalking scene; however, more harm than good will surely result from doing this scene badly and comically. Finally, one scene that is often missed in these dramatic readings because of the abundance of others is that between Malcolm and Macduff, ending with Macduff's learning the news of his family's murder and his vow to destroy Macbeth. A pivotal moment in the action, the scene acts well and ends with tremendous force.

Memorization is no problem in *Macbeth*. As in *Julius Caesar*, certain passages have been traditional favorites: "If it were done," "Is this a dagger," and "She should have died hereafter." All these we have recommended for paraphrasing, and all need heavy emphasis in discussion; further, they are certain to be included in the favorite acting-out scenes. The repeated attention given them should lead to clear understanding of them, and once they are wholly understood they are virtually memorized. Other passages in the play also deserve consideration: Macbeth's "Two truths are told," his "To be thus is nothing," Lady Macbeth's "Glamis thou art and Cawdor" and "The raven himself is hoarse," Lennox's sharply ironic speech that begins Act III, Scene 6, Malcolm's "Macduff, this noble passion." All these are fairly long single passages; but it should be noted that much of the most powerful dramatic verse in *Macbeth* (as, of course, in other plays) occurs in single lines and short passages of the great scenes. If students learn the speeches of Macbeth, Lady Macbeth, Banquo, or other major persons in order to take part in acting out a scene, their achievement should surely be looked on with as much favor by the teacher as if they had memorized any long, single passage.

3. A *Midsummer Night's Dream* (Grade 9 or 10)

Placement. In suggesting A *Midsummer Night's Dream* for grade nine or ten, we have followed tradition; perhaps, rather, we should question and possibly repudiate tradition. In schools that have no Shakespeare in grade nine, the most frequent play for grade ten is *Julius Caesar*; but in schools that follow the pattern of the anthologies, where *Julius Caesar* is offered in grade ten, and that go outside the anthologies to find a play for grade nine, that play is most often A *Midsummer Night's Dream*. In schools (including private schools) that study Shakespeare in grade seven, the play is regularly A *Midsummer Night's Dream*, which may be followed by *Julius Caesar* in grade eight. In schools that start Shakespeare with grade eight, the play is usually A *Midsummer Night's Dream*.

There is much in A *Midsummer Night's Dream* to recommend its placement as early as grade seven; there is also much in it to recommend its placement in grade twelve, when students have gained much in maturity and have read widely in drama, poetry, and literature generally. It is just possible that in recommending it for grade nine or ten we are placing it in the least appropriate years and that either extreme, grade seven or grade twelve, would be preferable.

It is attractive for grade seven for two reasons: the fairies, and Bottom and his wonderful company of players. Ninth and tenth graders have lost most of the capacity for childish delight in fairies and clowns that young children have; they are too old to believe in fairies, yet too young to take a sophisticated view of them. In short, they have neither the advantage of younger children who can delight in things as children, nor the maturity of older students necessary to appreciate and understand the rich artistic values of this truly superb work of art.

The fact is that A *Midsummer Night's Dream* is a sophisticated, subtle, elusive, complex work. Though children can laugh at the clowns and wonder at the fairies, the qualities that make it great are exquisite and are harder to grasp than are the qualities that make, for example, *King Lear* great. Nor do students grow up to these merely by growing older; they have to move through a period of literary maturation, during which they read much in first-rate books and refine their aesthetic sensibilities.

In placing the play in ninth or tenth grade, we are very probably, then, merely acquiescing to tradition, and to the virtual certainty that most teachers who have long been gratified by the fun that young students have with Bottom and his hard-handed crew will go right on, for a long time to come, teaching the play to ninth graders. We shall deal below with the problems of getting *even* ninth graders to appreciate more of the play than merely the Bottom incidents. It is no easy task.

Approach. The very first step is to find the best possible introduction. Earlier, we have said that the best "approach" to make to Shakespeare is to begin the play directly. Now, however, is A *Midsummer Night's Dream* an exceptional case that requires special introduction where other plays do not? It is possible that it does require one, or that in any event some very particular information initially presented will help to set the whole work in a perspective without which one entire dimension of its exquisite art will go unperceived.

A *Midsummer Night's Dream* was almost certainly written to celebrate a special occasion. That fact is in itself not unique; several of Shakespeare's plays, most notably *The Tempest* and *Macbeth*, were written for special occasions. Uniquely, however, in A *Midsummer Night's Dream*, the *real* occasion of the play (the marriage of a noble couple) frames the *dramatic* occasion (the impending marriage of Theseus and Hippolyta). Nor is this all. Just as, in the dramatic situation, Bottom's "rude mechanicals" come to present their tragedy of Pyramus and Thisbe before Theseus and his bride, so, in the real situation Shakespeare's own company of players have come to present their *Midsummer Night's Dream* before the noble couple whose marriage is being celebrated. Figuratively, in compliment, Theseus and Hippolyta *are* that couple, just as, satirically, Bottom's crew is Shakespeare's. During Bottom's play about Pyramus and Thisbe, Theseus and Hippolyta and all their guests sit as audience, just as, during Shakespeare's play, the noble couple and all their guests sit as audience.

The point of all this is that, to appreciate the extra and unusual dimension which is necessary to a full experience of the play, students need to have from the very start a sense of the play as being surrounded by its real occasion of wedding festivities and noble audience—for all these are, in an exquisite way, a part of the play and inseparable from the total experience. *Hamlet* presents a play within a play; but only *A Midsummer Night's Dream* offers, in effect, a play within a play within a play.

Again and again the dramatic experience is enriched from the sense of intricate relationships of ring within ring within ring. The lines separating participant and audience at times become confused and seem to dissolve. At the end, the reader or spectator who has become deeply involved will be unsure of just whose "dream" all this was—his own? the lovers'? Theseus and Hippolyta's? or whose? Shakespeare makes just enough crossplay between the dramatic situation and the "real" situation that the mind is delightfully teased. Consider, for example, the moon—an indispensable element that runs like a theme, as does the "dream" itself, throughout the play. Bottom's players make their own crude arrangements to present a moon, for a moon was needed in their play. But Shakespeare's players needed a moon, too, for their performance of *A Midsummer Night's Dream*. Did they, like Bottom's crew, provide their own moon? Or did they count on having a real moon shining through the window of the noble house on the Thames when they presented *A Midsummer Night's Dream?* Bottom, Quince, and Snout ask "Doth the moon shine that night we play our play?" and consult an almanac to find out that it does indeed:

> Why, then may you leave a casement of the great chamber window, where we play, open, and the moon may shine in at the casement.

But on second thought they decide to bring their own moon. Did Shakespeare's company trust the real moon to "shine in at the casement" of the house on the Thames, or did they, like Bottom, bring their own along? May it have been, then, that during the performance that noble audience was treated to the spectacle of three moons—Bottom's makeshift arrangement, Shakespeare's makeshift arrangement, and the real moon shining in at the great chamber window? It is with some sense of all these dimensions that modern readers need to experience the play, and accordingly a brief account of the "real" occasion that envelops the "dramatic" occasion, of the "real" play that envelops the rude mechanicals' play, and of the "real" audience that surrounds Theseus' royal audience would constitute a useful "approach" before a single line is read.

But teachers should experiment. We may be right in thinking that A *Midsummer Night's Dream* is unique in its need for the kind of introduction we have suggested, and yet we may be wrong in suggesting that this introduction *precede* the reading of any lines. Teachers may find that the better way, even here, is that which we have insisted on for other plays—namely, to begin reading the play with *no* "approach" and thereafter to "salt in" whatever information is needed at the time it is needed. Thus teacher and class might well read through the first twenty lines, to the entrance of Egeus and others, and *then* explain how Theseus and Hippolyta's preparation to be married "With pomp, with triumph, and with reveling" is, as it were, encircled by the real occasion for which Shakespeare's play—here beginning—is part of this same pomp, triumph, and reveling. And thereafter, when for example Bottom and his fellows first meet to cast their play, and, of course, again when they present it at Theseus' court, the sense of play within play and audience within audience should be reinforced by comment and discussion.

Emphases of Presentation and Discussion. We have earlier stated that Bottom and the fairies, especially when they are seen on the stage, are delightful even to young children, and that the play is often read as early as the seventh grade. But we have also stated that the play as a whole is anything but easy. The fact is that A *Midsummer Night's Dream* stands virtually alone, among Shakespeare's plays as a "highbrow" work of art. Nor is this fact disproved or altered in any way by the seemingly contradictory truth that young children delight in Bottom and the fairies; Bottom and the fairies are elements in which children can delight naturally, without knowing anything at all of literary tradition. Yet Bottom and the fairies are also elements of this "highbrow" art, and to see them, and other elements of the whole, in perspective requires a high degree of literary sophistication.

At least one high school anthology for grade nine reduces *A Midsummer Night's Dream* to only eight pages, with the title "A Midsummer Night's Play," the excerpt including only the play put on by Bottom and company—and even that heavily edited and "adapted." Though we have earlier deplored the practice of excerpting and "adapting" Shakespeare's plays, in this instance the elimination of everything from the play except the antics of the clowns counts as a frank acknowledgment of an unfortunate truth —namely, that ninth graders do not usually get much else from the play even though the whole text is used. When they do use the entire text, many teachers admittedly race lightly over everything except the Bottom scenes and give most time and emphasis to the performance of "Pyramus and Thisbe."

It is because of these facts that we have earlier suggested placing *A Midsummer Night's Dream* as late as grade twelve, when it will have a much greater chance of being read and perceived as a whole work of art. It is unquestionably a shameful waste to use it in the ninth grade if only Bottom and his crew can be appreciated. But since teachers will presumably continue to teach it as early as grade nine, our problem is to find how, even so early, it can be taught less wastefully than has been customary.

To begin with, one thing is certain: *A Midsummer Night's Dream* is not a play to turn over to ninth graders on their own; neither will it help to provide them with detailed "study questions" to be answered in writing or prepared for oral discussion, for the painful task of answer-hunting will assuredly destroy the exquisite pleasures that the art of this play especially affords. If any of these pleasures are to come through the reading, they will do so because an able teacher moves through the play with the class, reading and discussing line by line.

But let us see, now, whether we have been exaggerating the peculiar difficulties of *A Midsummer Night's Dream.* We have not denied that students can, from merely seeing the play, get the

most obvious "fun" that it affords: the antics of Bottom and his
crew, on the stage, get through to any kind of spectator. But "all
that is finest in the play," to invoke Hazlitt again, is subtle and
elusive; this is "highbrow" art, consisting of highly poetic language, loaded with mythological allusions, framed in classical and
Elizabethan conventions. The perspectives that we have already
mentioned, of the play within the play, the feigned occasion
within the real one—these are part of "all that is finest," and they
will invariably be missed by students on their own. Further, even
the Bottom scenes—the great Pyramus and Thisbe production
itself—contain subtle delicious touches of combined classical mythology and Elizabethan dramatic satire that will entirely escape
the unsophisticated reader: probably, thus, "all that is finest" even
in the "easiest" parts will be missed.

We may partially illustrate the difficulties by taking a few examples directly from the play; take the very first lines, spoken by
Theseus:

> Now, fair Hippolyta, our nuptial hour
> Draws on apace; four happy days bring in
> Another moon: but, O, methinks, how slow
> This old moon wanes! She lingers my desires,
> Like to a step-dame, or a dowager,
> Long withering out a young man's revenue.

What can the ninth grader do with this passage? By checking
footnotes, glossary, and dictionary, he can identify Theseus and
Hippolyta as legendary names, understand "nuptial hour," "apace,"
"methinks," "lingers," "dowager," and "revenue." And then by
diligently striving he may put together the main sense of the passage: that a legendary couple are to be married in four days, with
the change of the moon, and that, for Theseus, the time is dragging painfully. But the bare sense, painfully made out, will mean
nothing more, nor will Hippolyta's reply:

> Four days will quickly steep themselves in night;
> Four nights will quickly dream away the time;
> And then the moon, like to a silver bow
> New-bent in heaven, shall behold the night
> Of our solemnities.

Without a high degree of literary sophistication, the bare meanings of words and identities of persons, duly looked up, will convey no aesthetic experience. "Literary sophistication" in this case means having a "feel" for names like Theseus and Hippolyta; a "feel" for the significance of the moon in poetic convention; a quickness in apprehending the subtle image by which, in Hippolyta's lines, the moon is linked with Cupid's bow. And beyond these specifics, it takes a high degree of literary sophistication to recognize, with a thrill, the magnitude of the compliment extended to the noble couple whose own wedding "solemnities" are thus figuratively identified with those of Theseus and Hippolyta. Students to whom these names mean nothing, even after they have been looked up in a classical dictionary, will inevitably miss the magnificence that is evoked for the more sophisticated mind by the mere mention of these names.

Somehow, if this greatest single difficulty of the play is to be overcome even partially, the teacher will need to infect students with a feeling for the whole world of classic myth. In the ninth grade, it is too much to expect that a class will already have any adequate background in mythology. A "cram" course of two or three weeks prior to reading A *Midsummer Night's Dream* would help somewhat by supplying the details of names and places; but no one acquires in this way quite the kind of feeling for these wonders that the fully appreciative reader of A *Midsummer Night's Dream* needs. When, for example, speaking altogether casually, Hippolyta mentions a hunt she had taken part in—

> I was with Hercules and Cadmus once,
> When in a wood of Crete they bay'd the bear
> With hounds of Sparta . . .

—the names she drops are such as would make Homer's ears tingle, and the effect is lost on students to whom the line conveys no more than if she had said "I was with George and Bill once." So it is throughout the play, down to the very play of Pyramus and Thisbe itself—which is hilarious fun when seen only as the antics of clowns but is an infinitely richer artistic experience when it is perceived in all its dimensions, classical and Elizabethan.

The frame of classical mythology, then, in which the play is

encased, is one great barrier for students of inadequate background; this barrier alone is sufficient to make it evident that putting students on their own with A *Midsummer Night's Dream* is
sheer folly. By discussion, reading aloud from classical sources,
brief reports from students assigned to investigate names and
legends, the teacher can in five weeks, while the reading of the
play is progressing, at least build something of the sophistication
that is needed. But what is needed is more than sophistication in
the sense of "knowledge about" classical mythology; it is also a
certain sophistication of *attitude*, and this is unfortunately harder
and longer in the building. All that we have said, in short, argues
for a postponement of A *Midsummer Night's Dream* until the
later high school years when, hopefully, students will have gained
something of this sophistication.

Not only classical mythology, but also Elizabethan poetic
themes and conventions block the unsophisticated reader's way
to true enjoyment of the play. Classical mythology is itself, of
course, a major part of the rich complex of theme and convention.
Thus, for example, Hermia makes a promise to Lysander:

> I swear to thee, by Cupid's strongest bow,
> By his best arrow with the golden head,
> By the simplicity of Venus' doves,
> By that which knitteth souls and prospers loves,
> And by that fire which burn'd the Carthage queen,
> When the false Troyan under sail was seen—
> By all the vows that ever men have broke, . . .

But even without the ornamentation of classical allusion, this
poetry everywhere requires sophistication; thus Theseus urging
Hermia to marry Lysander—

> . . . earthlier happy is the rose distill'd,
> Than that which, withering on the virgin thorn,
> Grows, lives, and dies in single blessedness.

Such poetic expressions are much more meaningful against a background of Elizabethan lyric; in this particular case the teacher
might partially acclimatize students to the manner by reading

selected portions from Shakespeare's own sonnets, especially from the first ten or twelve, in which the poet urges his friend to marry and preserve his beauty in the features of his children. Poetic convention of this sort runs throughout the dialogue of the lovers; it is an artificial, self-conscious, special dialect that they speak; thus Helena, in soliloquy, discourses on Love:

> Love looks not with the eyes, but with the mind,
> And therefore is wing'd Cupid painted blind.
> Nor hath Love's mind of any judgment taste;
> Wings, and no eyes, figure unheedy haste.
> And therefore is Love said to be a child,
> Because in choice he is so oft beguil'd.

Nor is the highbrow art of this mannered poetry limited to the lovers; here, in one of the most famous passages, Oberon speaks to Puck:

> That very time I saw, but thou couldst not,
> Between the cold moon and the earth,
> Cupid all arm'd. A certain aim he took
> At a fair vestal throned by the west,
> And loos'd his love-shaft smartly from his bow,
> As it should pierce a hundred thousand hearts.
> But I might see young Cupid's fiery shaft,
> Quench'd in the chaste beams of the wat'ry moon,
> And the imperial vot'ress passed on,
> In maiden meditation, fancy-free.
> Yet mark'd I where the bolt of Cupid fell:
> It fell upon a little western flower,
> Before milk-white, now purple with love's wound,
> And maidens call it love-in-idleness.

To read A *Midsummer Night's Dream* and, for lack of sophistication, to miss such poetry as this is truly to miss "all that is finest in the play." To avoid missing it, teachers must clearly exhaust every resource in building sophistication as they go—and the lesson here is equally clear: that for A *Midsummer Night's Dream* teachers need to be "up" on classical mythology and Elizabethan convention to a degree that they hardly need be for any other play in the Shakespeare canon.

To this point we have concentrated on the special difficulties in teaching a play which, no doubt more particularly than any other of Shakespeare's plays, was written for a courtly audience and adapted to a special occasion. We have barely touched, not exhausted, the subject of difficulties; we have not, for example, examined the whole machinery of fairies and fairy lore, or the special quality of imaginative sophistication required in suspending one's disbelief in such creatures of illusion. The fairies, too, speak a "hard" poetic language. To enter into the experience, for example, of the fairy roundel sung in Act II, Scene 2, as a lullaby for Titania takes either a childish wonder, lost before adolescence, or a mature literary sophistication, acquired by few people before they are adults and by most people never:

> Philomel, with melody
> Sing in our sweet lullaby:
> Lulla, lulla, lullaby; lulla, lulla, lullaby.
>> Never harm
>> Nor spell, nor charm,
> Come our lovely lady nigh.
> So, good night, with lullaby.

Little children, fitted out with dainty costumes, can dance and sing these songs with delight even though they have no notion what the words mean, and an audience of children or adults can respond with delight to the charm of the music, movement, and color; but a classroom full of adolescents, in broad daylight, is very likely to find the aesthetic experience here quite inaccessible. Yet this, too, is unquestionably at the heart of "all that is finest in the play." For that matter, the celebrated quarrel scene of Oberon and Titania, done in mock-heroic high style and laden with classical and Elizabethan allusions, is one of the finest things in the play —and one of the least accessible to the unsophisticated.

In demonstrating why A *Midsummer Night's Dream* is difficult for most students to appreciate, we have at the same time identified the major points for emphasis in teaching. Unfortunately, the very areas that we have marked for special attention are also the areas most regularly slighted in the classroom because they are not, like Bottom and his fellow clowns, productive of instant mirth and similarly obvious responses. We may now boldly crystallize our argument, which is this: that if ninth grade teachers find it impossible to "get across" anything in the play except its grosser elements, they should either (1) choose another play and postpone this until a later grade, preferably the twelfth, or (2) choose another play and omit this throughout the high school years.

This is a harsh judgment. But it is not only for the sake of the "highbrow" art we have been discussing that we make it; it is for the sake of Bottom, too. To teach the play only for Bottom and his antics, without appreciation of the other, subtler matters, is to teach Bottom without his context, and hence to miss the best of Bottom as well as all the rest. For the cream of the jest is the presence of Bottom, like the well-known bull in the china shop, amidst all this "highbrow" machinery of classical mythology, poetic themes and conventions, lovers' fancies, and fairy lore. Bottom by himself is entertaining, but Bottom set incongruously amidst the fragile illusions of so much sophisticated art, blundering into fairyland unperturbed, grossly usurping the center of the stage at—of all times and places—the wedding of legendary Theseus and Hippolyta (and, incidentally, the wedding of a noble Elizabethan couple in a great house on the Thames)—Bottom so perceived is incomparable. There is no doubt that, after all, the very best of "all that is finest" to be had from A *Midsummer Night's Dream* is Bottom—but Bottom complete with context, and it is this context that needs the greatest care in teaching.

Accompanying and Following Activities. As before, we shall consider the foremost activity, after reading and discussion, to be writing; and, again as before, we shall assume that the greatest amount of writing will consist of short pieces, especially paragraphs, assigned as the outgrowth of discussion that has excited genuine interest.

We shall suggest some possible focal points for such compositions below; but first, to follow our previous pattern, we should identify some likely passages for written paraphrase. In this play especially, with the extravagantly lyrical character of its verse, the task of turning high poetry to plain, literal prose is difficult. The experience is, however, also highly rewarding. When the prose statements are set beside the original passages, the unique advantage of poetic expression is strikingly apparently. All that is beautiful in the finest poetic passages in A *Midsummer Night's Dream* is lost when they are converted—as far as they can be—to literal statement. Even students who are seemingly insensitive should be able to see the difference, and perhaps even be convinced by it that exquisite lines are irreplaceable.

It is here suggested, therefore, that paraphrasing exercises in this play be concentrated on the most memorable lyrical passages, with the aim of demonstrating the difference between poetic and literal statement. It should also be apparent that selection of such passages for the exacting task of paraphrase will help to involve students more deeply in the secrets of the "highbrow" poetic art described above as a formidable barrier to the unsophisticated. Paraphrasing is here a strong ally in the campaign to crash through this barrier.

Such passages as the following, moving quickly through the acts, would seem appropriate: Act I, Scene 1: Helena's long speech beginning "How happy some o'er other some" (the actual paraphrase might begin with "Things base and vile" and end with "showers of oaths did melt"). Act II, Scene 1: Titania's "These are the forgeries of jealousy" (or any portion of it); Oberon's "That very time I saw" and "I know a bank where the wild thyme blows." Act III, Scene 2: All or a portion of Helena's "Lo, she is one of this confederacy!"; Oberon's "Thou see'st these lovers" (a key passage for plot); Puck's "My fairy lord, this must be done with haste" and Oberon's reply "But we are spirits of another sort." Act IV, Scene 1: Hippolyta's "I was with Hercules and Cadmus once" and Theseus' reply "More strange than true" and "The kinder we, to give them thanks for nothing."

Turning now to the problem of identifying some representative points at which discussion may be expected to turn up subjects for short expository compositions, we must acknowledge a new kind of difficulty: A *Midsummer Night's Dream* does not lend itself as readily as *Julius Caesar* or *Macbeth* (or indeed any other play we have listed as especially good for study in high school) to analytical writing. Beside the solid mass of these plays, the substance of A *Midsummer Night's Dream* is so much gossamer. "Man," says Bottom profoundly, "is but an ass if he go about to expound this dream." We may well take this as a word of caution. The all-important thing in reading and discussing this play is to be caught up in its spell; heavy, plodding, workaday analysis will dispel illusion and destroy the dream.

This is all the more reason with A *Midsummer Night's Dream* to let composition take off from discussion. If students can capture some of the imaginative spirit of the play in their own writing, so much the better; perhaps writing in connection with this play can appropriately take on a lighter tone than usual. Lysander and Hermia, for example, engage in a kind of contest of "proofs" for Lysander's own woeful declaration that "The course of true love never did run smooth." Lovers, they say, are ever thwarted by being of different social ranks, or of different ages, or their choices are dictated by others, or war, death, or sickness severs them. Taking Lysander's line as their topic sentence, students develop a one-page paragraph in which they present contemporary obstacles to support Lysander's statement.

A *Midsummer Night's Dream* is by no means unique in containing many such "developable topic sentences" for paragraphs, of which some can be sober, some whimsical. "What fools these mortals be!" will certainly stand development out of contemporary experience. "The lunatic, the lover, and the poet are of imagination all compact" will give a springboard start to more imaginative students, though it is doubtful that any of them will excel Theseus' "paragraph" on the subject. Such starts prompt a kind of writing that turns out from the play and into students' own experience. We should now consider assignments to discuss aspects of situation, character, technique, etc.

We have earlier stated that, except for Bottom, A *Midsummer Night's Dream* lacks fully developed individual beings, mortal or immortal. But, taking Titania and Oberon together, students can assess the qualities that make these royal fairies resemble mortals. The subject might be treated briefly, using as basis only the first scene in which the two appear; or it might be treated more elaborately, using the evidence of their speech and behavior throughout the play. Puck can serve a similar purpose, used as the single subject of a paper, or all three of the principal fairies might be examined comparatively. The four young lovers, too, lack the

wealth of individualization that Shakespeare lavishes on Bottom.
They are clearly the creatures of situation; yet obviously they have
sufficient character to play their roles in this situation. One challenging task for a paragraph is to try to differentiate, on the basis
of actual evidence, between the two young men; another is to do
the same with the two young women. Yet another possibility is
to attempt to account—and the result may be whimsical—for
Helena's "failure" with young men in contrast to Hermia's success.
Helena is herself mystified and can give no explanation. Can
students?

Larger subjects for long papers completed at the end of reading
the play should normally, as with other plays, be found while the
reading is in progress. One major undertaking would be to discuss
the means by which Shakespeare makes a unified whole out of a
variety of actions. The play includes the following "plots": the
impending wedding of Theseus and Hippolyta—the "occasion" of
the action; the quarrel of the fairy king and queen; the problem
of the two pairs of lovers; and the theatrical production of the
artisans. The four groups constitute, one might say, four distinct
"worlds." One approach to the subject is first to consider the
points at which these "worlds" touch one another: the fairies, for
example, have come to the woods outside Athens in order to bless
the union of Theseus and Hippolyta; the artisans have in mind to
present their play as an entertainment at this same wedding;
Titania, bewitched, dotes on Bottom; Oberon and Puck intervene
in the lovers' dilemma. In these ways (besides others) all groups
touch one another except the lovers and the artisans and the
lovers and Theseus-Hippolyta. But the lovers' frantic nightlong
chase in the woods is precipitated by Theseus' command that
Hermia obey her father, and, at the end, the lovers and the royal
couple celebrate their several weddings together; thus the worlds
of royalty and lovers touch.

What of the lovers and the artisans? They, too, are brought
together at the end, when the artisans' play is staged with the
lovers as audience, and they share in the general blessing that the
fairies bestow on the household. But an essay on the subject of
unity should do more than show the meeting-points of the several
groups and lines of actions. It should consider, for example, the
use of the moon as a unifying element, and to do so requires

noting all references to the moon from the opening lines through to its very crude representation in the play of Pyramus and Thisbe. It should consider also the activities of particular actors, Oberon especially, as serving unifying functions. And, of course, the theme of love, with its frustrations, which runs through the affairs of all groups—including the artisans' lamentable comedy of Pyramus and Thisbe—is no doubt the greatest unifier of all.

Another subject of possible interest centers on royalty: what ideas of the nature of royalty can be gained from the study of its four representatives—Theseus, Hippolyta, Oberon, Titania? The question is not unimportant, since the play was intended to compliment nobility, to be acted before a noble audience, with Queen Elizabeth herself very possibly present. What qualities of royalty do these persons show? Are they equally admirable representatives? What, for example, of Theseus? Is he tyrannical when he commands Hermia to marry Lysander or suffer dire consequences? On the other hand, what of his exquisite graciousness at the end, when he gently reprimands Hippolyta for her unkind remarks about the artisans' play: "The kinder we, to give them thanks for nothing," he says at the start, and goes on with one of the noblest passages in the play. (Was Shakespeare, here, subtly teaching his own noble sponsors how royalty should respond to his own company's effort?) And later, when Hippolyta remarks good-humoredly, "This is the silliest stuff that ever I heard," Theseus utters an apologia for the whole world of illusion, Bottom's and Shakespeare's: "The best in this kind are but shadows, and the worst are no worse, if imagination amend them."

None of the foregoing suggestions points to an easy writing task. All are possibly too sophisticated for ninth or tenth graders. If the play is read at the earlier level, subjects for long papers will need to be found in the general area of summary and plot-recapitulation: How does Shakespeare contrive to get all four groups into the woods?—i.e., what reasons have the lovers for going there, what reasons have the fairies for being there, what reasons have the artisans, what reasons have Theseus and Hippolyta? Again: Bottom and Puck are the principal comic characters; what characteristics of each are "funny," what does each do that is funny, and, finally, what comic qualities (if any) do they share? Again: When does Shakespeare use prose, when blank verse, when rhyme?—and what probable reasons had he for this distribution? And, finally: Just how is the basic "problem" of the central plot solved? What are the steps in its solution? The "essay" here would involve some plot summary, but even so would offer a degree of challenge to young students even after careful reading. Reduced to simplest terms, the problem of the lovers' plot is merely *to restore Demetrius' love to Helena.* During discussion of the play, presumably teacher and students will find useful a succession of blackboard charts to keep abreast of the lovers' changing situation, with such headings as: Initial Situation, Second Situation, Third Situation, and Final Situation. In writing his paper, the student's problem is to *explain*—which means exposition and not merely narration—the situation at each step and the means by which one situation is changed into the next.

We turn finally to two remaining activities, oral reading or performance, and memorization.

With grades nine and ten (as with grades seven and eight, when the play is used so early), far and away the most popular undertaking has been (and presumably will continue to be) a classroom performance of "Pyramus and Thisbe." One great virtue of this choice is that every member of the class can be used as part of the dramatic situation, since those who form the audience will all serve as members of Theseus' court. Indeed, it is possible to go a step farther and have *two* audiences—one consisting of Theseus, Hippolyta, lovers, and guests, all watching "Pyramus and Thisbe," and an "outer" audience representing Shakespeare's noble audience (bride, groom, Queen Elizabeth, and all) watching both Theseus' party *and* Bottom's company.

But other scenes in the play make superb classroom acting fare also: all Bottom's scenes, obviously; the entire first scene, which brings in all characters except artisans and fairies; the quarrel scene of Oberon and Titania (Act II, Scene 1); the separate incidents in which Lysander's and Demetrius' eyes are anointed; and, especially, Act IV, Scene 1, which ties together all elements of the play before the denouement of Act V. But in fact, because the play is short and because its scenes are so sharply limited in number (only nine in all, unusual for Shakespeare), there seems no sound reason to omit any one scene, for all are eminently actable.

With the earlier high school years, it would seem unfortunate not to allow a considerable amount of time for preparation and acting, either of individual scenes or of the whole. Once the play has been read and understood, it should *all* be performed. With the upper years, it would seem more reasonable to limit the amount of performance, or even to omit it entirely, and concentrate on reading aloud for the subtler qualities of the poetic art and for meaning.

We need perhaps add nothing on the subject of memorization to what has already been implied. Any of the longer passages suggested for paraphrasing will serve admirably for memorizing; but since it is recommended that as much of the play as possible be acted, with time allowed for preparation, the special values of memorization will no doubt be realized through that major activity.

4. As You Like It *(Grade 9 or 10)*

Placement. Although it is possible to make a highly sophisticated play of As *You Like It* by delving into the pastoral traditions that it gently satirizes, it is also possible to read it without special reference to these. Of all Shakespeare's comedies, this can surely be placed with greatest confidence in the early high school years. If a teacher were to teach only two plays in grades nine and ten, there is little room to question the wisdom of choosing As *You Like It* for one, as there is little room to question the wisdom of choosing *Julius Caesar* for the other. These two are the most openly accessible of all the plays. Under "Presentation," below, we shall elaborate on this assertion.

Approach. Unlike A *Midsummer Night's Dream*, with its dramatic occasion enveloped by a "real" occasion, As *You Like It* can stand boldly on its own without any kind of frame that needs explaining before reading begins. The best "approach" to As *You Like It* is *no* approach except that provided by the dramatist in the first scene—indeed, in the very first speech.

To introduce this play, at whatever level it is taught, with lectures or reports on the age, the stage, Shakespeare, comedy, pastoral tradition, or any other historical or literary matters would be to begin less well than Shakespeare did, and to diminish the play's chances of being taken on its own terms and judged on its own merits. The time, for example, to comment on pastoral conventions will come when, in the course of reading and discussion, teacher and class arrive at Act II, Scene 4, where the weary trio from the court encounter Corin and Silvius, shepherds; with that first pleasant clash of urbanity and rusticity, the basic motif of pastoral literature is introduced.

If, on the other hand, teachers believe that some kind of introduction is preferable to none, we can suggest no better device than that described earlier: discussion on a theme, subject, or issue that, later, students will find treated in the play. Now, what might serve as a subject for this discussion and possible writing?

For generations past, most students, at some point in their public school education, have had to write a composition contrasting city life with country life. Some version of this topic is included in most composition textbooks, and most English teachers have used it repeatedly. Literature, from Theocritus to Thoreau and beyond, has kept it a fresh and living theme; it is the very root of the whole pastoral tradition. What is here suggested is that if ever there is any "right" time to engage a class in warm debate on the town vs. country question (and to get a full, solid paragraph of writing), it is during the hour or two immediately before the class starts reading *As You Like It*.

This is not to assert that the play is essentially "about" the subject of city vs. country, or that city vs. country is *the* theme. As with all the other romantic comedies, the theme is more likely expressed by Lysander's line from *A Midsummer Night's Dream*: "The course of true love never did run smooth." But the ancient debate of town and country pervades *As You Like It* in all its aspects: the central romance itself, of a royal princess disguised as a country youth and a heroic innocent whose upbringing, or lack of it, has left him unspoiled; the encounters of Touchstone with the inhabitants of forest and field; the songs of Amiens; the robust life of the usurped Duke; the shepherdess and her swain; the curative effects of the country on the visitors from the court. So if the play is essentially "about" the love of Rosalind and Orlando, yet it is the familiar old debate that provides frame and trappings for the "world" in which their story takes place.

But if students have become bored with the debate of town and country from too many admonishments in previous years to write "themes" on "Why I Like the Country Better Than the City" or "Why I Like the City Better Than the Country," *As You Like It* may itself be jeopardized by any new exhortation to debate the question. In that case, almost any other approach will be preferable. One possible alternative is to take up the subject of "heroes." Shakespeare, with tongue in cheek, drew in Orlando the most wonderful specimen of romantic, heroic, comic young masculinity in the world's literature: Orlando is the romantic hero "as you like him." If before meeting this prize specimen, students can be induced to pool and debate their ideas of heroes —wherever they have met them, in real life, the movies, television, or in fiction—and then to portray their heroic ideal in writing, they will have paved their own way to *As You Like It* without knowing it.

Emphases of Presentation and Discussion. The statement was made earlier that *As You Like It* is the most suitable of Shakespeare's comedies for high school study. The reasons are not hard to find. The play is written mainly in prose—nearly two thirds— and the blank verse is at dead center of the period that is freest from the characteristic difficulties that beset both the early poetry and the late poetry. Though there are some problem passages, it is a fact that Shakespeare never wrote a clearer language than in *As You Like It*. Nor is this all. *As You Like It* contains the least complicated of all Shakespeare's plots.

Orlando and Rosalind stand as the dominant figures on a great pastoral tapestry. Except for Oliver (to complete the bad older brother-good younger brother situation) and the two Dukes (one bad, one good), the plot truly requires no persons besides the lovers; it does not need Touchstone, Jaques, Amiens, Corin, Silvius, Phebe, William, or Audrey. This is not the same, of course, as to say that the *play* does not need these figures; the play would be bare without them, like a once-rich canvas or tapestry from which all but the key figures have been removed.

What is suggested above is that, of all Shakespeare's plays, *As You Like It* might most aptly be likened to a masterpiece of pictorial art; in it Shakespeare's dramatic art came nearer to painting or tapestry than ever before or after. If some such sense, or "image," of the play can gradually be brought to students' minds as they read, surely they will have come near to experiencing the ultimate satisfaction that this particular work of art can give. Dramatic art, of course, deals in action, and *As You Like It* is dramatic art; but the marvel of it is that, at the same time, it achieves a quality of repose that we think of as belonging uniquely to still art. A painter could more nearly represent the complete experience of *As You Like It* than that of any other play.

So much for the general "feel" of this pastoral comedy. Points of discussion can again be determined accurately only in the course of reading aloud with the class. Though we have stated that Shakespeare's language, verse and prose, is most open in this play, occasions for interpretation will arise regularly, in single words, lines, passages. The prose is everywhere direct—yet even Orlando's opening speech contains many expressions that need clarifying *right then and there*, in the colloquy of teacher and students: "he bequeathed me by will but poor a thousand crowns"; "Besides this nothing that he so plentifully gives me, the something that nature gave me, his countenance seems to take from me"; "He . . . as much as in him lies, mines my gentility with my education."

Such passing problems of reading will occur throughout the play, but there are no intolerably knotty problems. They need to be clarified in the least possible time, with the least possible fuss; but they must be clarified. Left "on their own" with such "easy" reading—or reading that *seems* easy—students rush right on by without bothering to examine the details that they imperfectly understand. This is the way to breed bad habits of reading. One excellent use of *As You Like It* in grade nine or ten is in the formation of good reading habits, the basic one of which is a personal commitment to understand *just what is said*. The teacher's own trained eye needs to detect the details of text that students' untrained eyes will skip over unless they are checked. The prose of *As You Like It* is just hard enough that students will not always quite understand it and just easy enough that they will suppose that they understand it "well enough." The highly figurative poetry of most of the plays does not offer quite the same danger, the same invitation to the development of sloppy reading habits. Confronted by it, students must, and know that they must, stop to "figure it out"; but with the "easy" prose of *As You Like It*, they need a lesson in pausing where they would themselves not think to pause.

Much the same may be said of the blank verse. It is so open that it seems more open than it is, so generally readable that when a phrase or line occurs that does demand a moment's hard thought before its meaning can be grasped, it may simply not occur to the reader to pause:

> But do not do so. I have five hundred crowns,
> The thrifty hire I saved under your father,
> Which I did store to be my foster nurse
> When service should in my old limbs lie lame
> And unregarded age in corners thrown.
> Take that; and He that doth the ravens feed,
> Yea, providently caters for the sparrow,
> Be comfort to my age. Here is the gold;
> All this I give you. Let me be your servant.

It would be a rare ninth or tenth grader indeed who, on his own, did not simply read through old Adam's speech without seeing a need to stop. It is the teacher's function to make him stop and look awhile at the lines, "When service . . . thrown." *As You Like It* abounds in such lines.

In connection with *A Midsummer Night's Dream*, the point was made that except for Bottom no one in the play is characterized in depth or becomes a fully realized human being. Lysander and Demetrius are figures who play their roles in the plot; Hermia and Helena are two lovely young ladies, one a little taller than the other, one a little fairer than the other, one more popular with young men than the other, and that is all. Like the heroes, they serve plot functions, playing their roles in a situation that is more important than they. The same is true of Theseus and Hippolyta and of Oberon and Titania. Bottom alone, though admirably designed to fit the needs of plot, breaks his mold and emerges a very special human being.

Accordingly, it was suggested that in the course of reading *A Midsummer Night's Dream* discussion would more often find starting points in situation than in character. Situation is important in *As You Like It*, too, but like the other supremely rich romantic comedies (*The Merchant of Venice, Twelfth Night*) it is also rich in character—not as rich as a mature history like *Henry IV, Part 1* or a mature tragedy like *Hamlet*—but rich. Much discussion can be expected to grow, therefore, out of Rosaland, Orlando, Touchstone, and Jaques. To illustrate, we shall begin with the heroine.

Rosalind is almost certain to be (in any event she should be) the first great heroine of Shakespearean romantic comedy that high school students meet; she is also the best all-around representative of an extraordinary species. Shakespeare started her kind with Julia of *The Two Gentleman of Verona*, his first heroine who doffs maiden garb and goes a-masquerading in the guise of a man. To the Elizabethan audience the exchange of roles had a double excellence, an extra dimension that is lost today; for, to begin with, a young male actor (like Flute of *A Midsummer Night's Dream*, who plays Thisbe to Bottom's Pyramus) played the heroine's part; so there was a young man, playing a young lady, playing a young man. The supreme accomplishment of Rosalind is that she adds yet another dimension, for as Rosalind she takes up the male role of Ganymede, and as "Ganymede" she takes on herself to simulate "Rosalind": so in the great climactic scene of *As You Like It* we have a case unique in Elizabethan drama—a young man playing a young woman playing a young man playing a young woman.

Just when, in the course of reading and discussing the play, should this especially delightful fact be pointed out to students? It is to be hoped that it will never need to be pointed out at all, but that it will be induced during discussion of Act III, Scene 2, when Rosalind first proposes to Orlando (who would never think of it by himself) that he "cure" his affliction by trying a daring remedy:

> ORLANDO. Did you ever cure any so?
> ROSALIND. Yes, one, and in this manner: he was to imagine me his love, his mistress, and I set him every day to woo me. At which time would I—being but a moonish youth— grieve, be effeminate, changeable, longing and liking,

> proud, fantastical, apish, shallow, inconstant, full of tears, full of smiles. . . . And thus I cured him, and this way will I take upon me to wash your liver as clean as a sound sheep's heart, that there shall not be one spot of love in't.
>
> ORLANDO. I would not be cured, youth.
>
> ROSALIND. I would cure you, if you would but call me Rosalind, and come every day to my cote and woo me.
>
> ORLANDO. Now, by the faith of my love, I will. Tell me where it is.
>
> ROSALIND. Go with me to it, and I'll show it to you. And by the way you shall tell me where in the forest you live. Will you go?
>
> ORLANDO. With all my heart, good youth.
>
> ROSALIND. Nay, you must call me Rosalind. . . .

If there is a finer moment in all Shakespeare than this, it would be interesting to know where it is. But only by going line by line in reading and discussing can the teacher prevent students from passing it by as if it were quite ordinary.

What is indispensable, surely, is to lead students to catch the spirit of *As You Like It*, as title and as attitude-to-life, and of Rosalind, who is its best exemplar. The moments when Rosalind is at her Rosalindian best are moments to exploit. Thus, as she tells Celia of her meeting in the forest with her father, whom she had not seen for who knows how long—

> I met the Duke yesterday and had much question with him. He ask'd me of what parentage I was; I told him of as good as he. So he laughed and let me go. But what talk we of fathers when there is such a man as Orlando?

Again when, as "Ganymede" she decides to make a game of poor Orlando in the forest:

> I will speak to him like a saucy lacky and under that habit play the knave with him. Do you hear, forester?

And again, when, still as "Ganymede," for whom Phebe has

cruelly rejected her faithful shepherd lover, she blasts the fickle shepherdess with all her might:

> For I must tell you friendly in your ear,
> Sell when you can: you are not for all markets.

The heroine of romantic comedy as exemplified by Rosalind is buoyantly alive, eminently capable, daring, able to carry off her imitation of man with bravado and finesse—and through it all to maintain (for the audience to see, not her deceived colleagues in the play) her exquisite femininity. And above all this heroine is intellectually brilliant, always the brightest person in the play, alert, ready for any situation that arises, wittier than a professional jester. It is some such Rosalind that high school students should come to see, not by the teacher's telling them that "this is how Rosalind is," but gradually, as this emerges from study of the text.

They should get a similarly full sense of the qualities of the hero Orlando, and by the same means. We have earlier stated that Orlando is the best in his line, as Rosalind is the best all-around representative of hers; that Shakespeare matched this pair of masterpieces in one play was a magnificent stroke; and that they are entirely "right" for each other is the ultimate wonder.

In Shakespeare's canon, Orlando's line begins with *The Two Gentlemen of Verona*, as, we have said, does Rosalind's. *The Two Gentlemen* has two heroes, Proteus and Valentine, who together foreshadow the tendencies of two contrasting sorts of romantic heroes that run through the comedies down to *The Tempest*. To set these contrasting lines before us abruptly, let us emphasize the extent of their difference by saying that the one line, founded by Proteus, inclines to the "black sheep" side and is capable of dastardly performance, and that the other, founded by Valentine, inclines to the side of intellectual and moral innocence and would never do anything in the least dastardly or mean.

Orlando of *As You Like It* and Bertram of *All's Well That Ends Well* represent respectively the best and the worst in the heroic lines begun by Valentine and Proteus, as opposed to the heroes of Shakespeare's other comedies who usually combine qualities of both sides but tend toward one side or the other.

Reading will not go far before occasion arises for a first discussion of Orlando. Perhaps the mutually contradictory accounts of him given by Oliver in the opening scene will be the starting point. First to Charles:

> . . . for if thou dost him any slight disgrace, or if he do not mightily grace himself on thee, he will practice against thee by poison, entrap thee by some treacherous device, and never leave thee till he hath ta'en thy life by some indirect means or other. For I assure thee—and almost with tears I speak it—there is not one so young and villainous this day living.

And directly afterwards in soliloquy:

> . . . he's gentle, never schooled and yet learned, full of noble device, of all sorts enchantingly beloved, and indeed so much in the heart of the world and especially of my own people who best know him, that I am altogether misprized.

Like Al Capp's L'il Abner, Orlando is naturally noble; Oliver's first description is as revealing as his second, because it defines everything that Orlando is not: guile is completely alien to him and to his kind.

One so good and guileless, and, as soon appears, so heroic, can, with just a touch of the dramatist's pen, be turned comic as well. Shakespeare makes Celia say of Orlando, "I found him under a tree, like a dropped acorn." What does this kind of remark do for his hero's heroic prestige? If it endears him to audience and reader, does it not at the same time make him slightly ridiculous? And what spectacle does this strapping hero make, running through the forest, hanging wretched love verses on trees? What was Shakespeare up to, in subjecting him to such witty thrusts as Touchstone, Celia, and most of all Rosalind herself dart at his absent person? Thus Rosalind of his verses: "O yes, I heard them all, and more too; for some of them had in them more feet than the verses would bear." And again, on hearing that there is a lover at large in the forest she says, "Is he of God's making? What manner of man? Is his head worth a hat? Or his chin worth a beard?" Much the grandest heroical speech in the play is Orlando's when, spectacularly, he bursts out of the forest with drawn sword to demand food for old Adam:

> . . . forbear, I say,
> He dies that touches any of this fruit
> Till I and my affairs are answered.

And more:

> If ever you have looked on better days,
> If ever have been where bells have knolled to church,
> If ever sat at any good man's feast,
> If from your eyelids wiped a tear
> And know what 'tis to pity and be pitied,
> Let gentleness my strong enforcement be.
> In the which hope I blush and hide my sword.

Orlando, of course, cannot possibly know that his heroic posture is vaguely preposterous; he mistakenly supposes that he is dealing with savages, when in fact he is addressing a duke. His heroics are grand—and quite unnecessary. "Of what kind should this cock come of?" asks Jaques.

Throwing down a professional wrestler and breaking his bones, later dispatching a hungry lioness who was set to devour Oliver, Orlando is as muscular as he is noble, as noble as he is innocent. We need not here comment—though a class should find much to discuss—on the comic figure he cuts in wooing "Ganymede" as though the latter were his "very Rosalind." The point of all this is that Orlando is a splendid tongue-in-cheek portrait of heroic, romantic young manhood.

Students sometimes laugh at Orlando while supposing that Shakespeare did not intend to make them laugh; and on the other hand they sometimes take him perfectly straight, seeing no fun in the portrait. But, of course, Shakespeare did mean for them to laugh, and at the same time to delight in Orlando. It is this latter spirit that, somehow, they must be led to appreciate; for if they take Orlando perfectly straight as a noble hero, they miss the fun of "as you like it," with its gentle ribbing of heroic heroes and the tastes of audiences.

One final point: to see Orlando so is not to diminish him but to find him personally even more charming and, as a dramatic achievement, even more remarkable. If any character in all the plays is more "right" for the dramatic world he moves in, it would be interesting to know where to find him. In putting his most brilliant heroine and exactly *this* Orlando together in a play, Shakespeare showed his genius and touched an ultimate in the genre of romantic comedy.

Like Rosalind and Orlando, Touchstone is one of a line, and like them he is the best of his line. Further, like the lines of heroes and heroines, the line of great professional fools had its beginning in *The Two Gentlemen of Verona*. Finally, like the line of heroes, the line of fools exhibits contrasting specimens. Where Proteus prefigures the "black sheep" hero and Valentine the nobly obtuse one, Speed of *The Two Gentlemen* points to the witty jesters and Launce to the duller clowns. Their common ancestor is, of course, the "witty slave" of classical comedy, first adapted by Shakespeare in the twin Dromios of *The Comedy of Errors*. For example, Launcelot Gobbo of *The Merchant of Venice*, though capable of being witty, is Shakespeare's great example of the fool who leans to the simple side, whereas Feste of *Twelfth Night* and Touchstone of *As You Like It* are always witty sophisticates.

The "logic" of Touchstone's wit is generally clear, but it will require care and discussion, especially with students who are meeting for the first time this specialty in which fools excel. Because the typical witty exchange in which the fool "proves" some outlandish conclusion to a cooperative "stooge" is a standard fixture of all the plays in which fools appear, the students' first encounter with it is important—and no play offers a better first encounter than *As You Like It*. Of course the wit-duel is a feature not limited to exchanges involving a professional fool. It is a game played not only by court jesters, but by servants and masters (for example, Gobbo and Lorenzo in *The Merchant of Venice*), heroines and heroes (Rosalind plays it as "Ganymede" with Orlando), bumpkins and scholars, citizens and tribunes.

Students should understand that these interludes of word play and wit are dramatic conventions of Shakespeare's time, evidently relished by audiences and no doubt willingly supplied by dramatists. Yet to identify them as conventions is not to apologize for them: as mental gymnastics they are still invigorating. In *As You Like It* Touchstone sparks several masterpieces in this exchange of wit—his interview with Corin (Act III, Scene 2), his one-sided exchange with William (V,1), and above all his encounter with Jaques (V,4).

A major subject for continuing discussion is the dramatic function of Touchstone. We have earlier pointed out that, like several other notable figures, he is insignificant in the development of the plot. Though he accompanies Rosalind and Celia on their move from Court to Forest, he does not influence the action that leads to the happy resolution of their problems. Nevertheless, the play would be infinitely poorer without him. In a sense, he serves the dramatic function merely by contributing entertainment. Yet dramatic function implies *use* made of a character, scene, and incident by the dramatist. To what uses, besides mere entertainment, does Shakespeare put Touchstone? What, for example, does his affair with Audrey do for the main romance? The same basic questions will arise, or should arise, in discussion of other characters in the play who are indispensable to the play as a whole, yet serve no plot function.

Other than Touchstone, the most notable of these persons is Jaques. *As You Like It* would simply be unthinkable without him —and yet, in terms of demonstrable dramatic function, what right has he to be in it? He is joined with Duke Senior somewhat as Touchstone is joined with the two princesses. Like Touchstone, he has a series of encounters with other persons—among them Touchstone himself, and the lover Orlando. He is also the subject of others' discussion, and the 1st Lord's description of Jaques and the stricken deer, for example, is unforgettable. The seven ages of man speech delivered by Jaques on the thinnest of excuses is recalled vividly by readers who have forgotten the main outline of the plot. But what are such passages, the character, and the incidents in which he is involved, doing in the play? What service do they perform in the dramatic whole?

This is the question with which we began discussion of *As You Like It*, and perhaps it will be the question with which teacher and class will both begin and end: *As You Like It* is abundantly populated with persons who perform no service in the plot itself; what services do they perform for the total work?

Accompanying and Following Activities. Some of the writing that grows out of discussion will no doubt focus on this question. It is possible that students can come to have supportable opinions, for example, on the larger functions of Amiens' songs before they have reached the end of the play, and can write a paragraph developing their ideas. But for the most part it may be wiser to wait until all the evidence has been seen, in which event students will wait until the end of the play before assessing the functions of Touchstone, Jaques, and others.

Here the possibilities will vary: the teacher might give students a choice of Touchstone, Jaques, Amiens' songs, or Phebe and Silvius as matter for single-paragraph compositions; or the teacher might suggest that the problem of the dramatic relevance of all these serve as subject for the final essay. Either way provides the teacher with opportunity to differentiate mere character sketch from analysis that sets a character in relation to the total play.

Now, what can the teacher do to induce students to go beyond a mere character sketch? One way is as follows: (1) Assign a one-paragraph, one-page, fully developed and well composed "character sketch" of, say, Jaques. (2) After this has been written, turned in, read, and discussed with the class but not returned, assign a second paragraph in which students are to discuss Jaques' function in the play as a whole—not merely to narrate what he *does* in the play, but to explain what he does *for* it, thus justifying his right to be a part of it. (3) When this has been turned in, read, and discussed with the class, return both paragraphs and assign a brief essay which is to present a unified discussion of Jaques and his place in *As You Like It.* The third assignment is not easy, and unless the teacher takes care in making it, most students will simply revise their two separate paragraphs and turn them back in—still two separate paragraphs and not a unified composition. But if even two or three students manage to write unified treatments of the subject, their performances can serve as models, and the way is paved for a more general success on the next occasion.

If we turn now to other sorts of writing subjects, we should note at once that *As You Like It* can be expected to yield somewhat more debatable issues than, say, *A Midsummer Night's Dream.* These may boil up through discussion at almost any point. Besides the major city-country issue are questions like these: Is

Rosalind too forward in her pursuit of Orlando? Is Rosalind truly in love with Orlando? (If so, why does she bait him so?) Does Shakespeare make the conversions of Oliver and Duke Frederick convincing? Does Touchstone always win his wit-duels with other persons? Is "melancholy" or "satiric" the better word for Jaques? Does Phebe deserve the ruthless treatment she gets from Rosalind? Does Silvius deserve the cruel rebuff he gets from Phebe? Does Orlando, or Jaques, come off better in their encounter?

Such issues, adequate for single, well-formed paragraphs in which students unite their own imaginations and the text, are virtually without number. The few that should be chosen for writing, as we have repeatedly suggested, will be those on which discussion has taken such hold that students can be counted on to write with fervor also.

Passages in *As You Like It* that lend themselves well to written paraphrase are so numerous that a teacher is more likely to overuse than underuse this kind of exercise. Less fancifully decorative and allusive than that of *A Midsummer Night's Dream*, this poetry is changed more readily to clear, literal, modern prose—but to say so much is not to say that it can be changed so easily that students will gain nothing by writing as many as half a dozen exercises. Not distinguished as poetry but appropriate for basic reasons (character, situation, plot) is Le Beau's speech at the end of Act I, Scene 2. This should make an admirable first trial. Later passages, in order, are as follows: Duke Senior's first speech in Act II, Scene 1; the First Lord's second speech in the same scene; Adam's speech beginning "I have five hundred crowns" in Act II, Scene 3, and Orlando's that follows it; Jaques' "it is my only suit" and his "Why, who cries out on pride" in Act II, Scene 7 (the "All the world's a stage" speech is long and needs almost no paraphrasing, except, perhaps, for the last portion beginning "And then the justice"); any ten or twelve lines from Rosalind's scolding speech in Act III, Scene 5.

Like *A Midsummer Night's Dream*, *As You Like It* is studded with lines that can serve as take-off points for the development of paragraphs in terms of students' own experience and imagination. Such are Duke Senior's "Sweet are the uses of adversity," (II,1), Touchstone's "We that are true lovers run into strange capers" (II,4), Jaques' "All the world's a stage" (II,7), Rosalind's "I had rather have a fool to make me merry than experience to make me sad" (IV,1), and her "Men have died from time to time, and worms have eaten them, but not for love" (IV,1), Orlando's "How bitter a thing it is to look into happiness through another man's eyes" (V,2), and Touchstone's "Your If is the only peace-maker; much virtue in If!" (V,4).

Some suggestions for long papers to end the study of the play have been made earlier. Beyond these, the best hope is that students will discover problems in which they have a genuine interest while the reading is in progress. Virtually any subject of discussion that can be developed into a respectable paragraph can, with fuller exploration of both the play and the student's mind, be developed into a respectable essay—and still without being exhausted.

Like *A Midsummer Night's Dream*, *As You Like It* abounds in scenes that lend themselves to classroom performance. The favorite is "Ganymede's" first interview with Orlando (IV,1), and next to this is the Duke's second Forest scene (II,7). One advantage of the latter is that it can involve the whole class as members of the Duke's party; another is that it includes Jaques' "seven ages" speech. But not to be overlooked is the last scene of the play, in which again all members of the class can participate as speaking actors or as interested onlookers to the ceremonies. But, indeed, any scene of substantial length, as in *A Midsummer Night's Dream*, serves admirably: none is dull, every one has its special charm. With Rosalind, Celia, Phebe, and Audrey, *As You Like It* offers abundant girls' parts. If a number of scenes are used, all girls in an average class can be involved in speaking roles, and this without any repetition of scenes. (But there is advantage also in repeating key scenes with different casts.)

As for memorization, there seems to be no good reason not to continue with the traditional favorite. The "seven ages" speech will no doubt figure in paraphrasing, in any character analysis of Jaques, and in classroom performances. It will take very little more to have every student in every class commit it permanently to memory.

It should not be memorized, of course, without being understood. The Jaques speech presents a view of man's life—Jaques' view. It should be understood as an expression of its speaker, an eccentric, jaundiced, whimsical, satirical fellow who can suck melancholy out of a song (or out of life) as a weasel sucks eggs. Whether Shakespeare shared any part of Jaques' view of life, no one knows. Often students memorize and speak these lines as though the speech were a gospel for their own lives; to speak them so is not to understand them. Before any memorizing is done, teacher and students should examine the speech word by word, line by line, to see what it actually *says* about life, and the whole thought should then be related to Jaques' character. Then, when students memorize and speak the speech, they will speak it in the context of Jaques' character, and of the play. Once in a great while a student may genuinely identify with Jaques; but no student should be allowed to do so without knowing what he is doing. He should not warble off these lines without knowing what they say. Curiously, it is possible to write a paraphrase in which every word and sentence accurately reproduces the original—and yet at last to have no real sense of the whole thought. A short paper by students evaluating Jaques' view of life will do the speech no harm and will do understanding much good.

CHAPTER 10

Special Notes on Four Plays

The preceding discussion has illustrated the basic problems of procedure broadly enough that no more of the same kind need be said about the remaining plays. We therefore will change our approach in this chapter in order to present a different sort of illustration. The comments that follow are meant to suggest a few special points of attack in each of four plays: *Romeo and Juliet*, *Hamlet*, and the two histories, *Henry IV, Part 1*, and *Henry V*. Important as they are, these special points represent only a fraction of the teacher's total task in conducting students through these plays. Where we shall be concerned only with selected aspects, the teacher will, of course, be concerned with the play as a whole.

Romeo and Juliet (Grade 10 or 11)

It is sometimes assumed that because *Romeo and Juliet* was Shakespeare's first tragedy and because it lacks some dimensions of the "Big Four," it must be one of the easier plays to teach. It is sometimes thought, too, that because it does not develop the tragic pattern that is characteristic of the later tragedies beginning with *Julius Caesar*, it is a "minor" work which does not merit the serious study given the others. In the following pages we shall take strong exception to both of these assumptions. *Romeo and Juliet* is not an easy play to teach; on the contrary, it is more difficult to teach than either *Julius Caesar* or *Macbeth* among the tragedies, than *As You Like It* or *The Merchant of Venice* among the comedies. Further, though it was indeed an early play, it is not a slight one; it deserves the fullest and most serious reading it can be given. This tragedy of young love can provide high school students, in particular, with an experience as genuinely moving as any that they are likely to get from literature. In what follows, we shall be concerned with just two aspects of the play—its poetry and its tragic pattern.

The Poetry. What makes *Romeo and Juliet* difficult is what, in general, makes all the early plays difficult: its poetic language. If the early plays lack the depth of characterization and other dramatic dimensions that make *Hamlet* and *King Lear* so formidable, they nevertheless spin out their ideas into fine, attenuated strands, in a poetic language that makes *it* formidable, too.

Romeo and Juliet, together with *Richard II* and *A Midsummer Night's Dream*, belongs to Shakespeare's extraordinary "lyrical year," probably 1595–96. Far richer music pours from them than from the earlier works, and yet, especially in *Romeo and Juliet*, the same early taste for playing with words and ideas together, for stretching out airy nothings to great length, is indulged. Thus Romeo, when he first encounters Benvolio after the street fray in Act I, Scene 1, says:

> Alas, that love, whose view is muffled still,
> Should, without eyes, see pathways to his will!
> Where shall we dine? O me! What fray was here?
> Yet tell me not, for I have heard it all.
> Here's much to do with hate, but more with love.
> Why, then, O brawling love! O loving hate!
> O any thing, of nothing first create!
> O heavy lightness! Serious vanity!
> Mis-shapen chaos of well-seeming forms!
> Feather of lead, bright smoke, cold fire, sick health!
> Still-waking sleep, that is not what it is!
> This love feel I, that feel no love in this.

Not only Romeo, but Montague, Capulet, Lady Capulet, Benvolio, Mercutio are capable of toying with figures, citing paradoxes, seizing on ideas that are often not much to begin with, and then attenuating, elaborating, embroidering until they have run out of breath. For example, in Act I, Scene 3, Lady Capulet describes young Paris:

> Read o'er the volume of young Paris' face
> And find delight writ there with beauty's pen.
> Examine every married lineament
> And see how one another lends content,
> And what obscured in this fair volume lies
> Find written in the margent of his eyes.
> This precious book of love, this unbound lover,
> To beautify him, only lacks a cover.
> The fish lives in the sea, and 'tis much pride
> For fair without the fair within to hide.
> That book in many's eyes doth share the glory,
> That in gold clasps locks in the golden story;
> So shall you share all that he doth possess,
> By having him, making yourself no less.

It is such poetry that makes *Romeo and Juliet* hard to teach. Students have an unflattering word for this poetry: they call it "icky," or whatever their local term is for what offends them in just the way this does. Holden Caulfield would instantly reject it as "phony." Less imaginative students simply find it "sissy stuff," and want to get on to a robust short story written in plain English.

What, then, is the teacher to do? To expound the virtues of this kind of poetry is to risk too much, for even if students politely acquiesce they will not really see any good in it. They may go along with the teacher, pretending to be affected by what does not affect them—and then, when the real poetry of the play comes, their dulled expectations may prevent it from reaching them.

It is surely better to be quite honest about such passages as those quoted, to represent them to students for exactly what they are—affected, fashionable effusions. But it is also necessary to get students to see that this "phony" poetry is *dramatically right*, suited to the speaker and the occasion. When Romeo speaks to

Benvolio in that first scene, he speaks as a *poseur*; he is the young man playing at the fashion of being in love, going through the verbal and physical motions of the conventional lover who sees himself as disdained by a mistress more imaginary than real, indulging in artificial expressions, sighing, pining, defining love:

> Love is a smoke rais'd with the fume of sighs;
> Being purg'd, a fire sparkling in lovers' eyes;
> Being vex'd, a sea nourish'd with lovers' tears:
> A choking gall and a preserving sweet.

It would be monstrous to let students suppose that Shakespeare could write no better love poetry than this, to blame the playwright for the affectations of the character. When Lady Capulet speaks, in the quoted passage, she too speaks in character. She is herself young, not more than twenty-six or twenty-seven, married to a man perhaps twice her age and no longer romantic. In describing Paris to her young daughter, she embraces the fashionable extravagance of poetic figure and is carried away by it. For the moment, possibly, she is fulfilling her own unrealized romantic dream. All things considered, it is dramatically "right" that she should speak exactly as she does. Though Shakespeare never emphasizes it, the Capulets' marriage is marked by defeated hopes. We learn incidentally of the great difference in their ages and sense, rather than learn directly of, their mutual disappointment. Much "character," thus, is suggested by her absurdly figured speech; but the absurdity is hers, not Shakespeare's.

It may be that when teacher and class have read through Romeo's "icky" poetry of the opening scene and found it not genuine, as it is not, they should immediately turn the pages to later scenes and read aloud a passage or two of Romeo at his best. They might take the short, blazing passage in Act I, Scene 5, which he speaks at the first sight of Juliet ("O she doth teach the torches to burn bright"), and the first dozen lines of Act III, Scene 5, the beginning of the marvelous lovers' duet at parting. They might finally turn to Act V, Scene 3, and read aloud a dozen lines from Romeo's last speech, beginning with "How oft when men are at the point of death." This demonstration will adequately make the point, without argument, that Shakespeare saw, at least as clearly as students, the difference between "phony" and "real" poetry, just as he saw the difference between affected and true love. Further, this preliminary dip into the splendid later passages will sharpen the appetite for what is to follow; and when at last, in the course of orderly reading, students again reach the later passages, now even richer for being understood in context, they will warm to them as to old friends.

The fact is that, like Richard II and Macbeth, Romeo improves as a poet as his experience of life deepens. This is the point that students must not be allowed to miss. It is the point that the dramatist himself makes through the startling contrast in the earlier and the later passages. The studied, empty affectations of the early passages turn to ecstatic lyrical outpourings during his first meeting with Juliet, and the music of these rises higher still during the first balcony scene. With the parting scene (Act III, Scene 5), the ecstasy turns to grief, despite his own and Juliet's forced bravado, and in the last scenes profound grief has turned the music to a dirge. Throughout the play, Romeo's speech is laden with poetic figures, from the first passages until the last. But whereas the early passages come from the lips only, and from the mind engaged in fashionable verbal play—

> . . . she hath Dian's wit;
> And, in strong proof of chastity well arm'd,
> From love's weak childish bow she lives unharm'd.
> She will not stay the siege of loving terms,
> Nor bide the encounter of assailing eyes,
> Nor ope her lap to saint-seducing gold:
> O, she is rich in beauty, only poor,
> That when she dies with beauty dies her store.

—the later passages come straight from the heart:

> O, how may I
> Call this a lightning? O my love, my wife!
> Death, that hath suck'd the honey of thy breath,
> Hath had no power yet upon thy beauty:
> Thou art not conquer'd; beauty's ensign yet
> Is crimson in thy lips and in thy cheeks,
> And death's pale flag is not advanced there.

It is not the excess of figures that makes the early poetry "phony"—the later fine poetry has just as many. The difference is in the fidelity with which the imagery bodies forth the passion— or lack of it—that lies behind.

Still, Romeo's growth as a poet is not without its apparent setbacks, and these are among the most interesting *dramatic* features of the play. For Rosaline, Romeo has cultivated a false language of love. But when he first sees Juliet, the language of the heart breaks through the falsity. Now genuine passion tries to speak, and it speaks in violent surges of extravagant metaphor—"O she doth teach the torches to burn bright" and "It is the East, and Juliet is the sun." Hyperboles that had been empty have quite suddenly become full with feeling. From then until Act V, Scene 1, when his process of "growing up" is abruptly completed at Balthasar's news of Juliet's death, Romeo is caught in an impossible situation: true passion fills his being to overflowing, but the language he has learned for its expression is false. Often the surges from the heart break clear of the mold and escape in the form of wildly exuberant metaphor, excessive, fantastic, and yet true because their very wildness exhibits the passion within:

> O, speak again, bright angel! For thou art
> As glorious to this night, being o'er my head,
> As is a winged messenger of heaven
> Unto the white-upturned wondering eyes
> Of mortals that fall back to gaze on him
> When he bestrides the lazy-pacing clouds
> And sails upon the bosom of the air.

But then, again, the "phony" language that lovers are "expected" to speak, like an old, bad habit, lays hold of the tongue, and Romeo (now not in soliloquy but speaking face to face with Juliet) speaks thus—as he might have spoken to Rosaline, when he was only playing at love:

> With love's light wings did I o'erperch these walls;
> For stony limits cannot hold love out,

> And what love can do that dares love attempt;
> Therefore thy kinsmen are no let to me.

And again:

> Alack, there lies more peril in thine eye
> Than twenty of their swords . . .

But Juliet's ear is as quick as Holden Caulfield's to detect the "phony." She acknowledges that she, too, might have played at the artificial game of love had not Romeo caught her unawares; but as it is, she will have none of it:

> O gentle Romeo,
> If thou dost love, pronounce it faithfully.

Romeo begins to swear a lover's oath—"Lady, by yonder blessed moon I swear—" and she cuts him off: "Do not swear at all." He tries again, "If my heart's dear love—" and then she cuts him off for good: "Well, do not swear."

Is it that, in this brief exchange, Romeo's passion is less genuine than it was a moment before, when it burst out in wild, ecstatic soliloquy? Or is it that Shakespeare, in 1595, absurdly thought that "Alack, there lies more peril in thine eye" was a perfect line for expressing genuine passion? It is surely neither. Romeo is trapped between a new, violent feeling and an old habit of artificial expression.

Probably no lines better demonstrate the lasting effect of this earlier habit on Romeo than two that he speaks in Act III, Scene 3. He has killed Tybalt, and now learns from the Friar that he is banished. The degree of the desperation that assails him at this word is best expressed by himself in word and action:

> Then mightst thou speak, then mightst thou tear thy hair,
> And fall upon the ground, as I do now.

He is never shown, before or after, in a condition so frenzied (later, he accepts news of Juliet's death not with frenzy but with a deathlike calm). At this point, the Nurse enters, wailing, and at once, in the midst of babbling, Romeo speaks this line to her:

> . . . and what says
> My *conceal'd* lady to our *cancell'd* love?

To any ear, sensitive or not, this obvious euphuistic trick with words, *at this particular moment*, must sound jarring and out of place. Is this a time to play with words? But this violence done to our sense of what is appropriate is not the only one. Just before the Nurse's entrance, while approaching the frenzy that ends with his falling to the floor and tearing his hair, Romeo had imagined how common flies could seize on "the white wonder of dear Juliet's hand" here in Verona, while he, banished, could enjoy no such privilege:

> *Flies* may do this, when I from this must *fly.*

We can justify Romeo's early poetic speeches as fashionable affectation, appropriate to the disdained lover's role he so consciously plays, and we can account for his extravagant outbursts at Capulet's ball and during the first balcony scene as appropriate artistic expressions of the passion he feels. But how can we account for his playing with "conceal'd—cancell'd" and with "flies—fly" at a moment of extreme desperation, when he lies on the floor, tearing his hair, threatening to kill himself? Must we not say that Shakespeare himself, unable to restrain his own youthful euphuistic impulses, was to blame here for these jarring notes?

Or are these, too, psychologically "right," subtly representing a trick of the mind which, in moments of deep crisis, will fall back upon familiar habit? Of course, we can never be sure. But it is always risky to underestimate Shakespeare. It is presumptuous to suppose that he would *not* have thought of just this. If he errs frequently enough in factual matters (giving Bohemia a seacoast in *The Winter's Tale*, confusing two Edmund Mortimers in *Henry IV, Part 1*), yet he is rarely wrong in dramatic matters. An hour, since the killing of Tybalt, is too short a time in which to grow up completely. In a frenzied moment, Romeo might well be expected to exhibit some aspects of his recent immaturity.

In these brief illustrations, centered on Romeo, we have left much of the play's poetry untouched; we have said nothing of Mercutio's great imaginative gifts, lavished alike on astonishing flights of poetry (the Queen Mab speech) and on the earthiest kind of talk; or of Juliet's outbursts of passion, unsurpassed elsewhere in literature, even by Shakespeare. They are all poets, as the essential spirit of the play demands—even the Nurse, whose account of the earthquake that tipped the infant Juliet off her unsteady feet is a rare thing; even old Montague, who begins with poetry that is as affected as Romeo's, but ends with an oblique expression of sudden grief, at seeing Romeo's body, that is unmatched anywhere:

> O thou untaught! What manners is in this,
> To press before thy father to the grave?

The teacher's problem, we have sought to suggest, is to get students to differentiate clearly between poetry that is extravagant because of a character's affectation and poetry that is extravagant because it expresses extravagant passion.

The Tragic Pattern. As is well known, all the tragedies after *Romeo and Juliet* establish and maintain a strong causal relationship between the character of the protagonist and the final disaster. Brutus, because he *is* Brutus, commits himself to a succession of actions that, in the given set of circumstances, lead inevitably to catastrophe. Though Cassius works shrewdly to bring about Brutus's first fatal decision and though Antony proves a mighty force in his eventual undoing, yet these two are only major items in the set of circumstances, and the ultimate *responsibility* for what happens is not theirs, but Brutus's alone. Or again, Macbeth, because he *is* Macbeth, takes the steps that lead to death and the frustration of all his ambitions. Though the Witches and Lady Macbeth similarly tempt Macbeth and though Macduff is similarly a mighty force in his eventual undoing, these, too, are only parts in the set of circumstances, and the final, full responsibility is Macbeth's alone. Both are authors of their own demise. This familiar pattern of Shakespearean tragedy is not the pattern

of *Romeo and Juliet,* and because it is not, this tragedy has sometimes been disparaged by critics and neglected by teachers. Traditionally, critics have tended to apologize for the play's failure to
fit the pattern of more typical Shakespearean tragedy, the implication being that a tragedy which does not fit this pattern is necessarily inferior and possibly does not even deserve the name
"tragedy."

Several critics, in attempting to defend it, have insisted that
Romeo and Juliet does, after all, fit the typical pattern. The tragic
protagonists *do,* they argue, have a kind of "tragic flaw" which
impels them along the road to catastrophe, even as the flaws of
Brutus and Macbeth push these protagonists on to disaster. They
maintain that Romeo and Juliet are too passionate and impulsive;
being so, they commit a succession of rash acts that lead to their
deaths and the deaths of others (Tybalt, Mercutio, Paris) who
are involved with them.

A major embarrassment, however, to critics who pursue this line
is the "accident" which precipitates the sudden deaths of the
lovers: Friar John, sent by Friar Laurence to advise Romeo that
Juliet is asleep, not dead, is detained in a house suspected of
plague, and therefore the saving word never gets to Mantua. Thus,
it appears, an irrelevant accident, and not the tragic flaws of the
lovers, brings on the catastrophe; hence the play as tragedy is
defective, or, worse, not tragedy at all.

Besides these two interpretations, there is another choice, and
perhaps it is the best one. This is the one which sees *Romeo and
Juliet* as having its own tragic pattern, different from but not
necessarily inferior to the tragic pattern found in Shakespeare's
subsequent tragedies. (Whether or not this pattern is inferior can
be a subject for debate after the play has been studied through to
the end. Obviously, to participate intelligently, students will need
to have read at least *Julius Caesar* and *Macbeth.*) Now, what is
this pattern?

The Prologue announces that the lovers are "star-crossed": they
were born to die so that the long and bloody feud of their respective houses would be ended. An *external* force—not, as in later
tragedies, the inner force of their own characters—controls their
destinies. Romeo calls this external force "Fortune"; the Friar calls
it "a greater power than we can contradict"; the Prologue men-

tions the "fatal loins" of the parents. The Prologue, as a whole, serves notice of what the play will represent: "The fearful passage of their death-mark'd love." At the end of the play, the lovers and three other young people who became involved in their "fearful passage" are dead, and so is the feud. The external force—which we may as well call "Fate"—has finished its work.

Just how did Fate do it? The whole play furnishes the answer, for what it represents is Fate at work, weaving the "tragic pattern." The very first scene shows Fate getting down to business, starting the machinery that will end with a pile of bodies in the Capulet tomb, and with the survivors mournfully asking how this thing came about. Rival servants, quarrelsome but cautious, come to blows; Benvolio, the well-intentioned, tries to stop them; Tybalt, mistaking (or pretending to mistake) Benvolio's intentions, joins the fray; soon all the street is brawling; the Prince enters, commands a halt, and shortly pronounces a categorical "sentence":

> If ever you disturb our streets again,
> Your lives shall pay the forfeit of the peace.

The next time the streets are disturbed (III,1), Tybalt kills Mercutio and is killed by Romeo. Romeo, after refusing to fight Tybalt, tries to prevent Mercutio and Tybalt from fighting, reminding them that

> . . . the prince expressly hath
> Forbidden bandying in Verona streets.

These lines also should underscore, for audience or reader, the fateful significance of the opening scene, when the servants' brawl led to the Prince's "sentence." Had that brawl not occurred, the Prince would not, as yet, have stated his ultimatum; and if he had not stated it, it is clear enough that Romeo would now go free—for Benvolio's admirably accurate account of the fray and of Romeo's conduct throughout it leaves no doubt that justice has already been served; the Prince himself states that the scales are balanced:

> Romeo slew him, he slew Mercutio;
> Who now the price of his dear blood doth owe?

If the servants' brawl had not occurred, it would presumably be only *now* that the Prince would say,

> If ever you disturb our streets again,
> Your lives shall pay the forfeit of the peace.

But because of the servants' brawl, he had already said it. He cannot now ignore his former pronouncement—but even so he softens the verdict by sentencing Romeo to banishment instead of death. But, of course, it is from this very banishment that both lovers die.

It appears, then, that in the opening scene Fate "uses" the actions of several persons in fashioning the tragic net: all four servants, Benvolio, Tybalt, and the Prince. It is notable that the tragic course of events has begun before the pair whom it is to destroy have met or, presumably, heard of each other. It is further notable that none of the persons who, in the opening scene, contribute to Fate's pattern has any knowledge of the fact; and it is finally to be noted that at the end of the play none of these persons is in a position to know that an action of his helped to create the terrible spectacle which greets the early morning visitors to the Capulet tomb. And though the Prince then seeks to

> clear these ambiguities,
> And know their spring, their head, their true descent,

none will ever guess what share in the total responsibility was his.

So it is throughout the tragedy. Fate's pattern is woven of the actions of persons who perform their deadly part on schedule, then go on about their business without knowing what they have done. One such person is Rosaline, the disdainful lady of Romeo's early infatuation. The audience never sees this Rosaline, yet her responsibility for the final catastrophe is as great as anyone's, for it is only to see *her* that Romeo agrees to attend the Capulet feast uninvited—where he sees, instead, Juliet, and will henceforth look at no other. The illiterate servant who bears Capulet's list of invited guests is another guilty one: had he not, by sheer chance (but, of course, it was not really chance, but Fate's intention), picked Romeo to help him "find what names the writing person hath here writ," Romeo would not have known that there was to *be* a party at Capulet's house. A second servant, presumably hired especially for this affair, plays a similar, seemingly inconsequential yet fateful part when Romeo, at first glimpse of Juliet, asks him her name.

> ROMEO.   What lady is that, which doth enrich the hand
> Of yonder knight?
> SERVANT. I know not, sir.

Considering the nature of each individual item of which Fate's pattern is composed, we do not strain too far in supposing that had this servant known Juliet's identity, and had he said "That, sir, is Juliet Capulet," Romeo would instantly have placed a hard clamp on his impulses, and would have turned away to search for Rosaline. But the servant did not know her, and so Romeo utters a ten-line soliloquy ("O, she doth teach the torches to burn bright!") after which it is too late; he can never turn back. (It is to be noted that Shakespeare makes both lovers comment on this very point. Thus Romeo says, when the Nurse, too late, tells him Juliet's identity: "O dear account! My life is my foe's debt." And Juliet, for whom also the crucial information comes too late, says: "Too early seen unknown, and known too late!")

We cannot here follow the course of events to show all the details of this kind, the "innocent" contributions to the fatal pattern made by unknowing persons; but at least two more are of so great interest and importance that we cannot afford to overlook them. The persons involved are Capulet and Romeo's faithful servant, Balthasar.

Capulet's contributions, unlike those of Rosaline and the servants, are born of his character—for Fate does use the characters of men, too, wherever these fit into the scheme. Capulet's moods swing like a pendulum between extreme joviality and extreme rage. His first action of dreadful consequence is performed at the ball, when Tybalt recognizes Romeo and, boiling with anger, wants to drive him out. Capulet, who has been presiding over the party with the gaiety that marks one of his extremes, swings instantly to the other extreme on having his authority challenged by Tybalt:

> He shall be endured:
> What, goodman boy! I say, he shall: go to;
> Am I the master here, or you? Go to.
> You'll not endure him! God shall mend my soul!
> You'll make a mutiny among my guests!
> You will set cock-a-hoop! You'll be the man!

Because of Capulet's mood, Romeo is allowed to stay, and, a moment later, speaks his first words—from which there is to be no turning back—to Juliet. But not less significant is that Tybalt's wrath, here bottled up by Capulet's authority, drives him to seek out Romeo on the following day, insult him, fight and kill Mercutio, be killed in turn by Romeo—and thus bring on Romeo's banishment, which sets the stage for Fate's final stroke.

We may skip over Capulet's obviously significant action when, ignorant that Juliet is already married, he commands her to marry Paris or die in the streets, and come to another action of his the significance of which is sometimes overlooked by readers. Here, again, the action springs from his mood of the moment. He had demanded that Juliet marry Paris (who, too, bears an "innocent" and heavy burden of responsibility for the ultimate tragedy) on Thursday morning; but when she returns from the Friar—with the magical potion secreted somewhere about her person—and humbly begs pardon for her former obstinacy, he abruptly advances the day to Wednesday. Why does he do so? Capulet loves his daughter beyond measure: "The earth hath swallowed all my hopes but she." So the pendulum swings back: Juliet has returned to him; her apparent obedience now elates him as extremely as, an hour before, her apparent obstinacy had infuriated him. The change of date seems insignificant—as insignificant, say, as the illiterate servant's asking Romeo to read the names of invited guests; but its effect is deadly. It means that the Friar has twenty-four hours less time in which to get word to Romeo in Mantua than he would otherwise have had, for now Juliet must take the potion that much earlier than was planned. Had the wedding date been kept at Thursday, Friar John could have been delayed, returned to Friar

Laurence for new instructions, and yet have reached Romeo with the truth before Balthasar reached him with false word of Juliet's death. Balthasar left for Mantua as soon as he saw Juliet laid in the tomb on Wednesday; had she not been laid there until Thursday, all would have been well.

We should comment, finally, on the part played by this Balthasar in Fate's deadly pattern. It has been remarked by all critics that the irrelevant accident which renders the play defective as tragedy is the detention of Friar John. But it is in fact not Friar John's failure to get through to Romeo that is decisive; *it is rather the success of Balthasar in getting through with false word*. Had Balthasar never reached Romeo with false word, Romeo would have remained at Mantua, knowing nothing of what was going on in Verona, and Juliet would have been saved. Friar Laurence, on learning of Friar John's mishap, would have hastened to Juliet's tomb (as, in fact, he does) and would have arrived there just before Juliet awakened (as, in fact, he does). He would then have taken her to his own cell, as indeed he planned to do. No harm would then have been done by Friar John's failure to reach Romeo; but as it is, the harm has already been done because Balthasar reached him: Romeo is dead when Friar Laurence arrives at the tomb.

Balthasar's contribution to Fate's pattern is thus of tremendous importance, and it is surely the most pitiful of all the unwitting acts in the play. "I warrant thee," Romeo had told the Nurse much earlier, "my man's as true as steel." True as steel he was indeed—yet it was he who, on the testimony of his own eyes, carried the false word that killed both lovers. His case is the more pitiful because, unlike the illiterate servant and the servant who could not tell Romeo Juliet's name, he is able finally to recognize what part his action played and to assess its enormity: "I brought my master news of Juliet's death," he tells all those who are blindly seeking the cause of the catastrophe, and his tone must, surely, be that of a man who is stunned and broken.

In sum, Brutus and Macbeth are destroyed by their own characters; Romeo and Juliet are killed by all who surround them—servants, friends, confidants, parents—acting unknowingly in the service of "a greater power."

This partial analysis of the tragic pattern of *Romeo and Juliet* may serve to suggest that teachers need, not, after all, apologize for the play's failure to fit the more typical pattern of Shakespearean tragedy: it has a pattern of its own that is just as moving, just as deadly.

Hamlet (Grade 12)

College teachers are often heard to say that they wish their freshmen had not read *Hamlet* in high school. Yet the very same teachers also raise their voices in the general chorus of complaint that their freshmen read far too little first-rate literature in high school. How is this apparent paradox to be accounted for?

It certainly does not signify that college teachers think *Hamlet* a second-rate work which should have been passed over in favor of a first-rate one. It may mean that they think *Hamlet* was read by students who had not yet been given sufficient grounding in works of comparable complexity, with the result that they made little of it and either "got it all wrong" or, worse, were turned against it. It may mean simply that students who have read *Hamlet* in high school see no point in reading it again in the freshman "Introduction to Literature" course and, accordingly, either act bored or behave like know-it-alls. It may mean that college teachers think that high school teachers have taught it "all wrong" and have filled students' minds with wrong interpretations. This last possibility is a likely one, because *Hamlet* is a unique case: no college teacher ever supposes that any other teacher understands it or knows how to teach it.

More likely, the explanation is a composite of all these elements and a great many more. *Hamlet is* complex, it *is* often badly taught and badly read, college freshmen's pre-conceived ideas of it *do* infuriate college teachers—though not as much as does their innocent, bland assertion, "Oh, I've already read it."

The question is whether, in view of such reactions by college teachers, we ought to recommend the use of *Hamlet* in high school. We have, of course, already committed ourselves by including it emphatically in the list of twelve to fourteen most appropriate plays, and we see no need now to recant. But we should reiterate a qualification made much earlier: *Hamlet* should not stand among the first plays that students read. If students have read only *Julius Caesar* in grade ten, they should not read *Hamlet* in grade twelve. In the discussion of *Romeo and Juliet*, we deplored the fact that that play stands in seventh or eighth place among plays read in high school; all things considered, it might well be the fifth or the sixth play that students read. As for *Hamlet*, we suggest that it should not be read until students have thoroughly studied at least six plays—possibly *Julius Caesar*, *A Midsummer Night's Dream*, *As You Like It*, *Romeo and Juliet*, and *Macbeth*; or possibly *Twelfth Night* should be added after *Macbeth*, and *then Hamlet*. What this means is that if only two plays or four plays, or even six plays are read in high school, *Hamlet* should not be one of them.

Whether it is the seventh play or the eighth, *Hamlet* unquestionably requires close, line-by-line study. One hears occasionally that *Hamlet* is read "outside," by students "on their own," while *Macbeth* is studied in class. Both plays very clearly require class study; but if for some reason one must be read outside, it should certainly not be *Hamlet*.

We have repeatedly insisted that the teacher's central problem in teaching any of the plays is to enable students to see for themselves "what is there." With *Hamlet*, this problem becomes peculiarly difficult. Most students will have drunk up from the very air, without laying an eye to the text, some basic notions of the play and its hero. One remembers the tale about a young student who reacted unfavorably to a performance of *Hamlet* because "it was so full of things I'd heard before." They will have heard of the "melancholy Dane," of Yorick's skull, of lines like "Something is rotten in the state of Denmark" and "To be or not to be." Nowadays, thanks to the Laurence Olivier movie, they may also have heard the bald statement that "this is the story of a man who could not make up his mind."

Teachers, before taking up the play with a class, will of course have drunk up a great many more ideas about the play. Directly or indirectly, they will have absorbed nearly two centuries of critical interpretation, from Goethe and Coleridge through the Victorians to the Freudians, and to Bradley, Knight, and T. S. Eliot. The main notion to which they will have been exposed, in many variations, is that of Hamlet's failure to "get on with the job."

One theme that is constant in the great stream of *Hamlet* criticism for nearly two hundred years is that his famous delay was caused by some inner defect. What was "wrong" with him? He was a man of thought and words, not action. He was irresolute. He was overly sensitive. He had a habit of procrastination. He was mad. He was afflicted with the disease of melancholy. His soul was sick. He resented his father, and guilt-feelings made him reluctant to attack his uncle. The precise diagnoses of what ailed him are nearly as numerous as the critics who have expounded them; the one common denominator is the idea that *something* ailed him. Something *must* have ailed him, or he would immediately have killed Claudius and had done with it.

In two centuries, this basic conception has become part of our atmosphere, and neither students nor teachers can come to the text of the play without having already breathed in a good deal of it. We do not mean to imply that a class would be better off if the teacher were ignorant of all that has been said about *Hamlet;* the more the teacher knows, the better. But *Hamlet* is a unique case, a work so deeply encased in critical tradition that we can hardly discern it by itself, apart from all that has been built up around it.

This, then, is the hardest problem in teaching *Hamlet:* how to approach it with an open mind. Because the most devoted teachers have a peculiarly passionate conviction about the nature of this very special hero and consequently a pet theory of why he delays, they labor under a strong compulsion to "sell" the class on their view: Hamlet is sick, or he does not want to hurt his mother, or he thinks too much and cannot act except when he has no time to think, or the idea of bloody revenge is intolerable to his sensitive soul, or he is weary of his own flesh and simply wants to die. It is an exceptional teacher who can successfully fight off the compulsion to "tell all," who can keep personal convictions tucked away out of sight and take students line by line through the play with no purpose but to have them see what is really there.

If even a little lecturing is to be done on *Hamlet*, surely none of it should be done until after the line-by-line study has been completed. If, before they read the play, students have heard only that Hamlet is a "melancholy Dane" and that "this is the story of a man who could not make up his mind," they have already heard too much. If, besides, the teacher instructs the students to watch for signs that Hamlet is mad, or resentful of his father, or in love with his mother, their already-difficult task of reading with completely open minds is made impossible. *Hamlet*, especially, is a play that needs to be studied with an open text; that is why it in particular should have the kind of reading-discussion treatment that we have recommended for all the plays. An open text offers the best protection against being merely told "what is there" and taking it for fact.

It may be that, as some teachers think, the best way to approach *Hamlet* is not with answers but with questions, and it is probably true that when a class has moved through the play with a good teacher, students have acquired, at the end, not a collection of answers but a series of unanswered questions. If high school classes could study *Hamlet* in this spirit, it is possible that college teachers would stop lamenting the use of the play in high school; if freshmen came to them not with "answers," but eager to renew the search, they might even be pleased.

To say that one will approach *Hamlet* with questions rather than answers is easy enough. But what questions? Unfortunately, even this way carries no guarantee that *Hamlet* will be studied freshly, without the influence of preconceptions. Such is the pressure of two hundred years of concern over this play and its hero that we can scarely even pose a question without already reflecting an attitude—without, in effect, already saying something about the tragedy. If we begin by posing the question that has been central to criticism through nearly two centuries, "Why does Hamlet delay?" we involuntarily commit ourselves to the view that he *does* delay. Now it is a fact, of course, that he delays, for he does not live up to his promise made to the Ghost—

> Haste me to know it, that I with wings as swift
> As meditation or the thoughts of love
> May sweep to my revenge.

He does not, that is, rush straight in from the battlements and kill Claudius within the hour. But in two centuries the question "Why does he delay?" has taken on a strong connotation of *blame*; it carries the suggestion that he delays *too* long and unnecessarily. But whether he does delay too long and unnecessarily is not a matter of fact, but of interpretation; to *assume* that it is a fact is immediately to allow a preconception to get in the way of honest search for "what is there."

If, again succumbing to critical tradition, we ask the next obvious question, "What is *wrong* with him, that he delays too long and unnecessarily?" we truly make an honest reading impossible, for this question sets students hunting for signs of what is "wrong," and each of his lines and actions becomes evidence of hypersensitivity, madness, melancholy, or an Oedipus complex.

Possibly Hamlet does delay too long, and possibly he does so because of something that ails him. But these are conclusions that should be reached—if they *are* reached—on the basis of evidence that was found *without being sought*. If one looks hard enough, feeling obliged to substantiate a prejudgment, one can find "proofs" for any view of *Hamlet*—even that he was really a woman in disguise, like Rosalind and Viola.

We are saying of *Hamlet* what we have repeatedly argued before —that the questions on which class discussion centers ought to grow out of the study of the text; they should not be planted beforehand. Unfortunately, with *Hamlet*, crucial questions are likely to have been planted beforehand in spite of all. The teacher must at least try to keep from compounding this misfortune. An admirable stunt for a teacher to try, in working through *Hamlet* with a class, is *to wait and see how long it is* before a student asks "Why does he delay? Why doesn't he just *do* it?" and before a student asks "What's *wrong* with him?" Teachers (and critics) may be in for a great surprise: a whole class of bright students could conceivably work very ably, line by line, discussing everything, through the entire play without ever asking either question. Unless they are told, it may not occur to them that these are *the* questions to ask about Hamlet. They were not *the* questions until just before the nineteenth century.

But questions that are based on fact, rather than assumption, will assuredly arise very often, and where they do not, they should be raised by the teacher. "Why does Hamlet put on an 'antic disposition'?" (For indeed he does put one on, and this is not a matter of assumption.) "*When* does he have it on, and when does he have it off?" (For indeed he does sometimes have it on and sometimes off, and a crucial problem in reading is to determine which is which.) "Why does he have a play 'like the murder of my father' acted before Claudius?" "Why does he take Horatio into his confidence while rejecting Rosencrantz and Guildenstern?" "Why is it that he does not kill Claudius in the 'prayer' scene?" "How is it that he can kill Polonius (did he really think the eavesdropper was Claudius?) a few minutes after he could or would not kill the King?" "Does he suspect that the fencing match with Laertes is really a trap? If so, why does he accept the challenge?" "Why is he able to kill Claudius at last, when he could not or would not before?"

Though we might go on indefinitely listing questions large and small, it is best to stop here with a few samples only. A complete list of the questions that should arise during study—supposing that any such thing could actually be devised in advance—would very likely do more harm than good, for in spite of efforts to the contrary it would be sure to betray the list-maker's "slant." And it is any and every sort of "slant" that, above all, the teacher should aim to avoid.

Henry IV, Part 1 and *Henry V* (*Grade 11 or 12*)

Of Shakespeare's major plays that are also eminently teachable at the high school level, *Henry IV, Part 1* and *Henry V* are the least frequently used. The purpose of the following remarks is to urge their more frequent use.

In view of both the critical esteem that has always been theirs and their relative "openness," it is not entirely clear why they should have been so generally neglected by high school teachers. It may be simply because they are histories, and not comedies or tragedies: Who wants to read, or teach, a "history"? It may be because they are not unfailingly included in one-term Shakespeare courses taken by teachers in college, as are *Hamlet, Lear, Othello, Macbeth* and their counterparts in comedy. It may be because of a suspicion that, since they deal with English history of the early fifteenth century, successful teaching would require an undue proportion of study in backgrounds. It may be that the title names, especially for Americans, lack the glamor of Caesar, Hamlet, Lear,

Macbeth, and Romeo. From this point of view, it is most unfortunate that a title like *Henry IV, Part 1* hides a name as glamorous" as any in Shakespeare excepting Hamlet: Sir John Falstaff, who is a luminary of the first magnitude.

Whatever the cause, *Henry IV, Part 1* and *Henry V* have certainly been neglected. Yet they are not as hard to get at as *King Lear, The Tempest,* and perhaps *Hamlet.* They are no harder than *Twelfth Night, Romeo and Juliet,* and, for that matter, *A Midsummer Night's Dream.* And at the same time they contain a richer abundance of exciting, wonderful things than any but two or three of Shakespeare's plays. If one were to apply to Shakespeare Dryden's remark on Chaucer, that "Here is God's plenty," one could not better demonstrate than by referring to *Henry IV, Part 1* and *Henry V.*

The Prose and Poetry. These plays are divided almost perfectly between prose and verse: *Henry IV, Part 1* has 1,464 prose lines to 1,622 verse lines; *Henry V* has 1,531 prose lines to 1,678 verse lines. The balance of prose and poetry in these two plays contrasts sharply with the balance shown by more frequently taught plays: *Romeo and Juliet* (405–2111); *A Midsummer Night's Dream* (441–878); *The Merchant of Venice* (673–1896); *Julius Caesar* (165–2241); *Hamlet* (1208–2490); *King Lear* (903–2238); *Macbeth* (158–1588). Among much-used plays, only *As You Like It* (1781–925) and *Twelfth Night* (1741–763) show a greater proportion of prose.

These figures prove nothing in themselves, but because prose tends to be less difficult for students to read than poetry, they are worth noting. What is much more to the point, as an argument for the relative "openness" of the plays, is the character of the prose, and particularly of the verse. Together with *Julius Caesar* and *As You Like It*, these two histories stand at the happiest point of Shakespeare's maturity in the mastery of dramatic language. Leaving behind him the youthful excesses of affectation, elaboration, and long-drawn out "conceits," Shakespeare achieved in these plays a language that gets directly at the business of communicating. On the other hand, he had not yet moved on to the later style which cramps distilled ideas into space too small for them, so that they are as hard to unlock as gnarled knots are to split. If there is a point of perfect balance between the extremes, it is found just here, where Shakespeare first crossed the line of his full maturity.

Besides its comparative "openness," the prose and poetry used in the *Henry* plays is extraordinary for its variety and appropriateness. In both plays, prose is regularly assigned to the more ordinary classes of society and to royalty only when it is either masquerading (as Henry V, muffled, moving among his soldiers at night) or hobnobbing with everyday people. This prose runs the gamut from the lowest argot of Elizabethan society—best illustrated in *Henry IV* in the exchange between the two carriers (Act II, Scene 1) —to the vital, eloquent, and moving prose of King Henry V expounding a subtlety of political philosophy (Act IV, Scene 1).

Between these extremes of lowly innyard slang and regal eloquence, the plays furnish many other levels of prose, a study of which should be both stimulating and profitable to the students. There is Gadshill's jargon of the Elizabethan underworld, Bardolph's childlike prose, Hotspur's blustering prose, Falstaff's witty prose. And in *Henry* V, there is the prose that exploits the dialects of soldiers who have come to France from up and down the isles of Henry's kingdom:

> FLUELLEN. What call you the town's name where Alexander the Pig was porn?
>
> GOWER. Alexander the Great.
>
> FLUELLEN. Why, I pray you, is not pig great? The pig, or the great, or the mighty, or the huge, or the magnanimous, are all one reckonings, save the phrase is a little variations.

Turning from the prose to the blank verse contained in these histories, we are soon struck by the absence of lyricism which was so prominent in Shakespeare's early plays, particularly *Romeo and Juliet* and *Richard II*. In the latter play (which Shakespeare wrote immediately before *Henry IV, Part 1*), everyone who speaks a passage of half a dozen lines breaks into song. Even the politician Bolingbroke, who represents the predominantly discordant counterpoint to Richard II's lyric melody, is sometimes carried away by the sound of his own voice. In *Henry IV, Part 1*, and *Henry* V the lyric voice is replaced by hard eloquence; the earlier exquisite music which obviously took delight in its own sounds turns severe and sometimes harsh. This is not to say that the new blank verse lacks music or that it avoids the figures of speech that characterize the rest of Shakespeare's verse. Music and figure are still here, but they are of a different·order, businesslike, severe, and hard as the substance they express. Take for example Henry's angry response to the Dauphin's jest of tennis balls in Act I, Scene 2 of *Henry* V:

> We are glad the Dauphin is so pleasant with us;
> His present and your pains we thank you for.
> When we have matched our rackets to these balls,
> We will in France, by God's grace, play a set
> Shall strike his father's crown into the hazard.
> Tell him he hath made a match with such a wrangler
> That all the courts of France will be disturbed
> With chances.

This is hard blank verse uttered between the teeth. But take a really extreme example now, which brings together all the granitic qualities. In Act III, Scene 1, Henry outlines the features of war in words and accents as severe as the portrait they draw:

> In peace there's nothing so becomes a man
> As modest stillness and humility.
> But when the blast of war blows in our ears,
> Then imitate the action of the tiger;
> Stiffen the sinews, summon up the blood,
> Disguise fair nature with hard-favored rage;
> Let it pry through the portage of the head
> Like the brass cannon; let the brow o'erwhelm it
> As fearfully as doth a galled rock
> O'erhang and jutty his confounded base,
> Swill'd with the wild and wasteful ocean.
> Now set the teeth and stretch the nostril wide,
> Hold hard the breath and bend up every spirit
> To his full height.

The honey-tongued Shakespeare of the Sonnets and lyrical plays has vanished from this verse, which is appropriately as hard as the man who speaks it and the action he is engaged in.

The Action and the Characters. Along with its consistently brilliant use of prose and poetry, the histories are eminently teachable because of their exciting action and vivid characterizations. Both histories bristle with action, and more specifically with action that grows out of, or into, conflict. The idea of conflict, in fact, pervades the whole substance of the two histories. It is manifest not only in the savage skirmishes of fighting forces and the deadly single combats of mighty opposites like Hal and Hotspur, Glendower and Mortimer (described as vividly by Hotspur as though it were witnessed directly), but in the deliberate contrasts of individual men, their attitudes and values.

Some contrasts, like that of Falstaff and Hotspur on honor, are black and white, but many are shaded. Henry IV and Worcester, for example, are alike in political shrewdness but contrasted in motive, which is personal with Worcester and (presumably) public with Henry. Hal and Hotspur are opposites until the errant Hal begins to ready himself for the transformation to the ultra-heroic Henry V, when he takes on some outward flourishes of his opponent. But these two are always opposites in their essential characters: Hotspur the slave of his own uncontrolled passions, Hal the cool master of himself and his situation. Henry's battle speech quoted above is no Hotspurian outburst, but a coolly calculated utterance meant to rouse soldiers to fighting fury.

The physical conflict of French and English on the battlefield is exciting, but no less vivid is the contrast of the two national characters—the French urbane, effete, overly civilized; the English sturdy, raw-boned, and blunt. The conflict of father with son, of Hal as a young man of pleasure with Hal as a prince and king, of the Boar's Head view of life with sovereign responsibility—these subtler conflicts furnish the base from which erupt the outright wars between factions and nations.

In speaking of action, we have mentioned some of the persons who are centrally involved in it. We need add only the observation that for their array of strong character portraits, these two histories are unsurpassed. Even the supreme tragic masterpieces, like *Hamlet* and *Lear*, do not exceed them in the number of memorable portraits or in the effortless skill with which the qualities of individual human beings are revealed. In *Henry IV*, not only the principal figures of Henry, Hal, Worcester, Hotspur, Glendower, and Falstaff come through as completely realized human beings, but such minor individuals as Blunt, Mortimer, Vernon, Gadshill, Bardolph, Lady Percy, Mistress Quickly, and even the "Welsh lady," Mortimer's weeping bride, manage to reveal themselves as distinct individuals. Their dimensions are real; they can be studied in depth. The same may be said of the following persons in *Henry V*: Henry, Canterbury, Gower, Fluellen, Macmorris, Williams, Pistol, Nym, the Dauphin, Montjoy, Katharine, Alice, and the Hostess, Pistol's wife, the former Mistress Quickly.

The Themes. It has been well said that the enveloping theme of all Shakespeare's histories is England, in war and peace, with her trials and glories, her joys and griefs, her indomitable spirit, remaining intact through all manner of disruptive assaults. Throughout the histories, England stands like a rock battered by warring elements. Men and events are, in the last analysis, judged by their relations to the common welfare of the land: men like Henry IV, who stand for the national unity, are prized even though they show some personal qualities that we find unattractive; men like Worcester, who represent divisive and disruptive forces, stand condemned; even the lovable Hotspur, the warmest human being of them all, is expendable and must be sacrificed for the greater cause: "Thus ever did rebellion find rebuke."

Within the enveloping theme are several subordinate themes. We shall speak of two that are of special interest because we are concerned with the teachability of the plays. It is improbable that the great theme of England can hold particular fascination for American students, upholding as it steadily does a principle of allegiance to one sovereign king as the symbol of national unity. But the theme of *honor*, which runs through the plays and receives its fullest treatment in *Henry IV, Part 1*, has an abiding claim on the imaginations of American as well as English students.

The great exemplar of honor is Hotspur, "Mars in swathling clothes." Hotspur's view of honor is a narrow one, but nonetheless shining. He conceives it as a prize to be coveted, a personal trophy to be won by valor:

By heaven, methinks it were an easy leap
To pluck bright honor from the pale-faced moon,
Or dive into the bottom of the deep,
Where fathom-line could never touch the ground,
And pluck up drowned honor by the locks—
So he that doth redeem her thence might wear
Without corrival all her dignities.

But this honor which expresses Hotspur's sole value in life is
examined around and around, from every point of view, for though
Shakespeare creates an adorable Hotspur, hot-headed, absent-
minded, boyishly ingratiating, he is not out to "sell" his audience
on a single, slanted view. Sir Walter Blunt, wearing a royal coat
on the battlefield to deceive the enemy and protect the king, dies
for a nobler idea of honor. Hal, quite ready to turn his back on
the intimate companions of his youth and the way of life they
represent, in order to embrace sovereign responsibility, exemplifies
Blunt's kind of honor also, and on a grander scale, because he is
a prince, whose duty is the country's good. But the views of Hotspur, Blunt, and Hal together do not encompass all the attitudes
toward honor that the total play expresses. The very notion of
honor, together with such virtues as courage and self-sacrifice,
Falstaff drenches with cold water:

PRINCE. Why, thou owest God a death.
FALSTAFF. 'Tis not due yet; I would be loath to pay him
before his day. What need I be so forward with him that
calls not on me? Well, 'tis no matter; honor pricks me on.
Yea, but how if honor prick me off when I come on? How
then? Can honor set to a leg? No. Or an arm? No. Or take
away the grief of a wound? No. Honor hath no skill in
surgery, then? No. What is honor? A word. What is in
that word honor? What is that honor? Air. A trim reck-
oning!

And later, seeing Blunt dead in the king's coat, he says, "I like not
such grinning honor as Sir Walter hath."
Not less compelling than the theme of honor, and surely as
fascinating to high school students as any in literature, is the

theme of Hal himself—the ne'er-do-well who becomes the most heroic king in English history. The attraction of this theme is as basic as any that writers have discovered. It is akin to that of the ugly duckling who becomes a swan, the poor boy who becomes a millionaire, the nobody who becomes the President. Shakespeare weaves this familiar theme through four histories. It starts at the end of *Richard II*, with the newly crowned Henry IV lamenting his son's wastrel ways:

> Can no man tell me of my unthrifty son?
> 'Tis full three months since I did see him last.
> If any plague hang over us, 'tis he.
> I would to God, my lords, he might be found.
> Inquire at London, 'mongst the taverns there,
> For there, they say, he daily doth frequent,
> With unrestrained, loose companions.

It is picked up in the first scene of *Henry IV, Part 1*, when the king contrasts his Harry with Northumberland's Harry Hotspur:

> . . . A son who is the theme of honor's tongue,
> Amongst a grove the very straightest plant;
> Who is sweet Fortune's minion and her pride:
> Whilst I, by looking on the praise of him,
> See riot and dishonor stain the brow
> Of my young Harry.

The theme is never dropped for long from this time on. Hal must prove himself again and again. In the moments before his death at the end of *Henry IV, Part 2*, the father still is unsure of his son and of England's fate under his successor's rule. In the opening scenes of *Henry V*, the clergy speak with amazement of what appears to be a miraculous transformation:

> The courses of his youth promised it not.
> The breath no sooner left his father's body
> But that his wildness, mortified in him,
> Seemed to die too; yea, at that very moment
> Consideration, like an angel, came

And whipped the offending Adam out of him,
Leaving his body as a paradise,
To envelop and contain celestial spirits.

The French scorn the danger he poses for them, and as a mock at his frolicsome youth send him a present of tennis balls. It is not until Agincourt and Harfleur that Henry gives the final proofs that dispel all the world's doubts.

But the story of Hal-Henry is not so straightforward as this sketch makes it appear. Very early in *Henry IV, Part 1*, Shakespeare gives Hal a soliloquy designed to assure the audience that it need have no doubts of his metal:

. . . when this loose behavior I throw off,
And pay the debt I never promised,
By so much shall I falsify men's hopes;
And like bright metal on a sullen ground,
My reformation, glittering o'er my fault,
Shall show more goodly and attract more eyes
Than that which hath no foil to set it off.
I'll so offend, to make offense a skill,
Redeeming time when men think least I will.

With this single speech, Shapespeare created the "problem of Prince Hal." Meant to clarify Hal's character and reassure the audience, the full soliloquy enormously complicates the question of Hal and makes this prince, next only to Prince Hamlet, the most debatable subject in all the plays. It is a subject that high school students should never have done with discussing.

At the worst, critics like Hazlitt and Quiller-Couch have pronounced Hal a calculating hypocrite and "a cold prig," who has no scruples about playing games with his intimate companions all the while he intends, and boasts of intending, to cast them off when the occasion suits him. The casting off, which Hal foresaw in the soliloquy at the start of *Henry IV, Part 1*, comes at the very end of *Henry IV, Part 2*, when he emerges from the coronation and is confronted by a jubilant Falstaff waiting at the door:

FALSTAFF. My king! My Jove! I speak to thee, my heart!
KING. I know thee not, old man. Fall to thy prayers.

> How ill white hairs become a fool and jester!
> I have long dreamed of such a kind of man,
> So surfeit-swelled, so old and so profane;
> But being awaked I do despise my dream.

He goes on for twenty more cruel lines, after which Falstaff goes home to die: "The king has killed his heart."

When Shakespeare wrote the first lines about Hal, at the end of *Richard II*, he knew, of course, what Hal was destined to become, and presumably he expected eventually to show him off as the super-hero of *Henry V*. Did the dramatist know what he was doing, in having his hero play the hypocrite with his Boar's Head cronies? Or did he miscalculate, and stain his "ideal hero-king" with a fault that audiences cannot forgive? When the new King cuts down Falstaff with cold, cruel words, Shakespeare appears to be making a point in the extremest terms he could invent; he seems to be saying: "Thus one must be, and do, to be a king." In saying so, he states no less than the cold reality. Obviously, the great king could no longer keep about him this great "bombard of sack" who stood symbolically for all that is opposite to what a great king must represent. But even if we can fully understand and accept Henry the King, are we not forever divided from Hal the man?

The Balance of Elements. We began by saying that one reason for the infrequent use of these histories in the schools may be the fact that they are histories, and not comedies or tragedies—clear dramatic genres the very designations of which are attractive. But it should be possible to make a strong case for the histories on the grounds of their balance of comic and tragic elements.

Now it is true that Shakespeare's comedies and tragedies, too, unlike the comedies and tragedies of classical tradition, have a certain balance of elements that contributes greatly to the pleasure that students find in them. No Shakespearean comedy fails to include, along with much that is fun, some serious, poignant, suspenseful moments. Even in a farce like *The Comedy of Errors*, the fate of pitiful old Aegeon overhangs all the comic incidents; and in the great romantic comedies, without exception, grief and danger enrich the effects of the most famous moments (e.g. Shylock with knife poised above Antonio's breast).

On the other hand, the major tragedies all have some comic incidents, situations, characters. *Romeo and Juliet* and *Hamlet* lead all the rest in comic proportions, but *Julius Caesar* is relieved by blunt Casca, *Macbeth* by the drunken Porter, and *King Lear* by the Fool.

But for a truly abundant feast of elements uproariously comic and profoundly serious, the histories of *Henry IV, Part 1* and *Henry V* are unmatched. The seriousness of the historical themes has already been touched upon; here, we need speak only briefly of the comic riches which engulf this seriousness and blend with it to make rare entertainment.

If one had to make a choice of comic characters and comic incidents to head a list of the "best" in Shakespeare, some of both would certainly be drawn from these two plays. The list would, of course, be headed by the peerless Falstaff, and the scenes in which he appears. Supported by Hal's wit, Bardolph's simplicity, and the Hostess's flustered bird-brain, his comic dimensions, like his physical ones, are without limit, "out of all compass."

Hazlitt said that the comic characters of *Henry V*, lacking Falstaff, are like satellites with no sun; yet they do very well on their own. Pistol, a grotesque caricature of the braggart soldier, all talk and no action, furnishes a preposterous counterpoise to the main heroic theme and to the sober heroics of Henry himself. Only Shakespeare would dare do such a thing—weave throughout his play a kind of subversive commentary on its main theme and its epic hero. Nym, Fluellen, and Macmorris, each somewhat mad in his own way, lend ample support to Pistol. Yet some of the best comedy is provided by persons who are not primarily comic figures at all. Katharine's English lesson under the tutelage of Alice and King Henry's wooing of Katharine rank among the finest comic scenes in all of literature. If the rollicking fun of these scenes is exceeded by any in Shakespeare, it must be only by that in which Fluellen makes Pistol eat the detested leek.

In the last analysis, perhaps it is the balance of elements that most recommends these histories for teaching: the balance of comedy and tragedy, the balance of prose and poetry, the balance of attitudes toward matters like honor and courage, the balance of many other elements on which we have not touched.

We have been supposing that these two histories will be studied one after the other. Each, of course, can be read alone, for each has a built-in wholeness; but the two together make a greater whole and offer a total experience that is too good to miss. In less than half an hour, a teacher can bridge over the intervening play of *Henry IV, Part 2* by touching on the main points of Hal's personal story that are there represented: his part in the defeat of rebel factions, the incident of the crown, which ends in his dying father's final acceptance of him, and above all, his repudiation of Falstaff.

CHAPTER 11

Special Notes on Six Plays: Outside Reading

SHAKESPEARE OFFERS AN EMBARRASSMENT OF RICHES. IN EARLIER chapters we have suggested specific procedures for teaching four plays and directed attention to selected aspects that deserve special consideration in the teaching of four others. And *yet* we are left with six plays—each in its own way too magnificent for high school students to miss—about which we have said nothing. The plays, with the years in which they might be taught, are *The Merchant of Venice* and *The Taming of the Shrew* (grade nine or ten); *Twelfth Night* and *The Winter's Tale* (grade eleven or twelve); and *King Lear* and *The Tempest* (grade twelve). What can we do about these?

Are they plays that students can read on their own? As a matter of fact, because of the prior claims of competing plays, they are most often used in this way—or not used at all. This is not to say that none of them is ever taught as "first choice" in a given year. *The Merchant of Venice* sometimes crowds out *As You Like It* and even *Julius Caesar* as the tenth-grade play; and when *Macbeth* has been taught in the eleventh grade, *King Lear* or *The Tempest* sometimes crowds out *Hamlet* as the twelfth-grade play. *Twelfth Night* serves very rarely as the play in grade eleven or twelve. *The Taming of the Shrew* rarely and *The Winter's Tale* probably never displace conventional choices.

Unfortunately, few of these plays that are often left to students on their own are particularly good choices for independent reading. *The Taming of the Shrew* is a strange jamming together (rather than a smooth blending) of two comic genres. The Shrew plot, all farce, is no problem, but the Bianca plot, with its romantic comedy devices of disguise, exchanged and mistaken identities, its linguistic quirks and situational mix-ups, and its added complication of the Christopher Sly frame, is a hard one to keep straight merely at the level of what is going on. The main argument for leaving the play for outside reading is that, as Shakespeare goes, it is a lightweight work which should not replace any of the plays conventionally studied intensively in the ninth and tenth grades. It could be taught in either of these years, but it does not make satisfactory outside reading for ninth graders, or for tenth graders unless they have already studied three or four plays. It could best be handled outside by eleventh or twelfth graders.

The Merchant of Venice belongs among the first three "most open" major plays. Unlike *The Taming of the Shrew*, it would make a worthy replacement for *As You Like It* or *A Midsummer Night's Dream*, which are more often taught in the early years. It can be read outside more easily than the latter. But one objection to reading it outside is that Shylock, who needs careful examination, may emerge for the immature reader as an ugly caricature of his race. Juniors and seniors who know how to examine and judge dramatic characters as dramatic characters might do well with Shylock on their own, but with sophomores it would be better to teach *The Merchant of Venice* and give *As You Like It* to independent reading.

Twelfth Night, having no Shylock and no peculiar difficulties, seems an admirable choice for outside reading, possibly in the eleventh grade but preferably in the twelfth. On the other hand, *Twelfth Night* is so rich in the poetic and dramatic qualities that distinguish Shakespeare at his finest that it is dangerous to assign it for outside reading, where all that is exquisite in the comedy is likely to be missed. It would be an entirely worthy replacement for *any* play that is more frequently used for close study in the upper years.

The Winter's Tale is probably the most appropriate of the six plays for outside reading. Though its verse is knottier than that of *Twelfth Night* and though as a "dramatic romance" it will confront students with a strange kind of experience for which their previous reading in the genres of comedy, tragedy, and history will not entirely have prepared them, yet, like *The Taming of the Shrew* and unlike *Twelfth Night*, it falls *outside* the group of "major" plays that leaving for outside reading seems wicked. Thus, though it is harder than *Twelfth Night*, students on their own will miss less in it because there is less in it to miss. Seniors, or juniors who have already read seven or eight plays, should do well with it independently.

Finally, *King Lear* and *The Tempest* make almost unthinkable choices for outside reading, the first because of its profundity, and the second because of its strangeness. They deserve, and need, to be taught.

But if these plays *cannot* be included in the tight circle of works that are to be studied in class line by line, is it better for students to miss them entirely than to risk misreading and misunderstanding them on their own? The very thought—of missing them—appears monstrous. Aside from exceptional students, probably freshmen and sophomores should not try any of these plays on their own; but juniors and seniors who have learned to read Shakespeare through close classroom study of five or six plays should certainly try the first four. *King Lear* and *The Tempest* should be recommended to exceptional seniors—and to any others who have closely studied a dozen plays.

Knowing that the going will not be easy, the teacher should guide the student's independent reading by providing detailed questions on lines, scenes, and acts. We have earlier deplored the independent-reading-with-study-questions method as a *substitute* for classroom reading with discussion. But it does not follow that, when one play is read closely in class, study questions are undesirable for a second play to be read independently. Or that if two plays are read closely in class, students should not be provided with study questions to them with a third play to be read on their own.

We have deplored the use of study questions with Shakespeare (and literature generally) because students so naturally fall into the vicious habit of reading for the purpose of finding the "right answers." It is impossible for the experience of literature to seep through any such straining device; and since it is the *experience* of literature that we value, we must deplore any method that blocks it. On the other hand, the experience of literature will certainly not reach a reader who does not understand the work, who does not read closely enough to permit any really intimate relation to grow between the work and himself, who may not even guess what is more and less important or at what points there is need to stop and ponder. It appears, then, that for many students reading on their own, a certain amount of guidance is necessary. But not too much, and not too soon.

The best kind of help *during* their reading can be supplied by the edition itself, which will gloss words and phrases and explain or paraphrase troublesome lines and passages. We have mentioned earlier a number of modern editions of Shakespeare that are authoritative and inexpensive. Clearly, an adequately glossed text is crucial for students reading on their own. Good editions can be counted on to provide not only appropriate textual assistance, but illuminating introductions which help as guides to critical reading. For high school students probably the least useful introductions are those that emphasize source, date, condition of text, and the like; and the most useful are those that raise critical questions and identify, without categorically solving, problems of interpretation. The best of the contemporary paperback editions keep an admirable balance of "scholarly" and critical matter.

So much for help from the edition. What more can, or should, the teacher provide? We suggest that *after* the students have read the play through once, the teacher provide them with a sheet that will (1) guide their second reading of the play; and (2) give them a means of reporting what they have read. This guide should include comments and questions (both general and specific), and it ought to suggest possible subjects for writing based on provocative aspects of the play.

The following pages may be of some help to teachers in preparing these guide sheets. The suggestions they contain are mainly intended for use with plays read independently, but they may also be of some use when any of these six plays is studied closely in class. Plays read independently provide excellent opportunities for composition. Thus, these suggestions call for at least one substantially developed, critically thoughtful paragraph on each act in the play, and, also, for a brief essay on one of several possible subjects. The intent is not that students should routinely report on their reading, but that they should seriously practice the art of composition.

The Merchant of Venice

Act I. Starting with Venice in Scene 1, moving to Belmont in Scene 2, and then returning to Venice, Act I fully establishes the foundation on which rests the action of the next four acts. Describe clearly the state of things at the end of Act I, including the situation in Venice, the situation in Belmont, and the significant relation of each situation to the other. (Paragraph)

Shylock and Antonio dislike each other intensely. On the evidence of Scene 3 alone, explain whether one or the other is wholly to blame. Or do both share responsibility for their mutual hostility? Study closely all that each man says. (Paragraph)

The worst thing that critics have said about Bassanio is that he is a fortune-hunter, eager to replenish his wasted means even at the risk of his dearest friend's life. Is this criticism wholly just? Too severe? Not severe enough? What can you say of Bassanio—the romantic hero of this play—on the basis of his conduct in this act? (Paragraph)

Act II. This is an unusually "busy" act, with its nine scenes that bring together incidents of great variety in both Venice and Belmont. Surveying these varied incidents, we might mistakenly think that we are watching two or three different plays at the same time, rather than a single one in which the central plot concerns the bond signed by Antonio and Shylock. Act II would truly be a poor piece of dramatic composition if its individual scenes—however entertaining they may be within themselves—should fail to bear upon this central issue. Take the three main actions represented by these nine scenes (Launcelot's change of place, Jessica's elopement, and the wooers' failures in Belmont) and show how each does in fact relate to the main plot. (Paragraph)

Act III. Unlike the nine scenes of Act II, the first four scenes of Act III relate very obviously and directly to the bond plot. The fifth scene of the act, showing Lorenzo, Jessica, and Launcelot enjoying themselves in Portia's fabulous villa, furnishes a breath of relief after the dark anxieties of the preceding four scenes. Thus the act begins with the direst predictions of tragedy to come—with rumors (soon to be confirmed) of Antonio's losses and of Shylock's determination to have his murderous revenge; but it ends on the gay note of happy honeymooners. Scenes 1 and 3 are particularly ominous, and even after the joyful scene that ends the act we cannot forget that Antonio must still face his implacable enemy. But this is, after all, a comedy, not a tragedy, and the total act (even in the most ominous scenes) keeps us reminded of this fact. How does it do so? (Consider, for example, the distinctly *comic* elements mixed in with dire moments; the hints—such as Portia's mysterious purposes that are half hidden and half expressed in Scene 4—that there may somehow be hope for Antonio after all; and, of course, the effect of the final scene.) (Paragraph)

Act IV. Very possibly no other single scene in all Shakespeare presents as full and varied a dramatic feast as the famous Court Scene, which takes up nearly the whole of Act IV. It serves up suspense, terror, humor both gay and grotesque (Shylock whetting his dagger on his sole), exhilaration, pity. In Portia's "quality of mercy" speech, it contains one of the three or four most famous passages in all Shakespeare. It presents an exciting confrontation of two powerful figures (Shylock and Portia), meeting in a head-on clash of contrasting human values. The scene might be said to be a whole play in itself, beginning with a deadly dangerous situation from which there seems no possible escape, and working its way to a happy solution (at least for Antonio and all his friends). The action accomplishes a complete reversal of the situation: Antonio begins doomed and ends triumphant; Shylock begins triumphant and ends broken. Following the scene closely, write a history *as honest and accurate as possible* of your own emotional progress throughout it, step by step. Make clear what affected you at particular moments. (For example, what effect on you did Shylock's whetting his knife produce? What effect did the "quality of mercy" speech produce? What effect did Portia's "Tarry a little. There is something else" produce? What effect did Shylock's "I am content" produce?) (Paragraph)

Act V. The fifth act is obviously needed to complete the "ring plot" which is begun in the final scene of Act IV. But setting aside that necessity, consider what function this final act serves in relation to the whole play. Would it have been as satisfactory to have Portia and Nerissa reveal their identities at the close of the Court Scene? What purpose is served by having the play end at Belmont? (Remember that the first four acts have involved a good deal of unpleasantness.) (Paragraph)

The Play as a Whole. The title of the play is *The Merchant of Venice.* Yet Antonio, the Merchant, does not stand out like Shylock or Portia, or perhaps even like Bassanio, the romantic hero. (Some readers have even mistakenly supposed that the "Merchant" is Shylock.) On what grounds can you demonstrate that Shakespeare did (or did not) name his play correctly? (Brief essay)

Shylock might be played as (1) a truly wicked villain who gets what is coming to him; (2) a grotesque, comic monster who makes us laugh rather than hate and fear; (3) a fellow human being, as much "sinned against" as sinning, whose suffering moves us to sympathetic tears; (4) a composite of these, not wholly blameless nor wholly to be blamed, who sometimes makes us fear, sometimes laugh, and sometimes sympathize. Using all the evidence that the play provides, present your own view of Shylock. (If it is approximately like No. 4 above, show at what times Shylock is a fearful villain, a comic figure, and a "tragic hero.") (Brief essay)

Is the judgment given Shylock at the end of the Court Scene (1) just; (2) too harsh; (3) too merciful? (Brief essay)

The Court Scene opens on a dark and apparently hopeless situation, for there seems literally no way for the gentle Antonio to escape Shylock's knife. Money, pleas, legal authority are powerless; Antonio must pay the penalty. But then, at the moment Portia steps into the scene, a change often occurs in the mood of the audience. People sit back more comfortably in their chairs, and emit a sigh of relief. All is well: Portia can deal with *any* situation. Study the character of Portia closely, from the time she is first mentioned until her appearance in the Court. Then see whether you can explain the "magic" of Shakespeare's skill in characterization: just why is it that the mere entrance of this heroine at a perilous moment can make a whole audience suddenly breathe more easily? (Brief essay)

The Taming of the Shrew

Act I. Elsewhere Shakespeare showed "players" performing a play, or part of a play, within the framework of the main play. Thus, for example, in *A Midsummer Night's Dream* Bottom and his fellow actors stage "Pyramus and Thisbe" before Duke Theseus and his court. Explain how the relation of the Christopher Sly "play" to *The Taming of the Shrew* differs from the relation of "Pyramus and Thisbe" to *A Midsummer Night's Dream*. (We think of "Pyramus and Thisbe" as being twice removed from reality, because it is a play *within* a play that is itself once removed from reality. But which play is here twice removed—Sly's, or the Shrew's plot itself? What implications can you find in this for the manner in which these two "plays" should be performed? Which, for example, should be performed more realistically?) (Paragraph)

Shakespeare never began another play with such a tangled situation as this which has developed by the end of Act I. Omitting Sly's situation (which is an additional complication), we have Petruchio, Gremio, Hortensio, Tranio, and Lucentio all caught up in a knot of intrigues. Explain the full situation as it stands at the end of the act—who is deceiving whom, who is aiding whom, who is aware and who is not aware of others' secret plans, etc. (This initial understanding is indispensable to an understanding of all that follows.) (Paragraph)

Act II. Christopher Sly is not so much as mentioned in the second act. But what elements in the action—in the opening incident involving Katherina and Bianca, in Petruchio's "wooing" of Kate, and in the bidding for Bianca by Gremio and Tranio—serve to remind us that what we are witnessing is twice removed from reality—a play within a play? (Paragraph)

Act III. This longest act of the play carries both main plots forward at a rapid pace. The two "affairs" going on (the taming of Kate and the wooing of Bianca) vie with each other for attention. Does one or the other win out? At the end of the act, are you more involved with the Shrew plot or with the Bianca plot? Or are you concerned equally with both? (Paragraph)

The act would be even longer except that Shakespeare contrives to tell much more than he actually represents by direct action. Specifically, on three occasions he supplements stage action in the Shrew plot by other means. What are these occasions, and what is gained (or lost) by this practice? Would you have preferred to *see* the action on these occasions? (You might begin by considering Biondello's account of Petruchio's arrival in town on his wedding day.) (Paragraph)

Act IV. Though the two plots have developed side by side, with a considerable number of direct connections between them, it is in Act IV that Shakespeare deliberately binds them tightly together by several means, beginning with the rather unexpected entrance of Hortensio in Petruchio's house. What means, in terms of persons and incidents, serve this unifying function—without which we should be in danger of having two plays rather than a single whole? (Paragraph)

This act also presents the most concentrated lesson in how to tame a shrew. What means (in detail) does Petruchio use? At the end of the act, what evidence is there that the task is finished? (As a start, you might refer to Petruchio's soliloquy at the end of III, 3.) (Paragraph)

Act V. Obviously, the main action of this act demonstrates the complete triumph of Petruchio in taming his shrew. But the fifth act of a Shakespearean comedy typically does much more than bring the affair of the hero and heroine to a happy conclusion. It achieves a universally happy ending—all persons, all lines of action join in the general harmony that will last "forever after." Thus, for example, at the end of A *Midsummer Night's Dream* Theseus and Hippolyta are married, the fairy king and queen are reconciled, and Bottom and his crew of players are warmly applauded and rewarded. Is everyone content at the end of *The Taming of the Shrew?* Consider each of the principal characters —not forgetting, for example, Gremio and Tranio. (At the end of Act IV, Vincentio threatened to be revenged for the tricks played on him. Will he deal harshly with Tranio and Biondello? And as for Gremio—unlike Hortensio, who won a widow, and Lucentio, who won Bianca—he wins nobody. Is he "left out" of the universal happiness?) (Paragraph)

The Play as a Whole. Whatever became of Christopher Sly? Should we not have expected a final scene, after the play is over, which would somehow dispose of him? (Write such a scene.)

Going back to the subject of your paragraph on Act II, reconsider what use the Sly device, which makes the entire action a "play within a play," is to the play as a whole. Would you expect —or even demand—that incidents and characters be more credible, less "wild" if there were no Sly? Which aspects of the play— characters, incidents, plot developments—here seem more appropriate to a "play within a play" than to a play? Does Petruchio, for example, seem more like a creature you would expect to find in the former than in the latter? (Brief essay)

The Taming of the Shrew is not especially noted for richly developed characters. There is no Bottom, no Falstaff, no Sir Toby Belch. But no doubt the characters are developed just enough to be "right" for the purposes of *farce* comedy, where the fun arises mainly from action and situation. Thus the plot itself requires the characters to be as they are, whereas in the later great plays it is because the characters are as they are that the plot develops along the lines it does. Choose at least three principal figures in the play and show how their characterization is made to serve the needs of plot. (Brief essay)

Twelfth Night

Act I. Two dramatic situations are already in existence before Viola, fished from the sea, lands on the shores of Illyria: (1) Duke Orsino is laying futile siege to the heart of the lady Olivia; but this is a stalemated situation because Olivia has vowed to spend seven years in mourning for her dead brother; (2) Sir Toby Belch, Olivia's cake-and-ale-loving uncle, is exploiting the wealth of his simple-minded friend Sir Andrew Aguecheek while pretending to promote Sir Andrew's love-suit to Olivia; this situation, too, is static and might continue indefinitely, or at least as long as Sir

Andrew's money lasts. Viola's arrival, with her sudden determination to masquerade as a young man, creates a third situation that is not static, but dynamic, and likely to break things wide open in Illyria. What is the state of things, with respect to all three situations, at the end of the act? (Paragraph)

Act II. In Scene 1, Sebastian, Viola's twin brother, arrives in Illyria. In Scene 2, Malvolio overtakes Viola, gives her Olivia's ring, and leaves her profoundly distressed over the hopelessness of her situation—hopelessly loving Orsino and hopelessly loved by Olivia. In Scene 3, Maria and her friends, furious because the pompous and high-handed Malvolio stopped their drunken cater-wauling, plot revenge. In Scene 4, Orsino and Viola hold a bitter-sweet interview ending with Viola's departure for a second attempt to win Olivia for Orsino. In Scene 5, Malvolio falls into the trap laid by Maria and shows every likelihood of making a great fool of himself. At least three of these are among the richest scenes in the play and in Shakespearean comedy, comically, poetically, and otherwise. But one of the five is loaded with the greatest significance for the entire play and all its situations. Which is this, and why? (Paragraph)

Act III. The act includes four scenes, of which three are rich and full, while the other (Scene 3) mainly exists to keep the audience posted on Sebastian's movements. But it is Scene 4 that is the Big One. Shakespeare regularly made the final scene of Act III (sometimes the first scene of Act IV) the climactic scene in his comedies, and this one deserves its place. If *Twelfth Night* represents the pinnacle of Shakespearean comedy, and if this scene is the pinnacle of *Twelfth Night*, then Scene 4 truly holds a unique position. It is formed of three distinct episodes: (a) Malvolio's mad appearance in yellow stockings and a ridiculous smile; (b) the "duel" of Sir Andrew and Viola-Cesario; and (c) the arrest of Sebastian's friend, Antonio. But none of these incidents could "come over" with any notable dramatic effect if they had not been *prepared* for in advance. (Someone has remarked that two-thirds of Shakespeare's dramatic art consists of preparation for such scenes as this one.) Take any one of the three incidents and show in detail how Shakespeare prepared in preceding acts and scenes for its exploitation here. (Paragraph)

Act IV. "Nothing that is so is so," says Feste, the Clown, and "Are all the people mad?" asks Sebastian when a total stranger (Sir Toby) strikes him in the street. Viola-Cesario has deceived all Illyria, with the result that the outsider, Sebastian, walking into the situation that his sister has created, suspects that all the inhabitants are mad, and even questions his own sanity. Sebastian's affairs take up Scenes 1 and 3 of this act. Between these, stands the scene in which the Clown and others bring their baiting of Malvolio to a hilarious, furious close. Show how the theme of "madness"—which is not really madness, but the result of deception—unifies the entire act, with the Malvolio incident complementing the major plot of the play. (Paragraph)

Act V. It sometimes appears as though Shakespeare wrote the first four acts of a romantic comedy in order to bring about a single, excitingly dramatic moment in the fifth act, when all the compounded mysteries are cleared away in an instant. In *Twelfth Night*, this instant is the face-to-face meeting of brother and sister in full sight of everyone. Curiously, the greatest astonishment is expressed by Viola herself, who seems to take Sebastian for a ghost: "If spirits can assume both form and suit,/You come to fright us." Can you justify Viola's apparent amazement? Has she not had good cause to suspect that her brother is not only alive but here in Illyria? Further, from the very first she was given cause to expect that he might have survived. Review the evidence and then, as best you can, explain her statement of disbelief. (Paragraph)

The Play as a Whole. Three main lines of action, or "affairs," make up the total play: the affair of Viola-Cesario with Orsino and Olivia; the Toby-Andrew affair; and the Malvolio affair. It would be a disunified, wretched play if these three affairs went on quite independently of one another. They are in fact woven together rather tightly, and have become inseparable after the first two acts. Examine their points of contact with one another. It is easy to see, for example, how Viola's affair runs afoul of the Toby-Andrew affair: Sir Andrew challenges "Cesario" as a rival for Olivia's hand. But how does Viola's affair connect with Malvolio's (which consists of his aspiration to be "Count Malvolio" and of the mistreatment brought on him by Maria and others)? And how does the Toby-Andrew affair connect with Malvolio's? (Brief essay)

Rosalind of *As You Like It* is robust, aggressive, buoyant, mischievous, capable, in her masquerade as a young man, of dealing with anyone she meets and with any troublesome situation that may arise. Portia of *The Merchant of Venice* is so brilliantly capable that she seems more like a goddess than a woman; it is unimaginable that any problem could be too much for her—and, in fact, none is. In contrast to these powerful heroines, Viola, on first realizing what a predicament she has got herself into, cries "O Time, thou must untangle this, not I!/It is too hard a knot for me to untie!" Rosalind or Portia would not have waited on time, but would have untied the knot with their own hands. Viola is the most completely feminine of the great romantic heroines. First, demonstrate the truth of this observation (if you find that it *is* true); and, second, show why, for the purposes of this particular play and its dramatic and comic effects, it is better for Viola to be as she is, rather than like Portia or Rosalind. (Suppose, for example, that Portia, not Viola, had been challenged by the feeble simpleton, Sir Andrew Aguecheek. How would the dramatic effects have been altered? Further, does this ultimate femininity of Viola partially answer the question asked about Act V, when she expresses astonishment at sight of Sebastian?) (Brief essay)

Though the play is a comedy, with boisterous moments and bellylaugh situations, and with outlandish characters with gross names like Belch and Aguecheek, its best effects are not all comic. Shakespeare at this point seems not to have been content with laughter alone, but chose to stir multiple emotions in the audience. Often he appears to aim at laughter and tears simultaneously. Take, for example, the interview of Orsino and "Cesario" in II,4. Here the *situation* calls for laughter—the Duke, all unaware of the real prize he has in his own household, sends Viola-Cesario off as love-emissary to another. But though the situation is basically comic, note the tone maintained by the poetry, and note also the haunting sadness of the Clown's song. What additional scenes seem also to strive for mutually contradictory effects, for such mixed emotions as these? By what means does Shakespeare accomplish these multiple effects? (Consider the quality of the poetry, the use of song, the character of the persons involved in the scene.) Finally, is the play better, or worse, for its blending of contrasting effects and contrary emotions? (Brief essay)

Not a few critics, readers, and spectators in the theater have expressed pity for Malvolio, chided his persecutors, and blamed Shakespeare for dealing too harshly with this "poor fellow," who at the end is the only one not included in the happy circle. (He says, "I'll be revenged on the whole pack of you!") Review the whole case of Malvolio and make clear your own verdict on him. Does he deserve the treatment he gets? Even if he does deserve it, *should* he get it? (Brief essay)

The Winter's Tale

Act I. The first scene exists to describe the closeness of the friendship that binds together Leontes and Polixenes. Archidamus sums everything up by saying, "I think there is not in the world either malice or matter to alter it." He proves a very bad prophet. After one hundred lines of Scene 2, Leontes has become suspicious of his friend and his wife, and after another hundred lines is ready to order Polixenes' death by poison. Nothing can shake his convictions that his wife is false and Polixenes a traitor. He questions whether even his son Mamillius (who looks just like his father) is truly his son. On the stage, the whole reversal, from Leontes as jovial friend and host to Leontes as jealous madman, takes less than half an hour. In that space, Shakespeare had two dramatic tasks to accomplish, both difficult: (1) to make the sudden change in Leontes appear credible to the audience; (2) at the same time, to make it perfectly clear to the audience that Leontes' suspicions are completely groundless. Here is a fine chance to study a master dramatist at work. How does he do each? (One paragraph if the subjects can be united; otherwise two)

Act II. Early in Scene 1, the child Mamillius says to his mother, "A sad tale's best for winter. I have one/ Of sprites and goblins." "Come on, then," says Hermione, "And give 't me in mine ear." At that instant, a furious Leontes enters and, it has been said, the "winter's tale" begins. What do you find in the words, movement, and events of Act II, that makes this little dialogue of mother and son an apt introduction? (Paragraph)

Act III. In Scene 1, Shakespeare gives Hermione three long speeches, made in an extremely trying situation, that stamp her as one of his noblest female characters. Using these speeches (and the entire scene as context), write a character sketch aimed at revealing her exact nature. (Paragraph)

Paulina enters unannounced in Act II, Scene 2, with no prior characterization and all but dominates the stage each moment she is present until the end of Act III, Scene 2. Like Hermione, she has extraordinarily well-defined qualities. Using all the evidence you find in Acts II and III, write a character sketch that makes these qualities clear and pointed. (Paragraph)

Act III contains one stage direction that is like no other in Shakespeare. It is famous, and has been used as the title of a book. Identify it, and then show how just such a stage direction befits the plot and "world" of this play. (You may want to remember, for example, the question asked about Act II.) (Paragraph)

Act IV. Except that we knew Polixenes and Camillo earlier and in different circumstances, Act IV introduces a totally new world; it is as though a new play, in a happier mood, begins when Time turns his hourglass at the opening of the act and sixteen years have passed. After the nightmare of Acts I, II, and III, much of Act IV seems like a pleasant dream. The idyllic romance of Perdita (a shepherdess who does not know her real identity as a princess) and Florizel (a prince who masquerades as a shepherd) is a delightful interlude. Autolycus, a rogue "littered under Mercury," sings charming songs; there is music, and shepherds dance. The sheepshearing feast of Scene 3—the longest single scene in Shakespeare—presents one of the most enchanting spectacles in Shakespearean comedy, rich in color, music, and movement. There is nothing else quite like it in any other play.

But, of course, it is also much more than a delightfully rich spectacle. All the while that the gaiety continues, an undercurrent of darker meanings flows on also, and this breaks suddenly into the open when King Polixenes throws off his disguise and confronts his son. At that moment the idyllic dream is shattered,

and the violent storm of Polixenes' threats against the old Shepherd, Florizel, and Perdita is bitterly reminiscent of Leontes
court in Sicilia. All the troubles of the first three acts, to which
this sudden turn of events is closely linked, surge in anew, and
the fresh, happy younger generation of Perdita and Florizel is
caught up in the old, bitter affairs of their parents.

Study the scene closely after Polixenes reveals himself, and
watch particularly the actions of two people—Camillo and Autolycus. Make clear not only *what* each intends to do, but the *motives*
of each. Are they motivated by loyalty to the King, to the lovers,
or by self-interest? The problem will involve a careful character
study of each. (Two paragraphs, or one if they can be woven
together)

Act V. The final act brings about two reunions: both Perdita
and Hermione are restored to Leontes. The first of these we
should certainly have expected, but the second is a complete
surprise, for Hermione was earlier reported dead, and the dramatist
provided us with no "aside" to tell us that she was not *really* dead.
Shakespeare handles the two reunions in markedly different ways.
Compare them, and decide which of the two is handled more to
your personal satisfaction. (Paragraph)

The Play as a Whole. Whereas *The Merchant of Venice, As
You Like It,* and *Twelfth Night* are called "romantic comedies,"
The Winter's Tale (along with *Cymbeline* and *The Tempest*)
is usually identified as a "dramatic romance." Since both groups
of plays are invariably "romantic" and end happily, and since
both have a good many similarities—use of disguise, hero and
heroine, clowns, etc.), it is not always quite clear why they should
be differentiated by name. If you know one (or more) of the
romantic comedies well, compare and contrast it with *The Winter's Tale* with the purpose of showing that there is or is not
reason for differentiation. (Brief essay)

If you know well the hero and heroine of one of the romantic
comedies, compare and contrast them and their roles in the play
with Perdita and Florizel and the parts they play in the total
drama. (Brief essay)

The romantic comedies were written from ten to fifteen years earlier than *The Winter's Tale*. In that time, Shakespeare's poetic style changed markedly. The poetry of this play well exemplifies Shakespeare's final style. Using passages of poetry from an earlier comedy and passages from this play, characterize the qualities of each. Is one more musical? More filled with imagery? More elaborate? More succinct? Metrically more regular? (Brief essay)

If the play had ended with Scene 2 of Act III, it might have stood as a three-act tragedy, with Leontes and all that was dear to him destroyed by a defect of his own character, as are Brutus and Macbeth. Discuss the first three acts of *The Winter's Tale* as tragedy, and Leontes as a tragic hero, using an earlier tragic play you know well for comparison. (Brief essay)

King Lear

Act I. The first act of *King Lear* moves with great speed, carrying the plot forward a considerable distance in a short space of time, as though Shakespeare wanted to get the preliminaries out of the way in order to come to what follows—the ordeal of Lear. Succinctly review the events of the first act (including the affairs of both Lear and Gloucester), ending with a clear statement of the final situation. (Paragraph)

Act II. One of the intriguing questions of this play is the conduct of Kent in II,2. If Kent is anything, he is a man of good common sense. Though in Act I he risked losing his head by standing up to the angry Lear, he did so in a good cause, knowing perfectly well what he was doing. But in the present case, he behaves so badly, first with Oswald and then with Cornwall and Regan, that he is put in the stocks. To stock a king's man—if one had respect for the king—was an unthinkable offense; yet Kent's outrageous behavior left Cornwall no other choice. Explain why Kent behaves so outrageously. Does he, carried away by dislike of Oswald and the emotions of the moment, lose control of himself? Or does he deliberately, for some calculated purpose, behave so badly in order to bring punishment on himself? If the latter, what possible purpose or purposes can he have had in mind? (Paragraph)

Act III. This act begins on a high note of hope: Cordelia and a French army are coming to the rescue of Lear's kingdom. But it ends on a low note of sheer bestiality: Gloucester's eyes are gouged from his head. In between Scenes 1 and 7 all is violence and villainy: the storm rages, Edmund betrays his father, Lear goes mad, Edgar as "Poor Tom" exceeds the wildness of both nature and Lear with an exhibition of the ultimate chaos in mind and universe. But in the very midst of this universal tumult, something happens to King Lear that marks the beginning of his redemption, of his becoming a wiser and better man. It is as though Shakespeare would demonstrate what he wrote elsewhere, that "there is a soul of goodness in things evil." Identify the moment, or moments, of change in Lear, and discuss their significance. (Paragraph)

Act IV. Three "main lines" run through this act: that of Edgar and Gloucester; of the wicked sisters' rivalry for Edmund and for power; and of Cordelia and Lear. Two of these lines progress toward a kind of triumph in the midst of tragedy; the other line is plainly headed for disaster. At the end of the act, the battle is imminent that will decide issues. But for the moment setting aside that battle, and all the events that will come in Act V, consider what elements in Act IV appear to be making toward a happy ending, as in a comedy. If the play ended with Act IV, in what sense could we say that the ending is "happy" for Edgar and Gloucester? For Cordelia and Lear? And if a happy ending may be thought to include the defeat of evil, how does the obvious direction taken by the Regan-Edmund-Goneril affair contribute to it? (Paragraph)

Act V. It has sometimes been said that Lear dies not "in pure grief," but "in pure joy." What argument can you make for either opinion? (Paragraph)

The Play as a Whole. King Lear presents one of Shakespeare's strongest portraits of savage man in a savage universe. One means by which the portrait is given force is the concentration on *beast imagery.* Study all the imagery of the play (there is other imagery, besides beast imagery, that also contributes to the dominant impression of savagery), and, having collected the evidence, show how it contributes to the drama—to its unity, its power, its "meaning." (Brief essay)

The story of Lear could exist, and make a strong tragedy, even if the entire story of Gloucester were pruned away. Edmund, for example, could function in the Lear plot exactly as he now does, without any relation to Edgar and Gloucester. True, with no Gloucester story we should miss the great moment of the "leap" from Dover cliff, and we should miss Edgar's theatrical exhibitions of madness. But the fact is that the whole story of Lear could easily be told without the Gloucester story. Further, it is sometimes said that Gloucester's affairs interrupt Lear's story in scene after scene, the implication being that such interruption is unfortunate. It is felt that we become involved in Lear's problems, only to have them laid aside for a scene or two while Gloucester's story is carried forward. Perhaps there are even moments when the reader or spectator asks himself in exasperation, "Whose story is this, anyhow—Lear's, or Gloucester's?" Did Shakespeare do his play a service or an injury, by telling the stories of both fathers? (Brief essay)

Among the words that are underscored by frequent repetition throughout the play are *nature, natural, unnatural.* What do these words mean? They are used not by one speaker, but by several persons. Do they mean the same thing to all who speak them? What significance do you find in the conspicuous emphasis Shakespeare puts on them? They seem like key words of the tragedy—but keys to what? Discuss the use, and dramatic usefulness, of these words in the play. (Brief essay)

We customarily say that in a great tragedy the hero is not static (i.e., unchanging), but learns and changes through the experience that he undergoes. He is a wiser and often a better man at the end than at the beginning. Nor is this kind of "learning" confined to the hero. In *King Lear*, the most conspicuous "learners" are Lear and Gloucester. Are there any others? Does Edmund, for example, "learn"? Does Cordelia? (In the case of Edmund, note, as one point, his "wheel is come full circle." Would the Edmund who, earlier, scoffed at the idea of great universal forces affecting men's natures and conduct have said this?) Are

there also any principal persons in the play who rather conspicuously do *not* "learn"? Treat the subject of learning, changing,
inner development, with respect to both those who do and those
who do not change. (Brief essay)

The Tempest

Act I. In *The Winter's Tale*, written immediately before *The
Tempest*, Shakespeare uses the first three acts to show the early
foundations of his story, then abruptly jumps over sixteen years
in order to come to the events of the final two acts. In *The Tempest*, such events as filled the first three acts of *The Winter's Tale*
are made part of the present time; though they occurred as long
as twelve years before, they are skillfully tucked within the frame
of the few hours represented in the entire five acts. Explain how
the dramatist accomplished this artistic feat. (Besides Prospero,
your account should involve three additional dramatic characters.)
(Paragraph)

Act II. In Antonio and Sebastian, some critics think that Shakespeare struck a new low in villainy. A villain like Claudius, in
Hamlet, is gnawed by conscience and tries vainly to pray. A
villain like Edmund of King Lear, wicked as he is, has a kind of
glamor about him—and, besides, in the end he tries to do good.
A villain like Iago carries off the worst of his deviltry with such a
boldly plausible manner ("Honest Iago") that we may find ourselves enjoying the "joke" with him. But this pair, Antonio and
Sebastian—are they not creatures of a different order? Study
closely every line they say in Scene 1, and then try to isolate the
secret of their unqualified baseness. (Paragraph)

Scene 2, in which Trinculo and the drunken Stephano meet
Caliban, is one of the comic high spots in all Shakespeare. But
the scene contains sinister implications also: this trio of drunken
beasts aspire to gain control of the isle—which, in the context
of the play, is the world. Do the sinister implications dampen the
hilarity (for spectator or reader)? Does the hilarity obscure or
negate the sinister implications? Do both effects manage, somehow, to work well together? (Paragraph)

Act III. Each of the three scenes in this act continues the experiences of the visitors on Prospero's island. In the first scene, the love of Ferdinand and Miranda ripens to a noble feeling that is blessed (secretly) by Prospero. In the second, Trinculo and Stephano, with their new-found friend, Caliban, plot a brutal murder and usurpation; in the third, Alonso and his fellows are driven to a frenzy of terror by Ariel and several "strange Shapes," who prey on their sense of guilt. The unifying force that runs throughout the act and manifests itself in each scene is Prospero's absolute command of every situation. It is evident that Prospero can, at any time, do whatever he wishes with and to all his visitors. What evidence is there, by the end of each scene, of his purpose and his intentions? What seems in store for Ferdinand, for Caliban's drunken, murderous crew, and for Alonso's party? (Paragraph)

Act IV. This climactic act represents two exciting spectacles: Prospero's "play-within-a-play" (a "masque") put on by spirits in celebration of the lovers' betrothal; and the ignominious defeat of Caliban's crew. The first is a gorgeous vision, filled with beauty, harmony, and promise of future rich blessings—but it is broken off abruptly and violently ("Prospero starts suddenly" certainly marks the climactic instant of the act, and perhaps of the whole play) and is succeeded by the ugly reality of Caliban's arrival and ensuing flight. To Caliban, at least, it appears that victory is lost because Stephano and Trinculo are deceived by the show of cheap, gaudy "trash" hung on the lime tree by Ariel. It appears very likely that Shakespeare meant the entire act to "say" something about man, life, the world, illusion, reality. There is surely no such thing as a single "right" answer about what this something is. But presumably the two main incidents of the act fit together to make a comment on life. (Note, for example, Prospero's famous "Our revels now are ended" and Caliban's disgust that his "army" is misled by worthless show.) What do you think the act, through its two parts, "says"? (Paragraph)

Act V. Usually (though not quite always), the last scene of a Shakespearean comedy brings a completely satisfactory solution to all the problems of all persons who are involved. What of the ending of *The Tempest*? Are the principal persons rewarded both to their own and to your satisfaction? (Paragraph)

The Play as a Whole. At a crucial moment late in the play, Prospero tells Ariel that "the rarer virtue" is in mercy than in vengeance—and he pardons all his enemies. Consider the play as a whole, from the first scenes on: Is this a decision that Prospero reached late, or was it a purpose he had in mind all the while? If the latter, why does he inflict such terror, grief, and general distress on the visitors? (Brief essay)

"Prospero is not merely a magician; he is more nearly a god." Consider what kinds of power Prospero has, how he demonstrates it, his command of mortals and spirits, his manner of dealing with his enemies as an indication of his providential character, and any other forms of evidence. (Brief essay)

Drama deals in conflict. Much of its excitement derives from the struggle of reasonably equal opposing forces—a villain and a hero, rival armies, etc. But in *The Tempest*, Shakespeare has created a figure of godlike powers, who is so strong that there can be no truly effective opposition. But even so, because it is so necessary to drama, Shakespeare contrives to give at least the *appearance* of conflict. How does he do so? (You should find not one but many ways.) (Brief essay)

Critics have written a great deal about what *The Tempest* means and what Shakespeare is saying through it. Although there is no single "right" answer, discuss what you think the play is essentially about. (Brief essay)

As lovers, Ferdinand and Miranda are sometimes compared with Romeo and Juliet. They might also be compared with some other pairs of heroes and heroines—Rosalind and Orlando of *As You Like It*, for example, or Bassanio and Portia of *The Merchant of Venice*. Take whatever other pair of lovers you know well and compare them with Miranda and Ferdinand. The problem is not only to show similarities, but differences between the two couples, and thus to establish whatever is *unique* in Ferdinand and Miranda. (Brief essay)

It is not easy to write an essay on the *poetry* of this or any other Shakespearean play. But *The Tempest* is obviously distinguished for its poetry, much of which, in its fine music, its imagery, and its economy of expression, matches or excels the best of Shakespeare anywhere. One possibility is to center on the *appropriateness* of the poetry to the subject and to the character of particular speakers. We can understand well enough why the lovers and Prospero should speak so splendidly, but why should Caliban be given some of the most effective passages in the play? (Brief essay)

CHAPTER 12

A Note on Teaching the Sonnets

1. WHY THE SONNETS?

A PERFECTLY DEFENSIBLE ARGUMENT FOR READING SHAKESPEARE'S sonnets is that the man who wrote them is so prodigiously great that any words of his which may conceivably "reveal" him are precious. "With this key," said Wordsworth, "Shakespeare unlocked his heart." But Browning replied, "If so, the less Shakespeare he." Browning, who venerated Shakespeare, meant no reflection on the quality of the Sonnets; he doubted that Shakespeare, always the dramatist, revealed any more of himself in the Sonnets than in the plays.

But even if it be true that the Sonnets get us closer to the personal ideas and emotions of Shakespeare than any other evidence that has survived, the fact must surely take second place as a reason for reading them. The most important thing about the Sonnets is *not* that Shakespeare wrote them. The great reason for teaching the Sonnets is that they are absolutely first-rate poems. Among them are many (some would say as many as 50) that belong in a restricted category of the finest poems in the language. And among the first-rate poems in the language that are eminently teachable and understandable, they have few peers.

2. WHICH ONES?

Knowing that no school can reasonably be expected to teach all of Shakespeare's 37 plays and knowing, too, that some have

278

better claim, for various reasons, than others, we rather brutally cut the canon to a list of 14 "especially appropriate" plays; and then this list itself, with decreasing certainty, we pared to 12, 8, 4, and even 2, the regrettable, irreducible minimum.

With the Sonnets, we start with a "standard" 154. One hears of teachers who teach them all, usually in a twelfth-grade "college prep" class, or in a class more highly selected still; and one often hears of teachers who use the entire Sonnets as "outside reading," again, usually in the twelfth grade English Literature survey courses. A fairly common practice is to offer the Sonnets as one "outside reading" choice to be completed while, in class, seniors are going line by line through a play.

There seems to be no wholly satisfactory argument that can be made against any of these ways of getting the complete Sonnets read, and there are very strong arguments for them. Time itself is no insurmountable barrier. A twelfth grader who reads fairly well can read through (though not "digest") all 154 in approximately the time it would take him to read through a play and in much less time than it would take him to read through a full-length novel. Further, there is a special advantage in reading *all* the Sonnets, in the order in which they are standardly printed. In a loose way, they tell a story of *experience*, real or imagined, over a period of years: the poet is young, and grows older; he has moments of exhilaration and of despair, feels anguish and finds consolation; he has relations with various individuals—men, women, friends, rivals, sweethearts; he moves about, philosophizes on the meaning of human experience; he praises and censures. There is no sonnet that is not a part of the total Sonnets; yet there is no sonnet that is not whole in itself. Can it be too much to propose that, by whatever means the teacher devises to get the feat accomplished, all students except the honestly incompetent should have read the complete Sonnets before they graduate from high school?

Here we are assuming that the reading of the Sonnets as an ordered collection will be an "outside" undertaking, probably for the twelfth grade. We do not propose that the full collection be studied line by line as we have recommended for individual plays.

But unquestionably a substantial number should be closely read and discussed in class. We cannot avoid the questions, then: How

many, and which?—otherwise we are implying that any one sonnet is just as good as any other, and that it makes no difference
which are selected for the special distinction of close reading in
class. To imply any such thing would be demonstrably absurd.
If every sonnet is fine, yet some deserve, and require, closer study.

Any selected list of the Sonnets, short of the total collection,
will encounter someone's disfavor. Indeed, the lister himself will
have been forced to omit many poems the omission of which he
may find impossible to justify. Fortunately, we get a good deal of
aid from anthologists—college, high school, and other; a "most
frequently reprinted" poem has presumably especially pleased
many editors, and perhaps it stands the best chance also of pleas-
ing the widest audience. In the list that follows, the most frequently anthologized sonnets are marked with an asterisk; others,
not so marked (though they, too, have been included by various
anthologists), can be assigned to the taste of this single list-maker.
The list constitutes the "irreducible minimum" number of Sonnets which should be given in-class treatment:

12   When I do count the clock that tells the time
15   When I consider everything that grows
*18   Shall I compare thee to a summer's day
23   As an unperfect actor on the stage
27   Weary with toil, I haste me to my bed
*29   When in disgrace with fortune and men's eyes
*30   When to the sessions of sweet silent thought
32   If thou survive my well-contented day
38   How can my Muse want subject to invent
49   Against that time, if ever that time come
53   What is your substance, whereof are you made
54   O how much more doth beauty beauteous seem
*55   Not marble nor the gilded monuments
*60   Like as the waves make towards the pebbled shore
*64   When I have seen by Time's fell hand defaced
*65   Since brass, nor stone, nor earth, nor boundless sea
66   Tired with all these, for restful death I cry
71   No longer mourn for me when I am dead
*73   That time of year thou mayst in me behold
74   But be contented: when did that fell arrest

89	Say that thou didst forsake me for some fault
90	Then hate me when thou wilt; if ever, now
*97	How like a winter hath my absence been
104	To me, fair friend, you never can be old
105	Let not my love be called idolatry
*106	When in the chronicle of wasted time
107	Not mine own fears, nor the prophetic soul
109	O never say that I was false of heart
*110	Alas, 'tis true I have gone here and there
*111	O for my sake do you with Fortune chide
*116	Let me not to the marriage of true minds
119	What potions have I drunk of Siren tears
128	How oft when thou, my music, music play'st
129	The expense of spirit in a waste of shame
*130	My mistress' eyes are nothing like the sun
*146	Poor soul, the center of my sinful earth

3. WHEN?

As experienced teachers of English know, such of Shakespeare's sonnets (usually six to eight) as are included in the most widely used anthologies of literature edited for high schools are placed mainly in the twelfth-grade volume, which typically surveys English literary history. There, with some "Songs from the Plays" and various examples of "Elizabethan Lyric Poetry," they serve to illustrate important characteristics of the Age and to introduce students to Shakespeare and, almost invariably, *Macbeth*. Irregularly, a Shakespearean sonnet or two will appear in a ninth or tenth grade anthology, but never in typical eleventh-grade anthologies, which are limited to American literature.

What is here to be proposed represents a drastic departure from the way of the anthologies, though it is by no means inconsistent with the practices of individual teachers who "run off" copies of sonnets (and other works) to supplement or substitute for readings found in ninth-, tenth-, and eleventh-grade anthologies.

Though we have earlier suggested that all the Sonnets be read as an outside, individual project in the twelfth grade, we emphatically urge that the 36 sonnets listed above for classroom reading and discussion (with such substitutions as individual teachers think best to make) be distributed among all grades from nine through twelve, and certainly not excluding grade eleven.

Can there be any sound reason for waiting until grade twelve before confronting high school students with a Shakespearean sonnet? Some of the best-known and best of these sonnets belong among the most "open," the most eminently "teachable" first-rate poems in the language. Accordingly, some teachers use them in making their first "approach" to poetry in the ninth grade. Indeed, some teachers begin to work deliberately with a Shakespearean sonnet during the first hour of the first semester in the ninth grade. By this means, they insist, they acquaint students at the outset with the nature of high school English and teach them what to expect in the next four years.

No purpose would be served here by attempting to distribute the 36 sonnets according to grade. A majority of Shakespeare's sonnets represent approximately the same degree of difficulty, and it would be absurd, on the basis of relative difficulty, to assign nine to each of four years. Thematically arranged reading programs will mainly accommodate particular sonnets according to their own structures, and such fitting is a local problem. In some ninth-grade programs there will conceivably be place for nine sonnets; but in others there will be place for only two. Some schools will manage to incorporate only half a dozen sonnets into their ninth- and tenth-grade programs, leaving thirty to be placed as they will best serve in the upper years. The sonnets are marvelously adaptable; if they center on only a few specific themes—love, friendship, beauty, the ravages of Time, carpe diem—yet the experience they reflect is widely applicable. Almost any sonnet will "fit" into practically any but the narrowest thematic arrangement a teacher has chosen.

Even so, some sonnets, like some plays, are more appropriate for the ninth or tenth grade, and others more appropriate for eleventh or twelfth. For grade nine or ten we should choose, among others, sonnets 18, 29, 73, 116; and for grade eleven or twelve, sonnets 105, 107, 119, 129, and 130. As for the rest, the setting—thematic or otherwise—that the program in a given year has or can make for them will presumably determine their placement.

4. APPROACH

As with the plays, we must insist that the best approach to a sonnet is to begin reading it. If a single sonnet is read, such information about its form, history, themes, and conventions as will enhance the student's experience of it as a poem should be introduced during the discussion that *follows* the reading. If several sonnets are read, such relevant information can be introduced *between* particular sonnets and *after* all have been read. *After* a sonnet has been read, students can be directed to count its lines, figure out its meter, determine its rhyme scheme and its divisions. *Then* the teacher may ask such questions as "Are *all* sonnets exactly like this one?" and "Where did this form of poetry originate?"

The important thing about a Shakespearean sonnet is not that Shakespeare wrote it, or when, or what its form is, or what its history is, or what the typical themes of sonnets are. To approach a sonnet by emphasizing any or all of these matters is certainly to prepare the way for the student to perceive the sonnet as an *example*, as a *specimen product* of author, age, history, genre. But this is surely not what is important. The important thing about a sonnet is the impact it can have as a highly potent work of art. Whatever is done by way of approach before reading should be calculated to improve the poem's chances to strike the student with full impact. If historical information does not help in this way, what justification can be made for introducing it "before the fact"? Better, surely, to approach a sonnet, like a play, by reading the first line.

For the plays we suggested an alternative, namely, involving students in discussion, before beginning to read, of a subject or theme which will later be found in the work. Because the study of a play may take from four to six weeks, an hour or two spent on this kind of warm-up approach would not be disproportionate. But if a single sonnet is to be read, it would seem ridiculous to spend one hour in discussing, say, the topic "friendship," and then half an hour at the next meeting in reading and discussing the sonnet. On the other hand, if the particular sonnet (say, 29) is one item in a "unit" of poems, short stories, essays, novels, plays, all of which develop the friendship theme, an hour or two spent in general discussion of students' ideas of friendship before *any* of the works are read might serve excellent purpose by making students receptive to literary treatments of the theme. There is another way that involves a certain amount of risk. Every teacher should no doubt try it once or twice; if it fails miserably, it should be abandoned. As every teacher knows, many students develop an antipathy to the very name of Shakespeare. No doubt, Shakespeare's reputation as the greatest English poet and dramatist, so often heard about, brings many students to him with a chip on their shoulders. The chip may stay on long enough to spoil the first two acts of, say, *Macbeth*, and of course it may stay on long enough to spoil all the two, three, or six sonnets that are read in that semester. Any way of getting this chip off early is surely to be praised.

Suppose, then, that the teacher proposes a game of judging some poems. Sonnets by unnamed authors are run off on sheets and numbered from 1 to 5. One sonnet is by Sidney, let us say, one by Spenser, one by Wyatt or Surrey, one by Rossetti or Edna St. Vincent Millay, and one—let us say number 4 on the list—is by Shakespeare (whichever one the teacher is personally devoted to *and can read best*). These sheets are distributed, and students are told that all five sonnets will be read aloud, after which each student will vote by number for the sonnet he honestly likes best— or dislikes least, if no more can be expected. The teacher then reads each sonnet slowly and carefully while students follow. Each student then checks one sonnet. Two students take the sheets to the blackboard, where the teacher has listed numbers 1 through 5, and the votes are tabulated. If all goes well, number 4 will soon begin to show an impressive lead, and when all votes are in, it should win by a staggering majority. The blackboard, hopefully, will look about like this:

1   xx
2   xxxx
3   xxx
4   xxxxxxxxxxxxxx
5   xxxxxx

The element of risk involved in playing this little game of

English teacher's roulette is obvious. But teachers can minimize the risk, if they think they need to do so, in two ways: (1) by selecting four comparatively knotty, muddy sonnets to compete with Shakespeare's magnificently open one; (2) by reading Shakespeare's sonnet with especial clarity and force—but certainly not ostentatiously, or the trick will deservedly boomerang. But after gaining confidence with a trial or two, teachers will find that they can trust Shakespeare's sonnet to win handily without special favor.

A shrewd modification of this game, to use with a particularly recalcitrant class, is to add a second sonnet of Shakespeare's— 130 ("My mistress' eyes")—and to have the class vote for two out of six. Many students will quite honestly vote for this one, and some others, suspecting a trap, will vote for it out of sheer perversity, thinking it cannot *possibly* be one that the teacher wants the class to vote for.

"And do you know who wrote this one?" asks the teacher, pointing to number 4, which has picked up, say, 15 votes out of 30.

"No," say the students.

"Shakespeare," says the teacher.

"And do you know who wrote *this* one?" asks the teacher, pointing to Sonnet 130, which has picked up, say, twenty or more votes.

"No," say the students.

"Shakespeare," says the teacher. This triumph, it hardly needs saying, is one of those rare moments that make an English teacher's lot bearable.

5. PRESENTATION

The select group of sonnets chosen for close consideration by teacher and class should be read aloud by the teacher with students following in their own texts. An actor's recording, with students merely listening, is an experience for later, perhaps, but certainly not for the initial presentation. Nor is the recorded voice of an unseen reader a satisfactory substitute for the teacher's reading, even though students follow the recording in their own texts. The initial experience of the poem is a thing between teacher and students; the intrusion of a third person by means of a mechanical box makes something different of it. Students cannot share an experience with a box, and no doubt the sharing is itself a vital part of the experience.

6. DISCUSSION

One problem that confronts teachers in using a combined reading-discussion method in presenting a Shakespearean play does not arise in dealing with a sonnet. This is the problem of when to stop, how often, how long, for what kinds of things, in order to discuss. In the initial reading of a sonnet, the teacher does not stop at all, however thorny the individual phrase or line, because the whole work is only 14 lines in length and can be read at a deliberate pace in about two minutes. With a play it is not possible to pack the "whole" into the mind and to hold it there while one goes back to examine the parts. But it is very easy to capture the "whole" of a two-minute sonnet and to hold it while details are re-examined.

As with other poems, especially short ones, the usual way to begin discussion is with the question, "What does the poem 'say'?" Shakespeare's sonnets are in this respect eminently teachable—in fact, perhaps the most teachable poems in the language—for they invariably say something that can be re-stated in a simple sentence or in a complex sentence with one subordinate clause that contains the gist of the first eight, or even twelve, lines. Thus Sonnet 29: "When all things else combine to make me discontent with myself and my lot, remembrance of your love once more raises my spirits high." And Sonnet 30: "When I brood over all my experiences past and gone, the thought of you restores all losses and griefs."

Next, the sonnets are eminently teachable because there is such a striking difference between what the sonnet says when it is reduced to a flat statement, and what the total sonnet *is*. Hence the usual second question can be answered with a good deal of clarity and substance: "Now, what is it that makes the sonnet itself so much more remarkable than the bare statement of what it says?"

This second question offers a guide into the discussion of the *means* by which the poet prodigiously enriched the bare thought: into the working details of imagery, sound and sense, musical cadence, vowels and consonants; into alliteration, assonance, personification, simile, metaphor, and all the rest. There seems little merit in routinely identifying "examples" of every kind of poetic device that can be found in a sonnet, or any other poem. A student's rudely voiced reaction is not without justification: "So it *is* a simile—so what?" But if discussion of these devices of the poet's craft is directed toward formulating at least a partial answer to the question "By what *means* did the poet make the total sonnet transcend the bare statement" then it has merit indeed. If what we truly want, beyond all else, is to have a great sonnet strike the reader with full impact, clear understanding of what it says is the first necessity, but only the first; appreciation of the *art*—all the poetic means the poet used in making the impact possible—is indispensable, too, because it is itself a part of the impact.

As with the plays, the cues to what is discussed about a sonnet should be given by the particular sonnet itself. It may well be highly relevant to discuss alliteration in one sonnet and to make no point about vowels; and in the very next sonnet, the reverse; and in the very next, neither consonant nor vowel sounds, but a unifying image. To point out routinely all items of the poet's craft in a given sonnet is not necessarily to have shed any light on the basic question that justifies spending time on pointing them out. It is necessary not only to identify this combination of sounds, that metaphor, this choice of word, but to consider why *this* particular combination of sounds or *this* particular metaphor is best suited to convey the poem's meaning, or to deepen the reader's experience of the poem.

Consider, for example, Sonnet 12. The sonnet's "statement" is approximately this: "Like all other things, your beauty must pass except as it is preserved in your children." The statement is the same, essentially, as that made in a dozen other sonnets in which the poet urges his handsome young friend to marry and have children to preserve his beauty from the common enemy of all earthly things, Time. (Time, of course, is the "villain" of the Sonnets.) What makes the sonnet itself so much more extraordinary than what it merely says? The first eight lines—moving along at a steady clip that brings to mind the inexorable march of Time—cite specific items open to ordinary observation, all testifying to Time's relentless passage: clock (the even beat of the lines suggests the ticking of a clock), day becoming night, violet fading, youthful curls whitening, leafy trees growing bare, green growth ripening and being harvested. The next four lines identify human youth and beauty with these passing things and with their fate. The final couplet flatly names the sole means of escape. (In Sonnet 15, Shakespeare suggests a second hope for Time's defeat: the friend's beauty may be preserved by the poet's verse.) It is noteworthy that no conspicuous figure of speech appears until line 8, when suddenly the green growth of summer is seen as "Borne on the bier with white and bristly beard"—and in a flash this image, bringing in the human form, identifies human fate with the fate of all other growing things. The shift effected by the startlingly vivid image is perfectly transitional, for this eighth line at once ends the series of non-human details and brings on the ninth line, "Then of thy beauty do I question make." It is as though the striking resemblance itself, between sheaves hauled in at harvest time and an old man carried on his bier, had *caused* the poet to think of his next thought, that men, too, pass: "*Then*," he says, "*Then* of thy beauty do I question make, That *thou* among the wastes of time must go."

If one reads this sonnet with just the slightest exaggeration of its predominant sounds, one finds that they are harsh, brittle. There is a prevalence of "b" and "d" and "g," along with a steadily hissing "s." Numerous words are harsh: *hideous, erst, heat, herd, girded, sheaves, bristly, wastes, 'gainst, scythe, breed.* Here if the teacher chose could be an elementary demonstration of the poet's reinforcement of sense through sound. In many of the finest sonnets, the golden vowels and the "m's" and "n's," set in a flowing meter, produce a gorgeous music. In contrast to the lyricism of these sonnets, Sonnet 12 has a core of hardness that is singularly appropriate to its blunt message: "Do this, or else."

The artistry of this sonnet is also clearly evinced in its repetition of the word *brave*, with its potent shift of meanings. In line 2 it means "fine, resplendent, glorious," and it carries a force of irony, for in a single phrase the "brave day" is "sunk in hideous night," and the sudden defeat of this "bravery" prefigures what happens to the violet, the youthful curls, the lofty trees, and summer's greenery. But in line 14—rightly, the last line of the sonnet—this ignominiously vanquished "brave" gets its revenge after all, for the poet has found a way to "brave" the destroyer, Time—that is to say, to "outbrave" him and put him down. Thus with a single play on a word at the beginning and end, the poet has thrown a final unifying loop of irony about his poem.

Such art as we have discovered in Sonnet 12 is present in any one of the 154 sonnets, and particularly evident in the 36 sonnets we have listed for classroom discussion. Let us now briefly discuss some of the more frequently-taught of these 36 sonnets, randomly noting a few remarkable features of each.

In Sonnet 15, one notes how the theatrical image of "huge stage" is sustained through the next lines with the words *comment, cheered,* and *check'd.* This is remarkable but not uniquely so: sometimes Shakespeare will start an image early in a sonnet and run it like a thread through to the end.

In Sonnet 18, one may select from a superfluity of superb images that of "summer's lease," which in an instant personifies a season of the year as a tenant, and makes its point that this tenant's lease has not very long to run. But even beyond this touch is the touch that completes it by subtle contrast. In line 10, the beauty of the poet's friend is called "that fair thou owest." "Owest," of course, means "ownest": the friend *owns* his beauty; summer has only a lease.

In Sonnet 29, one may first note the shift of vowels between the first eight lines and the last six; these vowels move forward in the mouth, and, as they move, the pitch of the sonnet is raised, with the sound going up like the lark that is soaring to the skies.

In Sonnet 30, one notes the court imagery that begins with "sessions" and runs through "summons," with echoes throughout the poem in words that might figure in a court suit: *cancell'd, expense, account, pay as if not paid, losses.* One notes, secondly, the conspicuous sound of "s." But, now, *why* is court imagery relevant to what this poem says, and *why* are "s" sounds appropriate? Here "rememberance of things past" is represented, in the figure, as a defendant before the court, hence the relevance of the court image. But also this is not a *real* court in session; actually, the poet is sitting quietly, soberly thinking of past experience: the steady "s" sounds are basic, as in the words "shh" and "hush," used to induce quiet. Thus the effect of the poem is to produce a doube image, of a court in session and a man in study, engaged in silent reverie.

In Sonnet 55, of particular note is the sense of hard and sometimes ugly solidity built up by words like *marble, unswept stone, besmear'd, sluttish, wasteful, broils, root, Mars his sword.* (If a class were to read *all* the sonnets, a point of note is the steady increase in the poet's confidence, from the first half-suggestion in Sonnet 15 that his verse will preserve his friend's beauty, on through such bold statements as that made by the couplet in Sonnet 18, to this sonnet, which boldly declares the poet's verse more durable than the hardest substance.) The sounds of the poem are as hard as the substances named.

In Sonnet 60, a question to pose for students is this: Since "toward" and "towards" are synonymous, would it do any harm to remove the "s" from "towards" in the first line? Students should shortly, on their own, see that the "s" sounds of the first two lines make up a pattern, and to remove one "s" would be to remove an item from this pattern. But the second question, thereafter, is this: But what is the point of *having* a pattern of "s" sounds? If the teacher then reads the first two lines aloud quietly, slightly emphasizing the predominant sounds, students should hear the waves hissing their way among pebbles on the shore—just as the lines say. (Surely these lines offer a more subtle introduction to onomatopoeia than, say, Poe's "The Bells.")

In Sonnet 64, worthy of note is the expression of a basic Shakespearean conception of life, nature, and the universe—an idea as basic as the physical principle that matter is not destroyed but merely changed:

> When I have seen the hungry ocean gain
> Advantage on the kingdom of the shore,
> And the firm soil win of the watery main,
> Increasing store with loss and loss with store . . .

In the great plays, all things are at last "evened out"; the turmoils of the histories and the tragedies, the struggles of Bolingbroke and Henry IV, of Hal-Henry V, of Richard III, Brutus, Lear, Othello, Macbeth—all ultimately come to this, like violent waves that are reduced to ripples and then dissolved in the eternal, unchanging sea from which they arose. If Shakespeare had what might be called an "ultimate perspective" on life and the universe, this conception must come close to it. Something of the sort seems suggested in Matthew Arnold's sonnet to Shakespeare:

> Others abide our question. Thou art free.
> We ask and ask—Thou smilest and art still,
> Out-topping knowledge.

In Sonnet 73, it is the *structure* of imagery that makes the poem memorable: season of year (Fall), time of day (twilight), glowing fire (embers)—these very directly, almost as if they were not poetic figures at all, spell out the poet's own time of life. This structure well supports the argument that the best art is the simplest, so simple that it seems not to be art at all. (But within the simple, obvious structure of the poem are some of the most haunting lines in the world's literature: "Bare ruined choirs, where late the sweet birds sang"; "When yellow leaves, or none, or few, do hang"; "Death's second self, that seals up all in rest." And add to this the biographical fact that proves what "art," both dramatic and poetic, went into the poem: when Shakespeare wrote the poem that speaks so splendidly of declining age, he was perhaps thirty, and may have been writing *Romeo and Juliet*, tragedy of the very young, with all the great histories, comedies, and tragedies yet before him.)

We skip abruptly to Sonnet 130, where students on their own will very likely conclude that the poet's "statement" is approximately this: "My love is plain, beside the greatest beauties, but she has other fine qualities, and she is mine." The sonnet, of course, says nothing of the sort. In an ironic manner, it sets the beauty of the poet's mistress above all the beauties that have ever been praised by "false compare." The poet has played a game of getting "one up" on other poets. This may be the only sonnet in the 154 that truly requires some historical background if even its basic sense is to be correctly understood. As background (though no doubt even this should be provided after, rather than before, the poem is read) the teacher may wish to cite early Elizabethan lyrics in which poets praise their loves with extravagant conceits; or if these are not immediately available, such passages as Romeo's "It is the East, and Juliet is the sun" will serve to illustrate the conventions of which Shakespeare took such gay advantage.

7. OTHER ACTIVITIES

As with the plays, discussion will claim first place among activities that accompany or follow presentation. Next in importance (again as in the plays) is writing.

There exist numerous possibilities for writing assignments. A paraphrase of an entire sonnet written in the student's own prose will help to teach the differences between poetry and prose. If several sonnets are read, excellent opportunities arise for paragraphs in which students compare the treatments of a common theme in two, three, or four sonnets, or examine some of the more subtle aspects of poetry, such as the relation of sound to sense, or the appropriateness of a dominant image to the whole thought. But in addition to these expository possibilities, we also would propose that every student should be encouraged—if not required—to try his hand at writing a sonnet. From this experience, the student will gain a sounder understanding of the sonnet form and, almost certainly, a respect for the achievement of the great sonneteers.

Third priority, after discussion and writing, belongs to memorization. Surely a sonnet or two each year will not overburden the memory of any student, for the best of them are comparatively easy to memorize. Their lines flow along with a word choice and a word order so absolutely right that one gains a sense of inevitable sweep, as though they could not possibly be otherwise than they are. Besides, the orderly development of the ideas in Shakespeare's sonnets, with their three quatrains and concluding couplet, facilitates the memorizing process.

We come finally to the use of recordings. Several famous actors have recorded readings of selected sonnets, and a prime virtue of their readings is that they bring out the music of the sonnets. No student should study the sonnets without coming at last to hear this music. If they can be brought to hear it by the teacher's reading, so much the better. (Every teacher has an obligation to practice reading the sonnets aloud until both their sense *and their sound* come through loud and clear.) Yet even if the teacher reads exceptionally well, students will profit by listening to other interpretations of the sonnets, rendered by other voices, as well. Again, however, as with the plays, the teacher's reading and the students' discussion should come first and the recorded readings afterwards.

If tape recorders are available, much will be gained by having students record their own readings, and probably there is a point in having these, too, played back to the class before the actors' readings are heard. Probably no great poem should ever be passed by until a class has heard it several times. If they hear Shakespeare's sonnet first read by the teacher, next by two or three students in turn, and finally by a professional voice, its magic will be theirs, one hopes, forever.

Suggested Bibliography for Teachers

Shakespeare's Age

Bindoff, S. T. *Tudor England*. Penguin Books, 1950. (The Pelican History of England, #5)

Byrne, M. St. Clare. *Elizabethan Life in Town and Country*. Rev. ed. New York: Barnes & Noble, Inc., 1961.

Ford, Boris (ed.). *The Age of Shakespeare*. Penguin Books, 1955. (The Pelican Guide to English Literature, #2)

Halliday, F. E. *Shakespeare in His Age*. Duckworth, 1956.

Tillyard, E. M. W. *The Elizabethan World Picture*. London: Chatto & Windus, 1943; New York: Macmillan, 1944.

Wilson, John Dover (ed.). *Life in Shakespeare's England*. 2nd ed. New York: Macmillan, 1913.

Shakespeare's Life

Adams, J. Q. *A Life of William Shakespeare*. Houghton Mifflin, 1923.

Chute, Marchette. *Shakespeare of London*. E. P. Dutton & Co., Inc., 1949.

Halliday, F. E. *The Life of Shakespeare*. Penguin Books, 1963.

Spencer, Hazelton. *The Art and Life of William Shakespeare*. Harcourt, Brace, 1940.

Wilson, John Dover. *The Essential Shakespeare*. Cambridge University Press, 1932.

Miscellaneous Criticism

Bradley, A. C. *Shakespearean Tragedy*. Macmillan, 1904.

Charlton, H. B. *Shakespearian Comedy*. Macmillan, 1938.

Shakespearian Tragedy. Cambridge University Press, 1949.

Clemen, Wolfgang H. *The Development of Shakespeare's Imagery*. Harvard University Press, 1951.

Granville-Barker, Harley. *Prefaces to Shakespeare*. Princeton U. Press, 1946–47. 2 vols.

Halliday, F. E. *The Poetry of Shakespeare's Plays*, Duckworth, 1954.

Shakespeare and His Critics. Duckworth, 1949.

Spencer, Theodore. *Shakespeare and the Nature of Man*. Macmillan, 1942.

Spurgeon, Caroline F. E. *Shakespeare's Imagery and What It Tells Us*. Macmillan, 1935.

Tillyard, E. M. W. *Shakespeare's History Plays*. Macmillan, 1946.

Shakespeare's Last Plays. Chatto & Windus, 1938.

Van Doren, Mark. *Shakespeare*. Henry Holt & Company, 1939.

Index

DATE DUE